Work Lessons 101

What they Don't Teach You in School

Year 1 (2019-2020)

Sabrina Woodworth

To Mike and Quinton, the loves of my life.

Table of Contents

Foreword

I met Sabrina at an Innovation Catalyst event in San Francisco in 2015, when we were assigned to the same work team. I had graduated from University a year prior with a Master's degree in Electrical Engineering and German. The team was intimidating to me. They were all so much more experienced, and I wasn't sure where my value or place was on this team. Sabrina was someone who inspired me from the second I met her. She was a woman in engineering – something that was hard to come by anywhere – but she could command a room like no one I had ever seen.

As we began working together, she made space for me and my opinions, listened and helped develop them. She had experience with our company and made time to teach me how to effectively pitch my ideas by aligning them with the company's baseline. We were only working together for a week, but we bonded, and I would trust Sabrina with anything.

As we got to know each other and worked on this innovation program over the next six months, she became a mentor not only in the workplace but in all aspects of my life. I've been through numerous personal challenges that impacted my career, but with Sabrina's advice, she taught me how to own these challenges, and my career has soared. When I decided to open up my own company, Engineer Your Mind Ltd, she was there to support me. No matter what direction my career has headed, she has always provided invaluable support.

Sabrina is well known within the industry for being a "go-to" person. She knows her stuff and makes it her business to learn as much as possible about a scenario and the people involved, leading her to be an effective Project Manager. She resonates with her team and clients.

Why? Because she listens. She takes time to sit and listen, then provides useful and practical advice.

I know my career excelled because of support from the right people, and Sabrina was one of them. When she told me she was starting Work Lessons 101, I was excited as I knew many more of you would benefit from her wealth of knowledge and experience. I've seen her mentor numerous people who have gone on to great opportunities. Sabrina's character comes to life when she is helping people; she has a genuinely kind heart.

I've spoken a lot about how Sabrina has changed others' career trajectories, but she also does it for herself. I witnessed her at this innovation program, developing herself. Asking questions, asking where she could learn more, and being nervous about putting some suggestions forward - we knew people would think we were ridiculous – but did it anyway and excelled because of it. She moved quickly from someone who was there to learn about innovation to being asked to come back and coach others on the process. Her success is a measure of how effective her strategies and advice are on this topic.

I can't wait for you all to read what she has in store for you in this book. Inside she has collected an incredible amount of advice to move the needle on your career. It's a book that can help you move forward and align with what you truly want out of your career. If you have a specific challenge at work – the likelihood is she will address it in the following pages.

Not only does Sabrina provide incredible tips to support you right now – but she helps you put together an effective plan to move up in your career. Having a strategy will always help you be effective in your actions – whether in your career or outside of it. A good comparison is, think about how you plan your commute to work. You don't just stand at a curb and pray for a bus to show up or sit in your car and expect it to take you exactly where you need to go. You develop a plan. You think about the time you need to leave, so you arrive on time; you think of obstacles that might make you late and adjust.

It's the same with your career. You need a plan to get where you want to go effectively, and Sabrina is here to help you on that journey with Work Lessons 101. She has helped me with my career, she has helped many others, and she has done it with her own career. Sabrina is a big reason I felt empowered to take a leap and start Engineer Your Mind Ltd. Without her, I may not have made the jump, and I know for sure, it wouldn't have been this successful.

The only person who can make the changes you want in your career is yourself, but Sabrina can offer the helping hand to get you started and assist with the bumps in the road. It's important to know that someone is supporting you because you're worth believing in. I regularly seek support for my development by investing in coaches for career guidance. Without it, I wouldn't be where I am today.

Where am I now? Happy. I'm happy and proud of everything I've achieved, and I'm aligned with my career and personal goals. Thank you, Sabrina, for all your support.

So, what are you waiting for?

Read the next few pages, and you'll see for yourself what I've been saying is true. I hope you enjoy learning from Sabrina as much as I have.

Sincerely,

Hannah Schaapkens

Founder, Director & CEO of Engineer Your Mind Ltd.
Consultant Senior Electrical Engineer

What I've Learned in the First Decade of My Career

I remember being in my last year of university and thinking about what job I wanted after graduation. At the time, I was only thinking of a job, not a career; I didn't know the difference between them. At that point, my goals were to graduate with my engineering degree and pay off my student loan. I hadn't spent the necessary time planning for my future career or what I wanted to spend the majority of my adult life doing. In retrospect, this was a mistake.

Reflecting on my academic life, I recognized that my higher education didn't prepare me for my career. Five years of education and over 150 college credits, not one of those credits was spent teaching me how to:

- Create a career development plan,
- Write an effective resume,
- Prepare for an interview nor
- Sell my credentials to an employer.

I didn't start Work Lessons 101 as a criticism of our education system; I founded it to share the work lessons I've learned from the first decade of my career that wasn't taught to me by the education system.

As I entered the second decade of my career, I came to a crossroads. Pursue the executive track and take a significant promotion leading a department team overseas or take a step back and start an organization that can help millions of aspiring professionals; I chose the latter. With the love of teaching, sharing my experiences and having a passion for mentoring, I founded Work Lessons 101, an organization that focuses on sharing experiences from the work environment by assisting, guiding and teaching people the essential work lessons to empower success in their careers.

My career started in Vancouver but has since taken me overseas, to several major cities and my Canadian corporate headquarters. Throughout all these journeys, I recorded my observations of the work environment, including life-changing conversations with supervisors, peers, and mentors; my own failures and mistakes; and those of others. Many of the lessons

I've learned are presented within this book. These are the lessons I wish I had known when I started my career.

Career's last decades and they don't become successful overnight or by accident. They take preparation, hard work, ability, patience and time. The road I've taken through my career has included: unexpected bumps, setbacks, and mistakes. Sometimes these obstacles sent me back a few steps, and sometimes they leapfrogged me forward. The question isn't whether you'll encounter setbacks in your career, but rather if you can prepare in advance, avoid the common setbacks you'll face early in your career, and prepare for the unexpected ones. Regardless of the bumps in the road, there are methods to better prepare yourself and navigate through smoother paths.

Many people struggle in progressing forward in the work environment, and I'm not surprised by these struggles. The old advice of work hard, put your head down, and you'll be promoted is terrible advice, and the education system has failed to adequately prepare students for their post-academic careers. Theory doesn't work by itself in an environment that requires you to be practical.

Work Lessons 101 provides practical advice and examples of how to:

- Learn an organization's unwritten rules,
- Manoeuvre around a bad boss,
- Build a bulletproof reputation, and
- Recognize and build an influential network that will help you.

This is the book they should be utilizing as a practical teaching guide within schools. It's applicable for students and career professionals who want the tools to launch successful careers. Graduates will face an uphill battle securing a position with the current employment climate. They don't need fluffy high-level sentiment; they need practical, no-nonsense career advice that will teach them how to create career opportunities and open their own doors.

Work Lessons 101 is dedicated to sharing the critical work lessons that they don't teach you in school.

Week 1 Theme: Be Selective in Choosing a Career

Careers can last decades.

At the start of your career, you'll be approximately 21 to 25 years old. You're most likely not married, have no children, and a mortgage. You may have a car and significant student loan, but for the most part, the people who depend on you will be at a minimum; this may be the best time in your life that you can genuinely be selfish and take on higher risk.

Choosing what you want to do in life is something that shouldn't be rushed. You should consider all your options and the benefits with each position before you make a final decision.

This is a time in your life when you can afford to be choosy, therefore, be selective.

Do you agree?

Work Lesson #1 – A job and career are not the same things; be mindful when you choose a job, thinking you can build a career. A career is the long game.

A job can be a stepping stone in your career. It can be temporary to gain specific skills necessary for your long-term goals.

A job and career can resemble each other, but they're not the same thing. A career can take years to build, while a job can serve an immediate purpose.

Ensure you have goals and a plan when you choose your first position.

What was your first position, and what impact has it had on your career?

Work Lesson #2 – Graduating is not about securing yourself a job right out of college; instead, think of building a career that can satisfy your passion and help you find your purpose. When selecting an employer, consider your long-term career goals and whether this organization can help you establish the steps to get you there.

Organizations usually take more than they give; you must think of yourself and your goals when selecting a position and career.

It's noble to think of your organization's needs, which will be necessary throughout your career, but you must do this within limits.

Don't sacrifice yourself, your dreams, your health, and your well-being for an organization that would not give you the same.

You must benefit from working at an organization. The relationship shouldn't be out of balance or one-sided.

If there is little benefit working at an organization, you should be looking for other alternatives.

Do you agree?

Work Lesson #3 – When selecting a position at an organization, always ask yourself:
- *Will you benefit from the position?*
- *Will you learn?*
- *Will you get closer to accomplishing your goals?*

If the answers are no, the position is, at best temporary.

Develop your check-ins and questions when making critical life decisions.

This is a method to ensure you're making the decision for the right reasons and thoroughly analyzing all the benefits associated with the decision.

What method do you use when making critical decisions?

Work Lesson #4 – *Do not assume that finding a job is all that matters, as long as you get a position, you will be fulfilled. This assumption is rarely the case. Do not make uninformed and rushed decisions about what you should be doing. Take the time to analyze what you want and prioritize the benefits.*

Choosing your career should not be rushed.

Choosing a career and what you want to spend most of your adult life pursuing is an important decision, and you'll need time to make this decision.

Important decisions should never be rushed or be emotionally compromised.

A clear mind and thorough analysis are required when making important, informed decisions.

Do you agree?

Work Lesson #5 – *The freedom you have at the start of your career may not be there in the future as your responsibilities, and financial commitments change. This may be a time when you can afford to be selective when choosing your future and take on higher risk.*

As you age, your responsibilities will increase; whether it has a spouse, children, mortgage, or aging parents, you may not have the same flexibility as you have in the early stages of your career.

You can probably take on higher risk with fewer consequences than in the future.

Take advantage of this flexibility and freedom.

What are your thoughts?

Work Lesson #6 – *Mistakes and failures are part of the learning process; you will make many, which is okay. The career game is built off of learning and progressing from your mistakes. Self-assess, learn, re-adjust, and move forward.*

No one is perfect, and we all make mistakes.

There is no possible way for each of us to understand everything we need to know in our careers. Accept the fact that regardless of the field you choose to enter, you will make mistakes.

Instead of avoiding risk, embrace the chance to learn and always conduct a proper assessment of your decisions. If you didn't get the results, you desired, instead of brushing this off, analyze and assess what you could have done differently to get a better result.

With successes, learn what worked and what didn't. Make assessing and analyzing your decisions, a daily hobby.

Do you agree?

Work Lesson #7 – *Short term career goals feed your long-term goals; these are the steps you climb to get to each floor in your skyscraper. Planning a strategy with proper set goals will assist you in achieving success; do not choose blindly.*

Careers take years to build and develop; they don't get made overnight...

Just like a skyscraper, it takes time for your career to take shape.

Plan your goals and list the accomplishments you want to earn. Use your short-term goals to feed your long-term career plan. Short-term goals are your stepping stones to the bigger picture of where you want to go in your career.

As you mature into your career, goals evolve, grow, and change; ensure you review your goals and career development plan regularly to guarantee you are executing your plan accordingly.

How do you establish your goals to have the most significant impact on your career?

Work Lesson #8 – Contemplate all your options when considering a position; evaluate your short- and long-term career goals and the benefits of the position before you accept it.

Before accepting a position, especially your first position, ensure you have adequately assessed the benefits and whether you can accomplish your goals within the position.

If you're accepting a position that doesn't fit your plan and doesn't offer the growth you require, it will be temporary.

Accepting a position, that you're aware of doesn't fit your career plan, and the benefits are few... don't get comfortable; if you stay and get locked into the simplicity of the position or money, this can end in regret.

Accept a job, if your immediate needs require you to, such as, the need to pay your bills, but don't settle if your goals are more prominent then this position can offer.

Do you agree?

Work Lesson #9 – Careers are journeys. They take planning and years to build. A foundation for a well-established skyscraper takes time to settle. You do not need to know it all or have all the answers. Plan and re-strategies when things do not work out; you cannot rush greatness.

Career development plans are always live.... They become outdated quickly.

Careers progress and move in directions and speeds that cannot always be predicted. Revisit your goals and career development plan regularly and pivot when required.

Sometimes your career will catapult, and sometimes you'll be given setbacks... the important lesson here, is you continue to move forward, whether it's a baby step or leap:

- Re-assess,
- Revisit and
- Re-strategies

Don't be scared with setbacks; every one of us will have career setbacks; this is normal, don't let it stop you from reaching your goals, ensure you learn from your mistakes and setbacks, and don't let it create unnecessary fear that can hurt you.

What do you do when you're given a setback?

Work Lesson #10 – *Careers are rarely a straight ladder with equal steps, instead they are a game of snakes and ladders; you will have leaps and setbacks in your career; ensure you keep rolling the dice.*

Your career can last over 40 years, a rather important decision to make at 22 years of age...

It's okay to make mistakes, just have the courage to restart.

Restarting takes courage; changing course takes courage.

When you're living your life and learning, you're progressing forward. You may not feel you're moving, but sometimes you must take a step back or make a lateral move to improve.

Like with snakes and ladders, you may be sent back 20 spots only to get a giant ladder on your next roll. Unlike the game, your role will be focused and planned; you won't rely on luck to get you through setbacks.

Use setbacks to re-focus yourself and learn the important lessons that will assist you in your career.

Stay determined to achieve your goals and make the necessary moves to continue to progress forward.

Do you agree?

Work Lesson #11 – *Will your career choice make you happy? Think of what is best for yourself when choosing a career. You must take full responsibility for your happiness.*

Your happiness is no one else's responsibility but your own.

Never depend on someone else to provide you happiness.

Have positive relationships in your life that contribute to your happiness but never delegate this responsibility away.

Choosing the right career for yourself can contribute significantly to your happiness... Choose the career you want that will add to your joy and help you feel fulfilled.

It may take a few restarts to find the right career, but when you find it, you'll know; it will fit.

Work Lesson #12 – *Selecting a career is a time to be selfish. Never rush in choosing a career that you think others want for you. This is your life, your time, your dreams, your happiness, and your choice. You sit in the driver seat; choose your road.*

You can spend over 70,000 hours of your life at work.

If given a choice, wouldn't you rather enjoy those hours and have them contribute to your happiness?

Well... the good news is... you have a choice; choose wisely, your happiness may just depend on it.

What are your thoughts? Do you agree?

Week 2 Theme: Pursue Your Passion to Find Your Purpose

Life is short.

Don't waste your precious time doing a job that doesn't fulfill you.

An average person works over 1,500 hours a year, which isn't counting commuting time. Approximately 25% of our year, we're either at work or commuting to and from work (at least 200 days a year, you spend part of your day at work).

Given that work falls for most people right smack in the middle of the day, the most productive hours of our day are spent at work.

If given a choice, wouldn't you rather spend that time on something you're passionate about, something that makes you want to get out of bed every morning?

Work Lesson #13 – Careers can last decades. If given a choice, wouldn't you rather do something you enjoy and find challenging? (Secret: You have a choice)

As we spoke in last week's theme, choosing a career for yourself is your responsibility. You're the one that will live with this decision; therefore, you should be the one making it.

Your happiness will likely be connected to your choice; therefore, choose wisely.

And if you choose incorrectly, dare to re-start and try again. You may need a few attempts to find your fit.

How many attempts did it take you?

Work Lesson #14 – *Think with the end in mind.*
- *What do you want to be thinking on the day you retire?*
- *What will you value on that day?*
- *What do you want to accomplish throughout your career?*
- *What will you want to leave behind when you are gone?*

Learn what you value and pursue it!

By thinking of what you want to be and what you want to accomplish by the end of your career, can help you choose wisely today.

Working backward can be an effective way of understanding what you value and what you ultimately want to accomplish throughout your career.

If you are stuck and unsure of what you want, ask yourself some of these questions, they may help you figure out your next move.

What questions do you ask yourself?

Work Lesson #15 – *Your career, your choice. Your life, your choice. You are the one that needs to live with the decisions you make; ensure they are your own.*

I have stated this a few times; what you choose to pursue for a career is your choice, and it's an important decision.

If you pursue a career to satisfy others, you may not be living the life you want and therefore, you may never reach the destiny you should have.

Don't be the person that dreads going to work every morning; if you aren't happy, dare to make the necessary changes.

Do you agree?

Work Lesson #16 – *A life with purpose is a life fulfilled.*

Choose your journey with self-awareness.

If you're not happy and fulfilled, make the necessary changes.

You never know how much time you will be given in life... living an unfulfilling life seems like a tremendous waste. Invest your time wisely.

What has given you fulfillment?

Work Lesson #17 – *An average person can spend approximately 50,000 – 70,000 hours at work throughout their life. Do you want to dedicate your time to someone else's dream? Or would you rather enjoy this time?*

Successful careers don't happen overnight, and they rarely occur without a plan and hard work.

We spend a lot of time at work; I'd rather enjoy this time.

Time is valuable, as we can never recover the time we have spent.

Make the right decisions for yourself today, so your time will be well spent throughout your career.

When you're starting in your career, think of the amount of time you will spend at work, wouldn't you rather enjoy this time?

Work Lesson #18 – *Given the amount of time you will spend pursuing your career, your happiness can be dependent on what you decide to dedicate your time to. Choose wisely and without fear.*

Pursuing a dream takes courage; don't allow fear to get the best of you. Choose the career you want.

If you choose to pursue a dream, my advice is to keep getting up and learning when you stumble. Failure is only permanent when you stop trying.

Do you agree?

Work Lesson #19 – *Find a career that makes you want to go to work every morning and build a life that makes you want to go home every night.*

I remember telling my future boss during my interview when asked what I wanted to get out of my career, and replied,

"Every morning, I want to wake up and be happy to go to work, and every evening I want to be happy to go home."

Fast forward, 13 years, and this statement is still valid. Given the amount of time I spend at work, work is a critical variable to my happiness.

Does work contribute to your happiness?

Work Lesson #20 – *Choose your career based on what you want to pursue and not merely what you're good at. Strengths are built with practice, hard work, and pure dedication to improving oneself.*

Many people choose their careers based on their strengths.

This may or may not be a wise decision; if you happen to enjoy a career that your strengths benefit, then this is ideal, but don't choose a career solely based on something you happen to be good at.

If you don't enjoy it, then don't pursue it.

When you enjoy doing something, you'll put the time into developing the skills, which will make you successful.

Do you agree?

Work Lesson #21 – *If you are trying to figure out what you want to do in your career, find out what you are passionate about. Then pursue that passion by putting together a career development plan and begin executing it.*

Make two lists:

- First, what you enjoy doing and
- Second, your strengths.

Analyze these lists and see if together, they can feed a career.

For example, you enjoy playing football and teaching; you're good at seeing your opponents' weaknesses, and developing exercise regimes… Potential careers from these two lists: Football coach, gym teacher, a Scout, etc.

Choosing a career isn't easy nor a quick process, you may even need to visit a career counselor for help.

Once you have an idea of what you may want to do, you'll need to develop a career development plan to ensure you gain the skills to be successful in your chosen field.

Being prepared with a career development plan will assist your overall success, as you'll have goals you want to accomplish and a plan to achieve them.

Do you have a Career Development Plan?

Work Lesson #22 – *If you have a plan, the drive, focus, and are willing to work harder than anyone else, success follows. Choose something you WANT and can see yourself doing; then put all your time, effort, and drive pursuing that goal and making it a reality.*

Career success doesn't happen overnight. It takes time, effort, help, and a great deal of planning.

Develop meaningful goals and a plan of how you'll achieve them.

Re-adjust when things don't work out or if priorities change.

Goals mature as you progress in your career, and therefore, so do career development plans.

Don't get discouraged when setbacks impact your career as this is part of the process.

Reaching a goal in the time you have allotted is not critical; what is vital is that you continue to move forward, allowing your goals to be achieved regardless of the timeframe.

What is your next milestone target?

Work Lesson #23 – As you progress in your career and learn more about what you want and enjoy, goals change, they mature and begin to take the form they should. You do not need to have all the answers today.

It's sporadic for a young aspiring professional to know what they want and how they will accomplish their goals.

You'll likely need help from peers and mentors along the journey.

You'll likely need additional experience that you'll gain as you mature through your career.

Be patient when you're gaining the necessary skills you require to be successful.

If you're entering new terrain and gaining new skills, you'll make mistakes. Take the time to learn the lesson and move forward.

What have you learned from a recent mistake?

Work Lesson #24 – Your parents, teachers, and friends don't always know the best career for you. Even the ones that love us are driven by their own motives and fears.

Sometimes the people who care about us, don't always know what's best for us.

Many parents want security for their children, to protect them from the hard life, this can make them blind and bias.

Chasing a dream takes courage; if you're chasing a dream that isn't supported by the ones who love you, then this takes a great deal of courage, as you may need to trek your journey without the support of the people who care the most about you.

This can be hard, and there aren't any great words I can offer. All I can say is, I had to do it myself for a time, and it wasn't easy, but it was necessary for my happiness and journey.

It is your life, and no one is entitled to live it but yourself.

Week 3 Theme: Do Not Postpone Pursuing Your Dreams

I met Tom at a career fair. We spoke for 30 minutes, and he left his resume with me. I gladly gave his resume to my boss.

Tom was full of life and an adventurer. He was the type of person never to waste a single night watching pointless television; he was always out in nature. Tom passed away in a rock-climbing accident in 2010.

I lost my neighbor in a vehicle accident. I cried for these friends and attended both of their funerals. Even though it's always a tragedy when a young person dies, a future that was not to be, I couldn't help but have a small smile at their funerals, as both these young men were living the life they dreamed of.

My neighbor was a talented musician and had a fantastic voice, one that will always sing on. He knew what he was going to be when he 'grew up'; he was working towards making his dream come alive. I know people who are twice the age of these men, who haven't lived nearly as fulfilling lives.

I learned from these two men that to never postpone fun, never to postpone working towards what you desire, that life is meant to be lived, by making your dreams come alive.

Are you working towards your dream?

Work Lesson #25 – "Nothing will ruin your 20's more than thinking you should have your life together already." – *Unknown*

Life is a journey filled with all types of days... the good, bad and ugly.

When you start in your career, be mindful that your plan is a guideline, as many variables may not work out the way you planned, this perfectly normal.

Many times, during my career, what I thought was a significant setback, was a hidden opportunity that catapulted me forward.

I remember working at the site in Mongolia and having the firewater system break down days before the government safety official was to visit and could shut down the entire plant... this got the attention of everyone at site, and everyone expected me to solve it, and you know what, I did!

This opened doors for me, but when the system first broke, I didn't know, I could solve it, I was scared.

During your career, your abilities will be tested; the fire system breaking was a test, I was put out of my comfort zone, and I stepped up and was rewarded.

Your career will present you with surprises... remember, sometimes you need to ride the wave.

Did your career face an early obstacle?

Work Lesson #26 – Careers are marathons... Most people cannot run 42 km without training; a career setback is simply a bad training day; start fresh tomorrow. Failure is only permanent when you stop trying.

Careers are marathons.

Some people may look like success has come easy, with a simple sprint, but this rarely happens.

Gaining experience and abilities takes time... Building your name and reputation takes time... It takes hard work, and many times, it takes more than one attempt.

If your first career development plan doesn't get you the promotion, you feel you deserve, analyze your results, and speak to peers and mentors. Conduct a proper assessment of your performance; maybe you missed something, or perhaps you were simply overlooked...

You'll have disappointments throughout your career; it won't always work out to your plan and schedule.

You'll need to learn from your mistakes, learn to re-adjust, learn to ask for help when needed, then move forward with the experience and lesson.

If you fall, keep getting up, keep learning and improving; if you build resilience and keep trying after adequately assessing your setbacks, you'll be successful throughout your career.

Do you agree?

Work Lesson #27 – *Not everyone has a tomorrow and gets to live out their bright future. You should spend the needed time preparing for your future but not always at the cost of today or at the expense of your youth. Learn the balance you need for your happiness.*

Many people have told me they wished they had worked harder in their twenties and had it more together.

On top of this, many people have also told me they wished they didn't buckle down so much in their twenties and enjoyed themselves more...

Career success will be in part to working hard and working smart; this is a guarantee; you'll need to work hard, but working hard doesn't always mean working endless hours and saying *"No"* to every party.

Learning what produces your best work, making you more productive, and learning what balance you want in your life will make you feel fulfilled and happy.

Don't worry too much when you start your career, that you need to have all the answers, and have it all figured out. As you gain experience, many of these answers will become clear.

Who was nervous on their first day?

Work Lesson #28 – *Following your passion and dreams takes courage, especially if it goes against the current of the river. It is easier to settle for the 'normal' life, be strong, and don't give in to the pressure of taking the 'safe' route. There is nothing glorious about unhappiness.*

Many people settle for the safe route or what they have always known.

They're too scared to pursue a dream, in case they fail and lose it; therefore, they don't branch out of their comfort zone.

When choosing a career, consider the length and amount of time, you'll spend pursuing this career. Does the thought exhaust you? If it does, this isn't a positive sign.

You should feel excited about planning and preparing for your career.

Do your dreams make you feel excited? If yes, then put a plan together and begin to execute it.

If you fear failing and losing your dreams forever, remember that you have lost them by default by not trying.

By trying, you may not reach them, but you'll learn along the journey, and I believe losing your dreams, is better than living in their shadow.

Do you agree?

Work Lesson #29 – *Use your youth, energy, and time to pursue PLAN A.*

Thinking of your future and career should make you smile, not create anxiety or stress.

Stress is a sign; you may not be pursuing your correct path; never ignore how you feel, especially when it comes to essential and time-consuming decisions.

The significant advantage you have at the start of your career is time.

You have time to gain the abilities to make you successful; you have the time to invest correctly and have the time to fail and start again with little consequence.

YOU HAVE TIME.

This is the time in your life that you should pursue what you want; go after Plan A. You can develop a Plan B or Plan C later.

Are you pursuing Plan A?

Work Lesson #30 – Recognize the signs when you are overly stressed, near burn out, or any other negative feeling. Your mind and body are trying to communicate with you. This may be a sign you are chasing the wrong path.

Your body is telling you how you truly feel, don't ignore these feelings under any circumstance.

Prolonged stress can damage and hurt you, not just your physical health but your mental well-being.

Unfulfilling careers can cause additional stress in your life and impact what you value the most.

What are your best tactics in dealing with stress?

Work Lesson #31 – Never postpone working towards your dreams and making time for what you value. Even if it's only a few hours a week, keep working towards your goals and dreams. A few hours a week is better than delaying and doing nothing because, as the years add up, nothing will still be nothing.

I had said goodbye to several friends before I reached my 30th birthday; you never really know how much time you have.

Many people aren't fortunate enough to live their bright future, so I believe TIME is our greatest possession.

Once a minute is gone, it can never be regained, even money, which has a set value, can always be re-earned.

The one thing money and time have in common, they're only as valuable, as we allow them to have and many people, especially if we break down our day to day schedules, prioritize money above time.

<u>For example</u>, *"I can go to the gym tomorrow, once I get this proposal out,"* or *"I can see my son's baseball game next week, I need to get this presentation done."*

On a day to day and week to week schedule, you may not see how you prioritize your life, but as the years go by, our misuse of our time can end up being our greatest regret.

Regardless of how busy you are, don't postpone what you value.

Take the trip you always wanted, say I love you when you feel it, write the book you imagined, stop postponing doing something that can make you happy in sacrifice for what you think you should be doing today.

What do you value above all else?

Work Lesson #32 – You will sacrifice weekends to build your dreams, and you will probably not mind. Time spent living someone else's dream can become a chore and won't end in fulfillment.

It always amazes me when I speak to happy people, especially those building towards their dreams, how they don't mind working the weekends, and many do this for free, knowing their hard work will pay off in the future.

As I have learned by building my own company, when you love what you're doing, you can work around the clock and still not feel tired.

Take these same people and put them in a career they don't want; they know exactly how much they make an hour, and they generally don't work overtime without being paid, and sometimes even paid overtime won't get them to give up their weekend.

As you start in your career, if you're finding yourself living for the weekend, you should question what you're doing and if this is indeed the right career for you. Don't waste your time doing something that doesn't make you feel fulfilled.

Have you ever worked for free? If yes, why did you? If No, why not?

Work Lesson #33 – Spend time at the start of your career to truly connect with your peers. They will follow their paths, move on to different organizations, potentially become high-level influencers, and contribute to your expanding network.

When you start your career, spend time building strong, trusting relationships with your peers.

Enjoy happy hour, plan activities together on the weekend; try to connect with your peers outside of work.

You tend to have more time at the beginning of your career before your work and life responsibilities increase. I say to do this at the beginning of your career, not merely because you tend to have more time but because your peers will disband and eventually move on to different organizations and industries.

If you've built trust with this group of people, many of them may become part of your inner circle, which is the heart of your network. The others can contribute to your business reach, which will make your network more effective.

With trusted colleagues, not only do you have access to your network, but you also have access to theirs.

Networks are like spiderwebs; every connection and ring increases your reach. Strong built networks are influential and expand to cover great regions.

Start from day one of your career to build your network, and this starts with your peers.

How did you build your network?

Work Lesson #34 – *Some of the most impactful and career-changing friendships occur when you are not looking or thinking of your career.*

I remember meeting the most influential mentor of my career; frankly, I didn't like him; I thought he was all business and had no interest in learning what I wanted and the person I was.

Well, I could not have been more wrong about this person.

At an after-work function, we got talking, and the conversation went on for hours; we spoke work for a bit, then got into sports, our dreams, and families.

By the end of the evening, I had a new friend; by the end of the year, I had the greatest mentor of my career. He brought out abilities in me that I didn't even knew existed; he got me to believe in myself and job shadowed me for months till I took over his position when he moved on. This all occurred because I got to know him, the real him. We connected.

Many of the most significant friendships and mentorships form organically and not under the official title of *'mentor.'*

Some of the most impactful relationships you'll develop in your career, may not happen during working hours.

How has a mentor impacted your career?

Work Lesson #35 — *Remaining Open Minded can influence your perspective of life, and the younger you are, the more impact it will have on your growth and future.*

Be open-minded throughout your entire career; this means you're adaptable and flexible.

Generally, as careers progress and we age, many people stop questioning the status quo, and their learning curve begins to plateau.

Don't allow this to happen to yourself; never get comfortable.

Remaining open-minded can influence our perspective and how we see everything from our work, our position in an organization, and our dreams.

Never settle and think you know it all; continue to question and learn.

Work Lesson #36 — *Learning who you are, becoming self-aware, and living your life, is never time wasted. Self-awareness is critical to career and life success. Spend time developing your self-awareness.*

Lack of self-awareness is one of the biggest culprits in poor leadership. Nearly everything stems from being aware:

- Awareness of your actions...
- Aware of how you make others feel...
- Awareness of your weaknesses and strengths...

Without accurate self-awareness, you'll never understand how you make others feel, and you'll never truly understand the critical feedback people give you so you can improve.

Without self-awareness, you'll have a harder time learning from your mistakes.

Do you believe self-awareness is essential in establishing a long successful career?

Week 4 Theme: Don't Assume Education Guarantees Success

Aspiring professionals entering the workforce can be discouraged when they learn how little the Corporate environment values their education.

Many times, a degree is simply a checkmark on a recruiter checklist that gets you in the door at an Organization.

Don't get me wrong; getting in the door is essential; it's the first step; just don't expect it to be recognized much after you're hired.

Most young professionals have a degree; therefore, it's not a differentiator; it's ground zero.

Your career skyscraper will be built by delivering on your commitments and acquiring high-quality tangible results that benefit your organization.

How much of your degree have you used during your career?

Work Lesson #37 – Having higher education doesn't mean you are adaptable. Being open-minded, flexible, and having the right attitude will help you create more opportunities in your career than relying on your education.

A degree rarely creates opportunities within an Organization; many times, it helps get you in the door, but once you're in, it has served its purpose.

Once you're hired, your resume needs to correlate to earnings and bringing value to your Clients, Customers, Team, and Organization.

Your boss will most likely not care about your education; they'll care about how good you are at your job.

The best employees can usually fill several roles by being adaptable. Being adaptable requires you to be open-minded and flexible.

The more flexible you are, the more roles you can do, and therefore, you'll acquire additional skills quicker, making your learning exponential.

The more skills you gain, the more value you can bring your organization.

Do you agree?

Work Lesson #38 – An education will not guarantee that you will be good at your job nor a good employee.

Many professions require a different skill set then school.

Being a good student doesn't necessarily correlate to being a good employee.

In the work environment, many times, there is no obvious path to the correct answer; it's not a physics problem that has a set number of steps to get to the one right answer.

Many times, in the professional environment, you need to discover the right questions, but there can be several answers and paths of discovery.

Employees that can bring value to their organizations, by solving difficult problems, will go further in their careers than a fancy education.

Do you agree?

Work Lesson #39 – There is no one defined path to career success. The equation is long and has many unpredictable variables.

Many variables contribute to a successful career; the equation can resemble many variations.

The path to career success is your journey, therefore be careful if you compare it to others.

If your peer wants to be a CEO and you want to remain in middle management, there is little value in comparing your progression with them. Your peer is most likely willing to make sacrifices that you simply aren't, and this is fine.

If you've spent the time planning and establishing your goals, you know roughly the steps and skills you need to complete to get there.

These steps and skills will become your variables and will feed the three significant variables that contribute to all successful careers: credibility, reputation, and network.

Building skills will establish your credibility, which will directly feed your reputation and build a sellable professional name for you.

A strong reputation will help build an influential network, as people will learn who you are.

What variables have contributed to your career success?

Work Lesson #40 – Finishing a degree may be a great personal achievement, but it means very little to recruiters and your organization. The minute you walk into a company's door on your first day is what you will be evaluated from there onwards.

Graduating from University can be your first step in your career achievements but recognize this as a first step; it will likely not mean a great deal once you start working.

I took nine credits of calculus during my education and used it once in 8 years while I was a practicing engineer.

Education helped me in specific ways in my career, but it didn't differentiate me from my competition (nearly everyone at my company is an engineer).

I differentiated myself by getting consistent, high-quality results. I delivered on every one of my commitments and responsibilities; by doing this, I gained skills exponentially while I built my reputation as a professional who delivers tangible results.

Delivering on my commitments, while I learned and gained skills, is the formula that helped me stand out from the crowd and get my organization's attention.

What got you noticed by your organization?

Work Lesson #41 – *Most career success will come from obtaining these critical variables: Gaining experience, getting results, being adaptable, being self-aware, being open-minded, establishing your credibility, building your reputation, building an influential network and securing strong mentors.*

Great leaders have many variables in their success equation, but they all at a minimum have:

- Self-awareness,
- Open-minded and
- Adaptable.

When you have all three of these traits, it means you learn from others and your mistakes.

When you continue to learn, you continue to improve, and when you continue to improve, you don't plateau. When you don't plateau, the sky is the limit to your success.

You'll continue to grow, and this growth can be exponential, it does not need to stop.

Do you think there are people who never plateau?

Work Lesson #42 – *When entering the workforce, ensure your expectations are realistic. Nothing will disengage a recruiter more than misinformed and entitled candidates. Research your industry and potential employer.*

When you first enter the workforce, you're untrained and have zero to little work experience.

You won't make a six-figure salary in your first year of employment unless you have a unique skill or are under strenuous working conditions.

When you enter the workforce, you haven't brought value to the company that has hired you, such as:

- Developed a new product or earned the company money.

You'll prove your ability and build your creditability by getting results and bringing value to your company.

Do you agree?

Work Lesson #43 – *Most young candidates entering the workforce are untrained and have little experience. An employer doesn't truly care about your degree; it's normally a checkmark to get you in the door. What they will care about is what value you can bring to their organization.*

When you start your first position after graduating, learn what business drivers your organization values, then go out and obtain them.

Bringing value to your organization will be the safest route to securing recognition and differentiating yourself from your peers; don't rely on your education to be a differentiator.

Work Lesson #44 – *When you enter the workforce, the young professionals who will increase their chances of succeeding will quickly learn to get the right experience, and results are far more important than education.*

Observe the employees, who climb the corporate ladder, and you'll quickly detect that education plays a minimal part in one's career success.

Learn what drives the business of your organization and obtain it.

Whether it's a new Client, a new account, or a new product, by obtaining it, you bring value to your organization, which will be critical in your career success.

Do you agree?

Work Lesson #45 – *Before you think a degree is a be-all, end-all, think… What does a degree tell a recruiter? Ensure you prepare appropriately for your interview, where you can truly differentiate yourself from your competition.*

A degree to some extent is a checkmark on a recruiter's checklist; it doesn't tell them a great deal about you.

It allows them to have a rough idea of your IQ and tells them you have completed something…

But to truly differentiate yourself, you'll need to have an effective resume and prepare properly, if you get an interview.

Sometimes the best candidate doesn't get the position; sometimes, it goes to the person who prepared and sold themselves the best.

How do you prepare for an interview?

Work Lesson #46 – *An effectively written resume and properly prepared interview can impress a recruiter far more than a fancy education. A degree rarely sells; it is YOU that sells your credentials.*

You differentiate yourself by showing and highlighting your accomplishments.

Link your accomplishments to the organization's business drivers to be effective.

If a Core Value of a company is Leadership, then highlight how you are a leader in your resume and discuss a situation, which amplifies leadership qualities in your interview.

Allow the recruiter or human resource representative to witness how you fit the company culture by aligning with their values.

Do you agree?

Work Lesson #47 – *Gathering and passing on information are different than gaining knowledge. Knowledge comes from both experience and information.*

As you enter your career, you're most likely untrained.

Degrees can help you in information-based industries but struggle to transfer applicable skillsets to many sectors; most of these skill sets you'll need to gain through experience.

If you lack experience, as you enter your career, this is ok, as no one expects you to have a tone of experience.

Your organization will expect you to ask lots of questions and learn quickly, then obtain results with these learnings.

Do you agree that experience is the best education?

Work Lesson #48 – *Nearly everyone hired by Fortune 500 Corporations has a degree; therefore, a degree will not differentiate you from the competition. Quality results will distinguish you, thus, get them often.*

When you enter the workforce, the young aspiring professionals, who will increase their chances of succeeding, will quickly learn to get the right experience, and high-quality results will differentiate themselves from their colleagues.

A degree can get you in the door at an organization, but that is generally all it does.

Get results and get them often!

Week 5 Theme: Have an Effective Resume & Be Prepared for an Interview

If you want career opportunities, especially opportunities you're not aware of, best to be prepared.

To be prepared for the unexpected, best to be overly prepared, and part of being overly prepared for your future career is to be able to sell yourself.

Part of selling yourself is having an up-to-date and effective resume, highlighting all your accomplishments.

Having an effective resume will assist in securing a job interview.

Once you have a job interview, preparing thoroughly for the interview will help you turn a job interview into a job offer; this week's theme will help you do this.

Do you agree that your resume must highlight your accomplishments first and not just your responsibilities?

Work Lesson #49 – Effective and sellable resumes highlight your accomplishments, not your responsibilities and duties.

When I worked in Business Development, I read countless resumes and nearly every resume that I reviewed, fell into the trap of highlighting their responsibilities and duties, instead of their accomplishments.

Your responsibilities and duties are your daily tasks that nearly everyone does.

You need to have your responsibilities in your resume; just ensure your accomplishments are there and stand out.

Accomplishments can vary from personal to professional.

A personal accomplishment or achievement could be a prestigious award you won, such as a scholarship or sporting trophy (e.g., MVP).

A professional accomplishment can be quantitative results you delivered, such as: Led the project under budget and saved our Client 2 million dollars.

You want your resume to be full of accomplishments, to assist in differentiating yourself from your competition.

Do you agree?

Work Lesson #50 – You must create differentiation throughout your entire career; it is your responsibility to sell your credentials to an employer or recruiter.

Differentiating yourself from your competition will first start with your resume.

Learn to highlight the right qualifications to differentiate yourself from your competition.

List your accomplishments throughout your entire resume, especially in your Executive Summary.

Many Human Resource staff won't read past your Executive Summary if it doesn't have anything unique.

Ensure you put something to grab their attention and then lay out all the accomplishments you have earned in each position.

By doing this, you'll create a common theme regarding yourself, that you bring value to anything and everything you do.

Do you agree?

Work Lesson #51 – *When you list your accomplishments and achievements in your resume, give specific details such as quantities and percentages. Specifically, it allows others to quantify your results and understand the value you brought to your role.*

Be specific, which one is more effective?

- Wrote a weekly blog for three years, or
- Wrote a weekly career development blog for three years that grew to have 1,200 hundred subscribers. Each blog entry got an average of 4,000 reads, 145 likes, and 40 comments.

The more accomplishments you list throughout your resume, the employer will begin to see a common theme: having you on the team, you will bring value to their Company.

Do you agree?

Work Lesson #52 – *Your resume can be your first impression to a future employer. Make it a strong and lasting one.*

Never underestimate the power and lasting impact of a first impression.

Many employers and recruiters don't know you; your resume may be the first thing they see regarding who you are; therefore, have a resume listing your accomplishments and credentials, highlighting why you're the best candidate for the position.

The best candidate doesn't always get the interview; the candidates who sold themselves effectively gets the interview.

Do you agree?

Work Lesson #53 – *An effective and sellable resume that attracts attention is an integral part of getting an interview.*

To secure an interview, you must have a well written and effective resume, highlighting the credentials the employer is looking for.

By listing accomplishments throughout your entire resume that apply to the position, you'll indirectly amplify the value you can bring to their organization.

No interviewer wants to interview dozens of candidates, make their job easier by having an effective and up-to-date resume, so they chose you.

Do you agree?

Work Lesson #54 – *A resume is not a time to be humble; an employer does not know you. They will learn this in your interview, but you first must secure an interview, therefore, brag a little.*

For your resume, this isn't the time to be humble, Albert Einstein could afford to be humble, for the rest of us mere mortals, we need to brag a little.

An employer doesn't know your hard-working and kind nature; they don't know your great personality.

They will learn all this in your interview after you sell yourself through your resume.

Spend the time and write an effective resume that differentiates you from the crowd.

The top and most qualified candidates may not get an interview, as they did not sell themselves the most effectively.

What accomplishments do you highlight to differentiate yourself?

Work Lesson #55 – *To turn a job interview into a job offer, best to be prepared. Learn absolutely everything you can about the Company and person interviewing you.*

Being prepared is the best tool you can have going into an interview.

Learning everything you can regarding your potential employer can assist in asking better questions and help you come off more naturally in your responses during the interview.

Preparing ahead of time can help remove nerves, so you don't spend the first few minutes of your interview warming up.

No runner enters a race without warming up ahead of time, and neither should you.

Ensure you have practiced and prepared ahead of time; you want to make a strong first impression. Enter your interview, ready to run the race.

How do you warm-up for an Interview?

Work Lesson #56 – *It is normal to be nervous, going into a job interview. Being prepared will assist in keeping these nerves under control.*

Most people are nervous about entering a job interview, which doesn't always lessen as you gain experience.

To help reduce your nerves, prepare thoroughly for the job interview, this will increase your confidence, and mitigate potential unforeseen questions the interviewer may ask.

Learn everything you can about the organization and their businesses; this will assist you in asking intelligent questions during the interview and show the interviewer of your general interest in the Company.

What's your go-to interview question?

Work Lesson #57 – *It is your job during an interview to sell your qualifications, skills, experience, and knowledge to the interviewer.*

It's your job to turn your interview into a job offer.

You do this by showing them that you'll be a suitable candidate for their organization; that you have the right attitude and motivation to fit their company culture.

Do you agree?

Work Lesson #58 – *Never interrupt an interviewer. Do not assume you know the question they are going to ask. Wait till they finish before you respond. Never be too eager to impress. Maturity is shown through patience.*

You may be nervous during your interview, but hopefully, you've thoroughly prepared, and therefore, can have more control over your emotions.

During your interview, be mindful of how fast you speak, the tone you use to convey your responses, and your body language.

Speak confidently in your responses; your tone should be positive, and body relaxed. Your voice will be more relaxed if your body is.

Don't interrupt the interviewer. Wait till the interviewer has stopped speaking before you respond.

If you're going to make multiple points that are not related to an interviewer's question, ask them if your response answered their question before you continue onto a different topic.

Work Lesson #59 – *Always bring supporting material to your interview. This can include extra copies of your resume, written references, transcripts, a sample of your writing capabilities, and any work portfolios that may be relevant to the position.*

Being prepared amplifies that you're professional and want the position.

Bring two sets of all supporting material, in case there is more than one interviewer.

Being extra prepared will assist in you standing out from your competition.

Do you agree?

Work Lesson #60 – *Steps in preparing for an interview:*
1) *Research the Company*
2) *Practice potential questions and responses*
3) *Prepare questions for the interviewer*
4) *Research salary expectations in advance*
5) *Perfect your verbal and non-verbal communication*
6) *Dress appropriately for your Industry*
7) *Bring supporting material with you*
8) *Send post-interview thank you*

If you follow these eight steps, your confidence will increase, and your nerves will reduce during the interview.

You've prepared questions, and you know how you'll answer potential questions that arise during the interview.

All this preparation will assist in standing out from less-prepared candidates.

How do you prepare for an Interview?

Week 6 Theme: Building Your Financial Future

You may be wondering why you need to be thinking about saving when you have no money?

You have recently finished college; you're most likely in debt and have little to no savings.

This is precisely why you need to learn basic financial terminology, understand the basics of investing your money, and know the worst kinds of debt.

The most significant gift you have is TIME.

You have the time to learn where to invest your money and the time to use the basic rules of compound interest to benefit your future.

This theme serves as an introduction to basic financial knowledge; it doesn't serve as an education in building an investment portfolio.

Work Lesson #61 – *Start saving for your future with your first paycheck, use compound interest to benefit you.*

Time is a gift when applied to compound interest.

It's simple when you're young; you have time to save money before you retire (Approximately 30 to 40 years).

To show why you should do this:

You're 22 years old and started your first position; you'll plan on retiring at the age of 55.

Assuming you can put away $4,160 every year for the next 33 years ($4,160 over 52 weeks is $80/week).

After 33 years with an Annual Percentage Rate (APR) of 8%, your savings will be $655,727.

If you wait five years till you're 27 years old to start saving and do the same amount, $4,160 every year for 28 years and retire at 55, your savings will be $428,338; a difference of $227,389 solely due to starting five years later.

Use compound interest to benefit your future.

Do you regret not saving earlier for your retirement?

Work Lesson #62 – *Utilize the time you have in your youth to learn where to invest your money.*

Capitalizing on your financial education when you're young is a wise investment that will benefit you and work in your favour, for the rest of your life.

Read books, speak to a financial advisor, and learn from others who have invested. Learn what worked and what didn't from them.

When you're learning, there is no such thing as useless information. Learning what worked and what didn't for people is useful information that can benefit you and increase your learning.

You may have no money at the start of your career to make significant investments, which is why it's the perfect time to learn where to invest.

Eventually, you'll have the money, and it would be ideal to have the proper knowledge along with the money to make wise investments.

If your formal education didn't teach you how to invest, ensure you put the time aside to educate yourself.

Did your education provide you with investment knowledge, or did you need to teach yourself?

Work Lesson #63 – *Create a budget plan, know how much money is coming in, and what's going out. There should be no surprises when it comes to your budget.*

When you start making an income, you should create a monthly budget plan to track the money coming in and the money going out.

When you're interviewing for your first position, you need to understand how much money you require to pay all your bills. Once you start and understand what you'll be earning with each paycheck, you should finalize your budget, including all loans, expenses, and bills.

The purpose of a budget plan is to understand where all your money is coming from and how much money you can be putting into savings and investments.

Do you agree?

Work Lesson #64 – *By having a current budget plan, you know the amount of money you have at your disposal, in case an unexpected opportunity arises.*

By knowing exactly how much money you have at your disposal allows you to take advantage of financial opportunities that arise.

I was two years into my career when the financial collapsed happened in late 2008.

This collapse crippled many industries and blue-chip corporations. In January 2009, many large Corporations shares such as Apple, and Starbucks were at an abnormally low price.

The young investors that had money saved were able to take advantage of these temporary decreases in share values.

Early 2009 was the rainy day we save our money for.

Are you saving for a rainy day?

Work Lesson #65 – *When you start your career, sit down with a financial advisor. Review your budget plan and work out where you can put your money to invest in your future.*

Part of learning is to seek knowledge from those who are more experienced then you are.

Discussing your future with a financial advisor is recommended before you make any significant investment decisions.

An advisor can help you know what type of retirement you want to have and how much money you need to save to ensure you get what you want.

It's recommended to meet with multiple financial advisors before choosing one, especially if you're not sure what you want.

By meeting with multiple advisors, will allow you to learn more and to have a better understanding of your options.

When choosing an advisor, ask them the hard questions and don't worry about offending them; this is your future, and you need to make informed decisions.

If you're not sure, ask, and learn. Do you agree?

Work Lesson #66 – *Debt should concern you; it's a trap. Avoid it at all costs.*

You generally don't want to go into debt building investments. When it comes to debt, the safest route to take is to avoid it at all costs.

If your financial education is minimal, this will be a safer stance to take. If you do go into debt for an investment, ensure you have done your research thoroughly.

Just like compound interest can benefit you for your retirement, it can also be a determent when applied to your debt.

For example, if your credit card has an annual percentage rate (APR) 18%, it will have a daily rate of 0.049315% (The APR rate divided by 365 days in a year).

With a cardholder balance of $1,000 at the 18% APR standard interest rate, the next day, interest has been added, and the balance will become $1,000.49, plus any additional purchases and minus any new credits or payments.

This process will occur each day until the end of the cardholder's monthly statement cycle.

To recap, at the end of the month, the beginning $1,000 balance becomes $1015 when interest charges are applied at 18% APR ($1,000 * 0.049315% * 30 days).

Based on your original balance of $1,000 and a minimum payment of $20 a month, assuming no additional purchases, it will take a cardholder 94 months to pay off the balance, including paying an extra $862 in interest.

Be mindful always to pay off your balance every month. Don't make unnecessary purchases you cannot afford, allowing your credit card interest rate to compound.

Work Lesson #67 – Always weigh the benefits versus the risk. Generally, higher risk, greater reward. If it's high risk with low reward, walk away.

Make calculated risks, use your instincts, and ensure you complete the smell-test if something seems too good to be true, it generally is.

General rules of thumb:

- High risk – high reward,
- Low risk – low reward.

If something is low risk, high reward, ensure you've thoroughly investigated, as these opportunities are rare and maybe a pyramid scam.

You always need to investigate where your money is going; this isn't a time to be lazy, ensure you've done your dual diligence.

If something is high risk, low reward, always walk away.

What's your most significant financial success?

Work Lesson #68 – All high-risk investments (e.g., Career or Financial) should produce great rewards if successful.

Walk away from the situations that are not worth your precious time.

As discussed in my earlier post, if something is high risk, low reward, always walk away.

Many things in life are risky, don't increase this, by choosing poor investments and chasing the wrong things.

You'll make mistakes throughout your entire life; walking away from high-risk/low-reward situations will help you reduce unnecessary risks from your life.

Do you agree?

Work Lesson #69 – There is no shame in walking away, as long as you are doing it for the right reasons. Fear of the unknown or fear of failure aren't good reasons.

Walking away from an opportunity, out of fear, can often lead to future regret.

There is nothing wrong with walking away from a situation or offer, after you've investigated the pros and cons, and have made an informed decision that something is not for you.

Not everything presented, you will want or have the time for, just ensure if anything appears to be an opportunity. Often opportunities are disguised as obstacles that you've given the situation proper attention before you walk away or pass it up.

Why have you walked away from something in the past?

Work Lesson #70 – Reasons to walk away:
- *Creates an unhealthy habit and lifestyle*
- *Absolutely zero benefit to you*
- *You have deemed the sacrifice or risk as too severe for the reward*

As discussed in my earlier post, walking away from an opportunity out of fear can often lead to future regret.

There are many reasons you should walk away from an offer or situation.

Anything that has a significant negative impact on your happiness and health is usually indicators you should move on; this can be an unhealthy work environment or relationship.

Your health is a top priority, as you're no use to anyone if you're sick. You must always take care of yourself.

Other critical reasons to walk away: If what is being offered to you has no benefit or the benefits are minimal, that the effort doesn't justify the time required.

Do you agree?

Work Lesson #71 – Purchase what you need, not what you want. Learn the difference between a need and a want.

When I was in my twenties, I was broke, along with most of my peers.

As we entered our thirties, the people who invested and made wise purchasing decisions were considerably financially ahead.

Upon reviewing why some of us were further ahead, there were several reasons such as career, annual income, timing on investments, etc.

But the one standard variable between the ones who had substantial savings and a robust investment portfolio and the ones who didn't were the people who purchased what they wanted instead of what they needed.

<u>For example</u>:

I want a four-bedroom house with three garages to park my luxury cars; I need a home for shelter.

I want a Starbucks coffee instead of making one at home.

I want a BMW when a Ford would suffice.

Making wise financial decisions can impact your financial future.

Five dollars a day at Starbucks can add up to over $1,000 a year and be invested or saved for a down payment.

Buying a house that takes over 50% of your household income versus a home that takes up 30%, that difference of 20% a month, can go towards diversifying your investment portfolio and lower your overall financial risk; as well as, you'll pay less money in interest.

Do you agree?

Work Lesson #72 – Questioning is a healthy habit to accustom yourself with. Learning what doesn't work for you is as valuable as learning what does.

Learning what works for you and what doesn't, requires you to try new things and requires you to question yourself.

If an opportunity is presented to you and your immediate response is *'fight or flight,'* you should analyze and question why this occurred.

Many career successes and our greatest growth occur when we leave our comfort zone and take on challenges.

This same process should be used with your investments. You should trust your instincts but not blindly, learn why some risks you flee from and why certain investments you jump at.

Learn what risks you're comfortable in taking and learn what doesn't work for you.

Being consciously aware of your decisions is critical, so you know exactly why you're making the decisions you are.

Do you agree?

Week 7 Theme: Have both Short- & Long-Term Career Goals

This week, I'll discuss how Goals can help measure where you are in your career and show that you're going in the direction you desire.

At the beginning of your career, spend some time thinking about where you want your career to go, the path you desire to travel.

Then put together a career development plan with targeted goals; these goals will serve as stepping stones to accomplish your career aspirations.

Work Lesson #73 – What do YOU want from your career? A question that must be answered before truthful and realistic goals can be established.

Never lie in answering questions that can impact your destiny and happiness, as they can hurt you and your future.

What you want to accomplish in your career is an important question that requires you to be honest in your answer.

If you're dishonest, you're more likely to travel down the wrong path.

If you begin to be dishonest with yourself, not only are you more likely to make poor decisions of where and how you spend your time, but it will most likely not result in fulfillment.

When determining career goals, be honest and realistic in establishing targets, so you can have check-in points, to ensure you are on your desired path.

Do you set career goals for yourself?

Work Lesson #74 – *Goals help you measure progress in your career. They are check-in points; without them, you pose the risk of trekking the wrong path.*

When establishing and developing goals, choose check-in points to ensure you're not straying off course.

The path to accomplishing your goals can take many routes. Deviate and pivot when required; goals mature and develop as you progress through your career as priorities change.

Well established check-in targets will assist in measuring your progress and whether a change is required to keep you on course.

Do you set check-in targets when assessing the path to your goals?

Work Lesson #75 – *Goals assist us in positioning our efforts to hit correct targets, ensuring we are spending our time productively to reach each career milestone.*

If you start your career without having short- and long-term goals:

- How will you measure your progress?
- How will you know if you're on the correct path?
- How will you know you're using your time productively?

Goals can help gauge where you are in your career and show you that you're going in the direction you desire.

Goals are the map and your steer the vehicle.

Do you agree?

Work Lesson #76 – *Having short and long-term career goals will assist in creating an accurate and realistic career development plan.*

Your career development plan (CDP) will address the critical questions you need to answer to achieve your career goals.

Properly developed goals feed a full CDP.

Your CDP will address where you want to be in your career at certain milestones:

- 1-year,
- 2-year,
- 5-year etc.

And what skills you will need to develop to achieve these career milestones.

If you don't have a Career Development Plan, start today!

Work Lesson #77 – *Your career development plan will address the who, what, when, where, why, and how to achieve your career goals.*

Questions to address in your Career Development Plan (at a minimum):

- Where do you want to be in 1 year, 2 years, 5 years, 10 years?
- Why do you want to be there?
- What motivates you about these career goals?
- What skills and knowledge gaps will you need to develop to reach your desired position?
- How will you gain the skills, knowledge, and experience to reach your goals?
- Who are the people that you need on your side to help get you there?
- What relationship do you need to build?
- By what time do you need to develop these relationships by?

Work Lesson #78 – *Knowing who you need to impress with your skills and ability is a massive part of being offered career opportunities that can be categorized as game-changers.*

Understanding why you want to accomplish a goal and whom you need to impress to reach your goals is critical information to acquire.

Many career game-changers come from being offered stretch assignments. Stretch assignments come from two methods:

- From requesting one, or
- From being offered one.

Developing your skills will boost your ability to perform more demanding roles and tasks.

By being organized with a detailed career development plan, you'll know what skills you need to develop; and you'll see whom you need to impress with these newly acquired skills.

With these two pieces of information, you can develop a strategy to ensure you're visible to these influential people.

Do you agree?

Work Lesson #79 – *Knowing your options within an organization is important in understanding the potential opportunities available to you.*

Many Organizations offer multiple career paths, such as:

- Finance
- Business Development
- Operations

Typically, larger companies offer more options.

When choosing an Organization, research what career options they have to offer and the growth potential you'll be exposed too; ensure they align with your career goals.

How many career paths have you taken in your career?

Work Lesson #80 – *Setbacks will happen throughout your entire career, do not be discouraged. Learn, re-adjust your goals, targets, and push forward. Setbacks are a huge part of success.*

Goals are designed to change and re-adjust as environments and prioritises evolve.

As you mature through your career, what you once wanted may not be what you want now.

Work experience will help you narrow down the career path you want, and your goals will become refined.

When I first started my career, I wanted to be an Engineering Lead. That was my first 10-year goal; when I accomplished it at year six, my sights grew to bigger and more ambitious goals.

Eventually, I moved into Project Management, which wasn't even on the radar for my career ambitions, till year seven of my career.

As you progress through your career, setbacks will occur. Everyone makes mistakes; learn from them and re-adjust if required, then move forward with the learned knowledge.

Setbacks are a massive part of success, as you tend to learn your greatest lessons when things don't work out ideally.

Embrace career challenges; they will make you better.

Work Lesson #81 – *Experts have become experts because they have practiced, set-targeted goals and prepared. There is no winging it. Never rush your Career Development planning; this is time well spent. Countless hours of preparation have gone into making something look 'effortless.'*

It takes time to become an Expert. Even if you don't want to be an Expert, it takes time to become good.

You'll need to be patient throughout your career, not everything you want will work out ideally or to your plan. You'll need to re-adjust when setbacks occur.

If you prepare and plan, this will assist in avoiding and maneuvering around some obstacles, but there will be those that are unforeseen; and you'll need to be patient and re-adjust if required.

If you think the best specialists in their chosen profession *'wing-it,'* think again; no one *'wings-it.'* The bests are the best because they have practiced, practiced, and practiced some more.

No one makes it to the NFL or NBA by *'winging-it.'* Countless hours of practice and preparation have gone into looking *'effortless.'*

Steph Curry makes his 3-pointers look effortless because he has practiced.

My old boss in Business Development made his speeches look smooth because he practiced and prepared accordingly.

If it matters to you and you care about something, always prepare and practice.

Do you put in the hours and practice your craft?

Work Lesson #82 – *It is nearly impossible to succeed when you don't have a plan. Acquiring the correct skills to ensure you get the desired results, takes preparation and time.*

Careers take years to develop, and they rarely become successful by accident or coincidence. They take planning, ability, and hard work.

New skills are developed by practicing and gaining experience.

If you haven't developed a plan to acquire these skills and improve your ability, how will you know if your career is progressing on target to reach your aspirations?

Don't rely on fate to get you what you want.

Set-targeted goals and develop a proper career development plan to secure you achieve what you want to accomplish.

What is your next goal?

Work Lesson #83 – *Be cautious when choosing career goals, don't make the mistake of wanting a title, and not realizing the responsibility that comes with it. Ensure you are chasing what YOU desire and not what your EGO wants.*

A Vice President and Executive titles sound glorious, but often, the responsibility and sacrifice that come with these positions, are not.

Depending on your industry, a VP title can take years and a great deal of sacrifice.

In my industry, it usually takes a minimum of 15 years to make it to a VP level and many sacrifices. Most VPs I know, have worked abroad and have worked countless weekends. They have sacrificed a great deal of their time to climb the Corporate ladder.

There is nothing wrong with wanting to be an Executive, Vice President, or CEO; just ensure you've done your homework on what responsibilities come with these positions, and you're aware of the sacrifices.

Work Lesson #84 – Ensure that your supervisor and boss are aware of your career goals. Never assume the path they see for you is the same as your own. Communicate your career aspirations to the correct people.

Your boss and supervisor aren't mind readers.

Ensure you communicate and align on your career aspirations with them.

People have different agendas; aligning with your boss on your career goals and aspirations, will assist them in supporting you. They can help you get the proper training and putting your name forward for stretch assignments that can assist in your career growth.

Have you communicated your career aspirations to your boss?

Week 8 Theme: Take Full Responsibility of Your Own Career

This week, I'll be discussing how you must take full responsibility for your career to ensure you're trekking the path you desire.

Successful careers require you to be in the driver seat, allowing you to change direction when needed.

Regardless of the journey you travel, you can re-adjust and change course; you control your actions.

The hands you hold can either keep you down or raise you up!

Work Lesson #85 – *Do not delegate responsibility for your career to anyone. No one will care more about your career, your dreams, and your destiny, then yourself.*

No one will care more about what you accomplish in your life, then yourself.

Your parents may be great supporters, but they will not be able to get you through all the difficult uphill battles you'll need to overcome to be successful.

Your dreams will be one of the most personal things in your life; if you want to make them a reality, you'll need to take full responsibility in making them happen.

Just like staff will never care as much for a business, as the business owner.

No one will advocate and care more about your career than yourself; therefore, your career is your responsibility.

Have you taken full responsibility for your career?

Work Lesson #86 – *Organizations and people have alternative motives; they may not align with your own. Taking full responsibility for your career, may mean you walk alone for a time.*

Not everyone will see what you have to offer.

If you're a *'big picture'* visionary:

- Don't expect the small-mind thinkers to understand you;
- Don't expect them to believe in you and by all means,
- Don't expect them to see your potential.

During your career, you'll come across people (potentially your boss) with conflicting priorities that don't align with your desired career path.

If you don't take full responsibility for your career and don't orchestrate and maneuver around these people, you'll be hostage to them, and as a result, you may not reach your goals.

Have you had to strategically maneuver around a boss to reach the next step in your career?

Work Lesson #87 – *For some people, words come easily, and without responsibility, they will tell you anything you want to hear to get what they want or to get you out of their office.*

Words spoken but not supported by actions, are meaningless. You cannot build a career from empty promises.

Be mindful of people that say lovely things like, *"I will help you"* but fail to support these words with the appropriate actions.

During your career, you'll meet many people that speak wonderfully. They have charisma, style, appeal, and are full of personality, but if these people tend to only speak of what they have done or will do, and don't back these words with results and actions, be cautious around them.

If someone appears to be the 'real deal' but never seems to deliver, they're not the 'real deal'; and probably a polished imposter.

Many people have agendas and may tell you what you want to hear, so you will help them and have no plans or desire to return the favour.

Honorable professionals always support their words and promises with actions. Do you agree?

Work Lesson #88 – *You are responsible for building your network. It is your job to source out career opportunities and build relationships with people who can help you.*

You'll be more successful in your career and less disappointed if you don't rely on others to open doors.

Keeping your head down and working hard is not the best advice these days; of course, always work hard, but you must also work smart.

Keeping your head down with the hope you'll be discovered, gives away your control and goes under the premise that you're not able to create your own opportunities.

Successful careers don't happen by accident; they require a plan and being strategic.

Learning who the influencers are within your organization is wise, and recruiting them for your network is a no brainer.

These are the people that can influence the decision-makers, and this is how you can secure stretch assignments that can catapult your career.

Learn who the influencers are within your organization and recruit them for your network. You can do this by:

- Being visible,
- Impressing them and
- Helping them look good.

Work Lesson #89 – *You are and will always be your biggest fan and supporter; if you are not advocating for your career, who else will?*

If you're not advocating for yourself, why would others want to invest in you?

Confidence is contagious; being confident in your ability makes you more likely to attract people's attention.

As you start in your career, you want to be labelled a *'safe bet.'*

If an Influential person invests in you, they want their investment to pay off and not disappoint.

Being confident and advocating on your behalf will help you sell yourself as a reliable young professional that delivers and shows others you believe in yourself.

What technics do you use to boost your confidence?

Work Lesson #90 – *Do not assume your boss will support your desired career path; they may not want to lose you. Recognize when you are being pigeonholed and put a plan together to escape their influence without burning bridges.*

People have conflicting priorities and their own agendas.

Never assume your boss wants what's best for you; sometimes, they want what's best for themselves, and losing you isn't part of their plan.

If you find your boss is trying to pigeon hole you, you'll need to develop a plan to maneuver around them, without creating an enemy.

The best way to maneuver around a boss that is trying to hold you back is to have your ability and results be visible to either your boss's boss and several influential managers/leaders.

It will be much harder to keep you from promotions if your credibility and reputation have begun to be known within your organizations.

Your boss will be more likely to go along with a promotion if you've helped them look good; if your network is reliable and keeping you back will be a harder battle then letting you go.

You're far more likely to be pigeonholed in your career if you don't advocate for yourself and build an influential network of supporters.

If no one knows what you are capable of, how will you be offered career opportunities or stretch assignments?

Work Lesson #91 – Being a Leader requires you to take full responsibility for everything you execute. Regardless of your team, organization, or career, to be successful starts with accepting responsibility for all your actions.

Credibility is your ability as a professional. You establish your credibility by consistently delivering high-quality results, which requires you to be skilled and accountable.

An established Credibility feeds a strong reputation. Your reputation will have a higher word of mouth and sellable name if you've first established a solid, credible presence in your field.

If you lack accountability, you may not take responsibility for your mistakes and follow through on your commitments. This will allow an opening for defamation of your reputation.

Accountable professionals are much harder to defame, as they back their commitments (words) with results (actions).

Accountable professionals commit to responsibility and follow through with the actions, which get the desired results.

This is the foundation in establishing your credibility. Do you agree?

Work Lesson #92 – *Setbacks, obstacles, mistakes, and failures, can be temporary. Failure is remaining stagnant.*

You control your hands, knees, and feet. It doesn't need to be a leap; it can be a baby step; what's important is that you have moved.

You'll have setbacks and obstacles in your career; you'll make mistakes in your career. These are guarantees and are part of the learning process.

There is no way for you to know it all, especially if you're regularly pushing your limits and boundaries.

Successful careers take years to build and require you to learn and re-adjust when things don't work out; whatever you do to move on from a setback, don't remain stagnant.

Failure is only permanent when you stop trying. Do you agree?

Work Lesson #93 – *Careers are marathons; you may fall behind at mile 14, only to recover by mile 19, and make up the lost time. Push through the setbacks and obstacles, learn what it takes to keep you motivated.*

There are marathons, and there are sprints.

To complete a marathon, you need to train. No one completes a marathon in a reasonable time without putting in the effort and proper training. Careers are no different.

Your career success will be a result of how smart and hard you work.

Part of working smart is to learn what keeps you motivated and performing at your best.

Learn what environments produce your best work.

Work Lesson #94 – *The greatest lessons come through difficulty. There are many lessons to be learned when building a career. Learn often.*

Your greatest lessons and growth usually come from painful setbacks and obstacles.

These obstacles force you out of your comfort zone, and when you succeed despite them, it builds your confidence and resilience.

Career success doesn't catapult in the good times; it catapults after you have succeeded through the bad times and are better because of them.

Do you agree?

Work Lesson #95 – "If opportunity doesn't knock, build a door." - *Milton Berle.*
Create your own opportunities.

Taking full responsibility for your career means that regardless of the hand you are dealt, you make the best of it.

You cannot control the cards you get, but you can control how you strategize your wagers.

A game of poker isn't based on one set of cards being dealt; it's how you calculate your risk versus reward, gauge your audience, and play the correct odds, over many hands.

Just like poker, there will be variables in your career that you cannot control, but you control how you react to every hand being dealt to you and adjust accordingly.

Create opportunities... You hold the hammer, and you can build your door.

Are you calculating your wages?

Work Lesson #96 – *It is your job to establish and develop your credibility. To improve, you will need to gain the skills you lack. You must develop a plan to acquire these missing skills.*

Taking responsibility means:

- Knowing what you want;
- Develop a plan;
- Execute the plan, which supports the path to accomplishing these wants.

These are the beginning steps to taking full responsibility for your career.

Week 9 Theme: Turn Obstacles into Opportunities

Most of us have heard the quote,

"In the Middle of Difficulty Lies Opportunity."

– Albert Einstein

I speak this week from my experiences from overcoming difficulty to building resilience in my character and how these obstacles catapulted my career forward.

Throughout your career, you'll be given obstacles that you must overcome, and some of these may turn into your most significant achievements.

Setbacks have the potential to disable you and to take you off your path permanently. This week I share stories of how I survived some significant setbacks in my career and life. Together, we can teach aspiring professionals, that setbacks, obstacles, and mistakes are a normal part of the career journey.

Work Lesson #97 – Setbacks and obstacles are critical variables in building successful careers. They assist in building resilience and resourcefulness.

You'll make many mistakes during your career. This is a critical part of the learning curve.

Making mistakes is a part of the career game, and don't be discouraged by this. Setbacks and obstacles will happen during your career for various reasons; this could be partly due to lack of experience, or timing that was out of your control.

Regardless of the reason, how you react to an obstacle is within your control. Overcoming setbacks in your career will build your resilience in getting up and trying again.

Providing solutions during trying and difficult times will build your creativity and resourcefulness.

A significant setback can turn into one of your career's greatest successes.

How have you turned a setback into a success?

Work Lesson #98 – *No one gets everything they want. Resilience will serve you throughout your entire career.*

Life can be unfair; it can be unforgiving.

You can be overlooked for promotions you've earned. You can be laid off when you're an excellent employee. Unpredictable things will happen to you in your life and career; this is nearly a guarantee.

My advice is, regardless of the career setback, learn from it, re-adjust if required, brush yourself off and try again.

You control how you react; your emotions are always within your control, as are your words and actions.

Resilience is built through difficulties, resulting in you becoming stronger, and, regardless of the setback, you'll overcome it and turn it into a strength.

How has resilience impacted your career?

Work Lesson #99 – *Resilience is built through difficulties; therefore, every setback can lead to greater learning, confidence, and success.*

A step back can lead to a leap forward.

Careers are not linear, and the Corporate ladder isn't straight.

A setback today can be your greatest achievement tomorrow.

When a setback is delivered, remain focused, stay calm, pull together your network, ask for help if required, but the absolute must-do is believe in yourself to solve it.

If you can deliver quality results through setbacks, through major difficulty... you'll become a *'go-to'* person; your reputation and name will become well known, and...

Career opportunities will come to you as a result.

Do you agree?

Work Lesson #100 – The most efficient way to prove yourself as a young, resourceful and talented employee is to have high visual obstacles presented to you and knock them out of the park.

High-quality results are your best references and testimonies for your qualifications as a professional.

Results are the proof and evidence of your capabilities.

When you're given a hard problem to solve and provide a tangible solution that has been visible by upper management, it's the ideal situation to be in, as...

This is how you build your reputation as a talented individual who produces solutions. You advance in your career by proving your capabilities.

How have you advanced in your career?

Work Lesson #101 – Opportunities are often disguised as obstacles. The secret is to recognize the hidden opportunity and build your reputation as a resourceful and talented professional.

Another word for *'obstacle'* can be *'opportunity.'*

Your credibility is your ability as a professional. These are the skills you bring to a team.

When unmanageable problems arise, don't run from them. Embrace the challenge and solve it.

When you solve challenging issues, you get labelled as resourceful, and this begins to build your reputation as a credible, resourceful, and talented professional.

The harder the obstacle, the greater the success, do you agree?

Work Lesson #102 – Embrace lifelong learning as a career goal. The more you learn, the more you can accomplish. Face obstacles as they arise, they can be a gift in disguise.

Obstacles are simply unplanned career opportunities.

There will always be things you cannot thoroughly plan for, just like your car breaking down on a rainy day.

Develop your skills and embrace lifelong learning; you can minimize making mistakes and getting the desired results by being prepare.

Just like you carry a spare tire for your car, developing your ability and continuous learning will help prepare you for the unexpected obstacles that can arise and help you succeed.

Do you believe obstacles can be a gift in disguise?

Work Lesson #103 – When you succeed through a difficult obstacle, your ability increases, and you reach a higher potential. Talent doesn't need to plateau.

Talent doesn't need to plateau; it can continue to grow if you allow yourself to push through adversary and learn.

When you prematurely give up, the learnings, the new abilities, will elude you.

To build a strong reputation as a *'go-to'* person who can solve difficult problems, you'll need to finish what you started...

You need to deliver on your commitments.

Obstacles are often career game-changers; don't run away from your responsibilities; step up, learn, re-adjust, and deliver.

Do you think talent plateaus? Or with the right attitude and determination, it can keep going?

Work Lesson #104 – *When obstacles rear their ugly head, be the solution, not the problem.*

The world is full of people that can discuss and complain about a problem; there are far fewer who can solve it, be the latter.

If you're a person who can solve difficult problems and deliver high-quality results, you'll always be in high demand.

This is the best job security you can have.

Do you agree?

Work Lesson #105 – *Embrace obstacles and bring a positive attitude to every challenge. Be the level-headed person, when everyone else is panicking.*

Part of developing your reputation as a *'go-to'* person will be your ability to solve severe problems.

Before you turn down or walk away, view every challenge thoroughly, and see if there is a hidden opportunity to show your resourcefulness and creativity.

Solving difficult problems makes you effective, and productive people get recruited first.

Do you agree?

Work Lesson #106 – *It's in our challenges that give us our greatest accomplishments.*

Obstacles can be career highlights and can build your confidence in your ability.

As you diffuse each challenge, your reputation will grow stronger, and you'll become more confident in your ability.

Embrace challenges; they will have you reach a higher level and improve at a quicker rate.

Did your greatest accomplishment start as an obstacle?

Work Lesson #107 – *The secret to addressing obstacles that arise in your career is to become comfortable with being uncomfortable. Never reside in your comfort zone.*

When you become comfortable in being uncomfortable, you'll rarely be caught off-guard.

You'll subconsciously be prepared as you've trained yourself to embrace challenges.

The more you challenge yourself, the greater your ability will become, allowing you to reach a higher level in your career that eludes so many others.

Never reside in the comfort zone. When addressing challenges, where do you reside?

Work Lesson #108 – *Obstacles will expedite your learning. Embrace challenges, a career built on solving difficult problems, is reinforced with confidence and an attitude that will benefit you.*

When you embrace obstacles head-on, you build your credibility at a faster pace.

Building additional abilities early in your career will give you a head start on your peers and competition.

Your attitude and mindset influence your perspective and how you see the world.

Therefore, train yourself to be comfortable being uncomfortable.

This will allow you to be capable of taking on greater challenges and developing skills that can benefit you throughout your entire career.

How has your mindset impacted your perspective?

Week 10 Theme: Don't Let a Bad Boss Undermine Your Plan

Bad bosses can genuinely dampen your mood. A bad boss is hard to avoid, as they are there each day.

When you start your first position, you'll quickly learn that a bad boss is not hard to point out, and most of the evidence you need will be how you feel when you are around them.

Don't be discouraged if you have a bad boss; you may not be able to control who your boss is, but you can control how you react to them, and you can put a plan together to maneuver your way out of their reach.

Have you ever had a bad boss?

Work Lesson #109 – Your first boss can strongly influence how you view your organization. Don't be discouraged if your first boss is terrible; this may or may not be a reflection of the company.

If you're unfortunate to have a terrible boss, before you decide to leave your organization, you need to make a thorough investigation.

You'll need to observe if poor leadership is a common theme at your organization; this is step one.

If poor leadership is uncommon at your organization, create a plan to maneuver around your boss without creating an enemy.

If poor leadership is common at your organization, this is probably a sign of a deeper issue within the company culture, and you may be best to leave.

Before you decide to stay or leave, ensure you complete a thorough investigation; never be too quick to jump to conclusions.

How have you maneuvered around a bad boss?

Work Lesson #110 – *POOR LEADERS tend to blame and belittle others. They can TAKE CREDIT for others' work. Trend CAUTIOUSLY around these types of people, especially if one of them is your boss.*

Remember the mirror versus window analogy if you have a hard time recognizing a weak leader and boss.

I read the book Good to Great, in college, and I'll never forget, their mirror versus window description of leadership.

A strong leader will only look at a mirror in times of failure, blaming only themselves. A strong leader in times of success will only look out a window, recognizing their team and everyone else for their contributions.

In poor leadership, the story is reversed. Learn to recognized signs of poor leadership; these types will rarely help you.

What signs of poor leadership have you witnessed?

Work Lesson #111 – *The first step in dealing with a bad boss is first to identify them as an ineffective leader. The second is to assess their influence and reach at your organization.*

If your boss is an ineffective leader and you want out from under their influence and grip, you need to know how far it goes.

- Do they have powerful contacts?
- Do they seem to have the respect of their peers and colleagues?
- Do they hold a grudge?

If your boss has powerful contracts and influence, you need to be extra careful in maneuvering yourself away from their grip. You don't, and I repeat, don't want to create an unnecessary enemy nor burn a bridge.

If you have decided to stay with your organization and maneuver from your boss's grip, you need to develop a plan to do this.

Every step needs to be planned; there is no winging it when avoiding a hazardous situation.

Do you agree?

Work Lesson #112 – *One way to maneuver around a poor boss is to build a strong relationship with your boss's boss. It will be harder for your boss to hurt your reputation or pigeonholed you when their own boss thinks highly of you.*

Whatever method you choose to do to maneuver around a bad boss, it must be done discreetly.

If you're a high potential employee who delivers consistent, high-quality results, your boss won't want to lose you off their team.

You must operate discreetly and tell very few, if anyone, of your plans. You don't want your boss to learn of your plan; if they do, this can hurt you.

If you choose to build a strong relationship with your boss's boss, build this relationship discreetly.

How have you maneuvered around a bad boss?

Work Lesson #113 – *To maneuver around poor bosses, you will need to be discreet, strategic, and have a thorough plan that details your path out of their control and influence.*

You'll be far more likely to be successful in your career when you're executing a plan.

I cannot stress this enough, if you're potentially working in a hostile area, such as, working for a bad boss, to maneuver out of their control discreetly. Keep your plans and moves to yourself.

Don't, and I repeat, don't publicly bash or discuss your boss's poor performance.

You don't want your boss as an enemy. Avoid discussing your boss in public; if you don't know how to maneuver out of a conversation when your boss's performance is brought up, remain silent.

If your boss is unaware of your plans, then they cannot stop it. Just like Sun Tzu stated in The Art of War,

> *"The supreme art of war is to subdue the enemy without fighting."*

The less your boss knows, the easier it will be to execute your plan. Move with lightness in your feet.

Work Lesson #114 – *Always develop a detailed plan to escape an undesirable situation; you are not a hostage to your current circumstances. As long as you have a plan that you're executing, you are in control.*

From my experience in the Corporate Environment, there are many types of employees, but nearly all of them can be separated into two categories.

First, you want them on your team, and second, you don't want them on your team. A maybe, in this case, is a NO.

The people I want on my team are people who never settle for their circumstances, who are always aware, that the hands they hold can either rise them up or hold them down.

If you know you aren't happy with your current work situation, you're the one that needs to take action to improve this.

Don't allow yourself to be in the same situation a year down the road; don't be a hostage to your current circumstance, put a step by step plan together, and execute it.

How have you gotten out of an undesirable work situation?

Work Lesson #115 – *Avoid burning bridges, especially at the early stages of your career. Burning bridges can hurt your reputation before you break out of the gate.*

I will sound like a broken record throughout this week's theme; when maneuvering out of an undesirable work environment...

Always be discreet!

Creating an enemy and burning a bridge, risks hurting your reputation; avoid this at all cost.

Do you agree?

Work Lesson #116 – *Always, and I repeat, always protect your reputation. When it comes to your career, very few things are more valuable than a strong reputation.*

Your reputation is your brand. Once it's tarnished, it will be hard to get it shiny and clean.

A tarnished reputation can be permanent.

The strength of your reputation can be the difference between you being offered a fantastic opportunity and you being overlooked.

If you can help it, never and I repeat, never risk damaging your reputation.

Do you agree?

Work Lesson #117 – *You will encounter a poor boss at some point in your career, remember they are temporary; don't allow them to influence your attitude and goals.*

You can't control who your boss is, but you can control how you allow them to make you feel.

People will come and go throughout your career, whom you don't like or respect, and you may need to work with them at times.

Regardless of the situation, always act professional and mature:

- Never allow another person to change who you are;
- Never allow someone to reduce your standards and ethics.

Your destiny is in your hands and is far too important to allow a self-serving person to disrupt you off of your path.

Work Lesson #118 – Never, never, never allow a poor boss to have control over your career progression. Build relationships with the people that can protect you from your boss's reach and influence.

1. Plan, plan, plan.
2. Maneuver, maneuver, maneuver.
3. Network, network, network.

A bad boss with selfish motives can hurt your career progression. If you're a high performer, they may not want to lose you off their team.

If this is the case, plan your escape.

One way to secure yourself from being withheld from opportunities and being pigeonholed, is to network with influencers within your organization.

The more well-known and visible you are, the harder it will be for your boss to keep you hidden under their clutches.

Do you agree?

Work Lesson #119 – *If you're executing your plan to maneuver around your boss; it's wise to have them like you, sometimes working discreetly, means your true motives are hidden.*

If you don't like your boss, only you should know your true feelings.

Being likable can often be a highly underrated variable in career success. The truth is, it's harder to hurt well-liked people.

When you're well-liked, you tend to have more fans, and people are more likely to help you and defend you.

If your bad boss likes you, then they may be less likely to try and stop a promotion or another opportunity from reaching you.

Do you agree?

Work Lesson #120 – *Never bad mouth your boss. This doesn't mean you need to promote or speak highly of them, just never speak poorly of them in public. You don't need any unnecessary enemies.*

Regardless of your boss's competency level, it's unprofessional to belittle or bad mouth them publicly.

As an employee, you represent your company, whether you're at work or not. Always be mindful when you're discussing your organization or company personnel when you're in public.

You never know who is listening. It could be a Client or a network contact of your boss.

Because of this, it's safer not to discuss troubled work matters in public.

Have you ever overheard, what should be a confidential work matter, being discussed in public? If yes, what were your thoughts on the subject?

Week 11 Theme: Say *"Yes"* Often

It's a three-letter word that has the potential to be a career game-changer...

Therefore, Say it often:

- *"Yes, I'm up to the challenge."*
- *"Yes, I can deliver on my commitments."*
- *"Yes, I will be the solution."*

Say it... Yes! Yes!! YES!!!

Career successes often build off each other; each one serves as a step to the staircase that will take you to the top of your skyscraper.

At the start of your career, say yes to opportunities, and say yes to leaving your comfort zone. It's a simple word that can be powerful.

Did your career game-changer result from saying Yes?

Work Lesson #121 – By saying "Yes," *we invite possibility into our careers.*

How will you ever learn what you're capable of if you always play it safe?

To reach new levels, you must branch out of your comfort zone. If you find yourself resisting leaving your comfort zone, take small steps.

Never underestimate the power of taking small steps. Small steps can add up to a giant leap.

The critical point here is, to branch out of what you've always known. Learn something new.

Say Yes to a small task or assignment and grow gradually.

People who don't leave their comfort zone will eventually become stagnant, and their careers can stall as a result.

What technics do you use to help leave your comfort zone?

Work Lesson #122 – *Saying* "Yes" *opens a door. Saying* "No" *closes it.*

There may be times in your career when you need to close a door; this generally doesn't happen at the beginning.

Saying *"No"* doesn't invite opportunity into your career.

To establish your credibility and build your reputation as a *'go-to'* person, saying yes will assist in being labelled this.

Saying *"No"* too often at the beginning of your career may have you labelled unfavourably as a person who is:

- Not willing to help, or
- Not able to leave their comfort zone.

Keep the door open at the beginning of your career, say *"Yes to opportunities,"* even if it scares you. Do you agree?

Work Lesson #123 – *You don't get endless career opportunities. Saying* "Yes" *increases the potential of getting more.*

When you venture out into your career, try to say *"Yes,"* to the first few requests of your time.

When you say, *"No,"* right out of the gate, it doesn't give the right atmosphere you want for your reputation.

Think of it this way, when someone asks you to join them for happy hour, and you say, *"No,"* the first two times; what are the odds they will ask you a third time?

The same goes for career opportunities. You won't be given endless career opportunities, and this will be more likely if you continue to say *"No"* to people.

Do you agree?

Work Lesson #124 – *Greater growth is possible by leaving your comfort zone; this can start with you saying "Yes" to an opportunity.*

Stretch assignments get offered to High Potential Employees.

You get labelled *'High Potential'* by being a *'go-to'* person who solves difficult problems.

Solving difficult problems often requires you to leave your comfort zone.

As Richard Branson said, *"If somebody offers you an amazing opportunity but you are not sure you can do it, say yes – then learn how to do it later!"*

Do you agree with Mr. Branson?

Work Lesson #125 – *Career progression comes in all sizes: small and minuscule, to large leaps. Saying "Yes" can start a ripple effect of career opportunities that you cannot quantify.*

Saying *"Yes"* can get the momentum started in your favour.

Success builds on success; Opportunity builds off of opportunity, and a strong reputation is assisted by being pushed by momentum.

Think of the Butterfly Effect; a small YES can give rise to a big OPPORTUNITY. Flutter your wings to start your tidal wave.

Work Lesson #126 – *Building a strong reputation means you have been labelled favourably.* "Yes" *is the vocabulary of a* 'go-to' *person—a label you want.*

YES, can develop your presence as a *'go-to'* person, someone who is always willing to help and is always willing to provide a solution.

There are countless <u>examples</u> from my career that helped me advance more than I could have ever predicted, just by saying YES!

A countless number of fantastic opportunities, advancements, and recognitions have been awarded to me, simply by using that little three-letter word.

Saying YES can have a strong reciprocal effect that by helping others, the more likely it is that you'll develop a network of supporters.

Do you agree?

Work Lesson #127 – *Never walk away from a career opportunity because it scares you. Being scared is normal when you are entering unfamiliar terrain.*

Your fear will keep you alert; use this as a strength instead of a deterrent.

Allow it to keep you curious, keep you questioning, so you can see a problem from all angles.

This is how fear can be turned into a strength; instead of stopping you from pursuing your goals, you have made yourself more inquisitive and able to dig deeper into a problem.

If you feel fear is getting the best of you, take a breath, regain your composure, then take a step forward.

How do you prevent fear from getting the best of you?

Work Lesson #128 – *Don't ask yourself why? But instead, ask yourself, why not?*

Influence your perspective to question the possible, instead of succumbing to the impossible.

Your attitude and mindset can influence how you see the world and how you see yourself.

Change your perspective to see the opportunity in every challenge and allow it to motivate you.

Abandon your fears, and proceed forward.

Is there a process you use to influence your perspective to remain positive?

Work Lesson #129 – *A greater number of opportunities, advancements, and recognitions can come from saying* "Yes." *Say it often.*

Saying *"Yes"* indicates you're a person willing to help and want to be part of the solution.

When we say, *"Yes,"* we invite possibility into our careers.

Open that door by saying *"YES."*

Build a strong reputation by helping and being the solution.

Do you agree?

Work Lesson #130 – *You gain new skills, knowledge, and experiences by trying something different. Saying "Yes" will not only help you gain skills; it can help you build your confidence and self-worth.*

The first step in the learning process is often by saying, *"Yes."*

The truth in the matter is, you learn more from trying new things then remaining in the comfort zone of status quo.

If you never branch out of what you have always known, your *'true'* potential will elude you, and you may prematurely plateau.

When you succeed at something you didn't believe you could, you build confidence in your ability, and as a result, you increase your professional worth.

What have you done recently to increase your professional worth?

Work Lesson #131 – Saying "Yes" can help you gain more skills, help you meet additional people, and your business reach and influence can grow at a greater speed.

If you have ambitious career goals, you'll need to leave your comfort zone; this is a fact.

You want to create an exponential learning curve so that you can gain skills at an exponential rate. You do this by:

- Saying, *"Yes,"* and
- By being open to challenges.

Throughout my career, I found some of the most memorable and rewarding experiences came from the ones that required overcoming challenges.

The reward and feeling of accomplishment came from knowing these challenges didn't stop me from succeeding.

These challenges made me a better leader and improved my ability as a person who delivers high-quality results regardless of the situation.

Saying, *"Yes,"* invites challenges and opportunities into your career!

Work Lesson #132 — *The quickest way to end opportunities presented to you, is by shutting down people.*

I will end this week's theme, by summarizing it, in one sentence:

"The quickest way to end opportunities being presented to you is by shutting people down."

When you say, *"No,"* you're closing a door. Whatever possibility you had by saying *"Yes,"* is gone.

Success often builds off momentum; to start this momentum, you must take the first step.

Just like a snowball at the top of a hill, once it's pushed and begins to roll, it grows bigger and bigger.

Remain open-minded and flexible and allow your snowball to gain traction.

Week 12 Theme: Build Your Network

There will be very few variables that contribute to your career success more than an influential and diverse network.

When you enter your career, you'll soon learn:

- The most qualified people don't always get the promotion;
- Word of mouth can help you build a sellable name; and
- Many advancement opportunities aren't advertised.

A strong network will increase your business reach and assist in building a strong reputation where your name sells and helps open doors for you.

Work Lesson #133 – Don't be naïve. The most qualified people aren't always given promotions and growth opportunities. Many times, it is the person who is more well known.

You've worked hard; you completed your degree, and now you've entered an organization on your first day.

From this day onwards, you'll be assessed on the results and value you bring to your organization.

Part of producing results is to have them visible. When they're visible, they'll be associated with you.

When you're associated with delivering high-quality results, this begins to build a sellable name and reputation...

...You become well known.

You can't be offered growth opportunities and stretch assignments:

- If no one knows you, and
- If no one knows what you're capable of.

Do you agree?

Work Lesson #134 – *Well-connected people have access to information that isn't normally advertised.*

Many opportunities, such as new positions, are not advertised.

You hear about them through your network of contacts.

If you want to hear about these opportunities before the general public, build an influential and diverse network.

A strong network will increase your business reach and increase your chances of hearing about these hidden opportunities.

Have you ever been given a heads up on an opportunity because of your network?

Work Lesson #135 – *Before you can get followers, effective mentors, and influential leaders to be a part of your extended network, you first must attract their attention.*

When you enter your career, you may feel overwhelmed. There will be many things to learn.

Careers take years to build and don't become successful by accident; they take effort, hard work, preparation and planning.

So, where to start?

Start with establishing your credibility as a talented solution provider. Build your abilities as a professional.

When you begin to achieve high-quality results that are visible, you will attract attention.

When this happens, you've begun to build a strong reputation.

What was your first achievement in your career?

Work Lesson #136 – *It's not what you know, it's who you know... this is an incomplete statement. The full statement is what you know, who you know and who knows you.*

Many people believe it's who you know and not what you know that makes you successful; I am not one of them.

What you know is extremely important... A network can open a door and open a big door, but you won't be standing in the room for very long if you don't bring anything to the table.

- What you know, allows you to take a chair and sit at the table.
- Who knows you, allows you to receive an offer to sit down.
- And who you know, allows you to see the table and know of its existence.

Always and I mean, ALWAYS, bring credibility with you to any opportunity.

How important is *'what you know'* in a person's success?

Work Lesson #137 – *What you know is your CREDIBILITY. Who you know is your NETWORK. Who knows you is your REPUTATION.*

I want to expand from my earlier post. I believe these three variables play critical roles in a successful career.

- What you know is your CREDIBILITY; this allows you to take a chair and sit at the table.
- Who you know is your NETWORK; this allows you to see the table and know of its existence.
- Who knows you is your REPUTATION; this allows you to receive an offer to sit down.

These three together, complete the saying, *"what you know, who you know and who knows you."*

Do you believe these three variables, Credibility, Reputation and a Network, play critical roles in career success?

Work Lesson #138 – *Your Credibility feeds your Reputation.*

Your credibility is your ability as a professional.

Credibility is both your hard and soft skills, as well as, your character.

When you first start your career, start with establishing your credibility.

Develop the hard and soft skills that will make you a desired professional, whom people want on their team.

Solve hard problems and bring a solution-based mindset to every challenge you're given.

Work with pride and integrity.

Establishing your credibility early in your career is important because it can directly feed your reputation.

Essentially your reputation is what others say about your credibility.

Are you building your reputation?

Work Lesson #139 – *A strong reputation will assist in selling your name, your brand. Never underestimate the strength in word-of-mouth.*

When you have a strong reputation backed by credibility, you become known as a *'safe bet.'*

People want *'safe bets'* in their network; because you're a guarantee.

You've become a smart investment:

- Low risk / High reward

When you have a strong reputation, you have a sellable name and people know who you are.

Since people know who you are and that you're a safe bet, they'll recruit you for their network.

The most influential networks have people coming to you voluntarily, for recruitment.

Do you agree?

Work Lesson #140 – Who you know and who knows you, is the substance of a strong network.

Your REPUTATION feeds your NETWORK.

If you build a strong reputation, you'll, in turn, build an influential network.

Both your reputation and network will be critical elements in building a successful career full of growth and opportunities, therefore, build them with REINFORCEMENT.

Establish your credibility early in your career, allow it to feed and build a strong reputation, which will, in turn, feed and build an influential network.

What do you think is the safest method to build a strong reputation?

Work Lesson #141 – You can first start building your network with your peers, classmates and professors. Keep in touch.

Many classmates will move onto different industries and organizations that can assist in extending your business reach and influence...

...Therefore, keep in touch.

Make it a habit of checking in on people. Remember, their birthdays, send a card, or give them a call.

Checking in with your extended network is a good habit of becoming accustomed to; you never know when their help may be needed.

Never allow your extended network to forget about you.

Work Lesson #142 – If you're not sure who you need to impress when you enter an Organization; start with intelligent, interesting and ambitious people. Many times, you get labelled based on who you associate with.

It's perfectly normal when you start at a new Organization that you won't know who's who.

It's hard to impress the influencers of your organization when you don't know who they are.

Don't worry too much about this.

Before you can be strategic on who you recruit for your network; establish your credibility.

Be helpful, bring value and solve difficult problems by bringing and developing solutions.

If you do this, you'll impress people and get the right type of attention.

Start your network with your peers; choose intelligent, interesting and ambitious people to be around.

They will help you develop skills, and influence your mindset, which will transfer into your credibility.

You often become what you surround yourself with; therefore, choose wisely.

Work Lesson #143 – The best stretch assignments and opportunities come from asking or from someone recommending you. Build your reputation, so your name and abilities do all the heavy lifting.

Just like you want your money to make money while you're sleeping...

...Build your name, so it does the selling.

You want people to recommend you for opportunities that you're not aware of.

You want your network to help you find opportunities that will lead to career game-changers.

Since most stretch assignments aren't advertised, you get them by either asking for one or by being recommended.

The only way you'll be recommended for one, is if you built a strong reputation, backed by a network and name that carries some weight.

Build your reputation, so your name sells and brings you opportunities.

Do you agree?

Work Lesson #144 – *Networks are like spiderwebs, the more 'connectors' and 'links' you build, the stronger it will be, the larger distance it can span, and the greater storms it can weather.*

I will end this week's theme with a simple statement:

An adequately built network will cover all generations and levels of an organization.

Strong networks have a far business reach and influence.

And, they never and I repeat, never, have missing gaps.

Missing gaps in a spiderweb cannot weather all storms.

Your network will be built to withstand a hurricane, as you'll put in the time, effort and attention to detail to ensure you have no missing gaps.

Week 13 Theme: Find Effective Mentors

As you begin your career, accept that you'll need help along your journey, as:

- No one knows it all, nor do we have too,
- No one makes it to the top without assistance, and
- No one can see everything they need to learn to make them better.

Once in a while, we need people to teach and show us our weaknesses, strengths and help bring out our best versions of ourselves.

Mentors play critical roles throughout our careers, and their influences can be significant.

This week's, I'll be discussing the importance of finding effective mentors.

Work Lesson #145 – *Effective mentors are willing to teach and share their experience, skillsets and knowledge.*

An effective mentor is:

- Someone you can learn from,
- Someone that will provide critical feedback you NEED to hear, and
- Someone you can trust.

A mentor can play many different roles throughout your career; just ensure that they meet the above criteria at a minimum. If they don't, they're not an effective and trustworthy mentor.

What criteria do you believe builds a productive mentoring relationship?

Work Lesson #146 – *A mentor can influence your perspective, which, in turn, can influence how you see your potential.*

The influence of a mentor can be significant; therefore, choose someone who:

- Sincerely wants to help you,
- Believes in you, and
- Wants to bring the best out of you.

Choose a mentor that wants to see you succeed in your life and career.

Have you had a mentor bring the best out of you?

Work Lesson #147 – *An effective mentor will help you identify your weaknesses and help you turn them into strengths.*

Effective mentors will tell you what you NEED to hear, not what you WANT to hear.

An active mentor doesn't feed your ego; they help keep you grounded and working on self-improvement.

You want mentors that will tell you the truth, even if it hurts your feelings.

Weaknesses can hold you back from reaching your potential.

Ensure you choose mentors that will never lie to you.

Do you agree?

Work Lesson #148 – *In many cases, the best mentoring happens without the formal label of* 'mentoring.'

Don't get hung up with having a mentoring relationship being formally labelled by your organization.

Inner circles are built on trust and can form organically.

The most effective mentoring relationships I've had in my career, have formed from a friendship.

I consider all my mentors, friends, and some family.

Not one of them was considered a mentor when I met them. The relationships formed and developed from a friendship to a mentorship.

Be patient when building relationships; some of the most impactful relationships form organically and in their own time.

Were your mentors, friends first?

Work Lesson #149 – *Learn the difference between a mentor and a sponsor. They play different roles in your career; don't mix them up.*

A sponsor is formally assigned to you by your organization.

- Their responsibilities are to advocate and open doors for you.
- They are generally in senior roles with authority.
- They are not responsible for mentoring you.

A mentor can advocate for you, but their primary responsibilities are to:

- Advise you, and
- They don't need to be a senior employee with authoritative power.

Mentors provide more of the day-to-day learning and critical feedback you need to hear to progress forward in your career.

Do you believe the role of a mentor and sponsor is different?

Work Lesson #150 – *An effective mentor is someone you trust and can go to them for advice in nearly all situations.*

Mentorship is built off of trust.

You shouldn't need to walk on eggshells with your mentor.

If you find yourself holding back information from your mentor, you should question the relationship's effectiveness.

You must allow time for the relationship to progress to mentorship. But even after a sufficient amount of time has passed, if you're still holding back information from them, the relationship may not be an adequate fit.

You can continue a good working relationship with this person, but they shouldn't be considered a mentor. Effective mentorship must have trust.

Do you believe you can have an effective mentorship without complete trust?

Work Lesson #151 – *The goal should be to build strong, trusting relationships with people, not to simply find a mentor.*

You'll need mentors throughout your career, but the ultimate goal isn't to secure effective mentors but to build trusting relationships.

Before you can attract effective mentors, you must first get their attention; therefore, go out and establish your credibility as a reliable and trustworthy employee.

You'll rarely need to ask someone to be your mentor; this happens naturally. Focus on establishing your credibility and building strong relationships based on trust.

If you do this, your mentor will find you.

Did you choose your mentor, or did they choose you?

Work Lesson #152 – *An effective mentor may not have an impressive title nor be a senior employee. A mentor is someone who teaches and shares.*

A true leader doesn't require a title, and neither does a mentor.

A mentor may not have influence or be well known. When picking effective mentors, don't get hung up on a title.

The best mentors guide, support and help you through difficult career obstacles; they assist in bringing out your potential by developing your skillsets that will improve your ability.

None of this requires a mentor to be a senior employee with authority.

Never underestimate the strength of peer mentorship. People develop at different speeds, and you can learn critical work lessons from people younger and at your level.

All ranks and levels can bring value to your work.

Do you agree?

Work Lesson #153 – *If you want influencers in your organization to recognize you, then find ways to impress them by bringing value to their work.*

As discussed yesterday, before you can attract effective mentors with influence, you must first get their attention; therefore, go out and impress them.

You can do this by:

- Delivering on your commitment,
- Bring a positive solution-based mindset,
- Solving difficult problems that are visible and
- Consistently producing high-quality results.

If you do these things, while remaining humble and kind, you'll attract influential people.

When you're the solution to difficult problems, you become valuable and can bring value to people's work.

This correlates to: You have become a *'safe bet,'* and influential people will invest in you.

How have you, impressed influential people?

Work Lesson #154 – *Engage senior employees; many want to transfer their knowledge to energetic, willful protégés, who are willing to listen, work hard, and learn.*

Don't hesitate to approach people and ask for advice. We all need help, and it takes courage to ask.

Of course, be mindful of their time and come prepared for the conversation, but don't be scared to engage in a conversation; this is how relationships start.

To better prepare for a discussion with a potential mentor, research their career history and ask yourself:

- Does their career path match your objectives and goals?
- What can this person teach and share with me?
- How will this relationship benefit both our careers?

By being prepared, you'll make a better first impression and will make the best of both of your time.

How have you approached, asking for career advice?

Work Lesson #155 – *Mentorship is a two-way street; it's not only about looking ahead for yourself; it's a team effort. While you're setting your career into motion, help junior employees reach their next career goal.*

Mentorship is a two-way street, a give and take, where both parties gain from the relationship.

Part of effective mentorship is for you to receive guidance but also to mentor others.

While you're receiving mentorship, ensure you're mentoring others, always pay it forward.

Every one of us has something to offer. Always help others if you can; some of our most significant experience comes from giving.

Do you agree?

Work Lesson #156 – Be cautious if your organization doesn't appear to support mentoring. Effective mentoring is part of building a company's future.

Mentoring is an effective way to secure a bright future; this goes for all organizations.

Preparing and developing a company's future is its lifeline.

Without it, an organization will seize to have a pulse and will perish.

A company that doesn't support its future is a company that doesn't value its greatest investment, its people. If they cannot understand the importance of this investment; they may not understand other critical investments

People strategize, people invent, people produce, people design... Regardless of the business, it's their people that deliver and sustain their growth.

If a company doesn't invest in you, your place within their organization is temporary.

Week 14 Theme: Prepare for Lifelong Learning

As Henry Ford stated,

> *"Whether you think you can, or you think you can't,*
> *you're right."*

Whether you're given a significant setback, or a great stride forward, how you react and feel regarding a situation, is ultimately, how you will perceive it.

Mindset is critical when it comes to how you approach difficulty and how you can grow as a person.

When you start your career, the aspiring professions who dedicate their life to lifelong learning will create a mindset that can influence their perception and attitude.

When you dedicate your life, regardless of the situation, to lifelong learning, you grow, improve, and evolve.

Allow yourself to learn the lessons that life delivers you, and you won't remain stagnant.

Work Lesson #157 – The person who can continue to remain open-minded and learn, who can remain flexible, will continue to improve and grow.

Continuous learning contributes to constant growth.

This is the simplest method to reach the best version of yourself.

You don't reach the best version of yourself by remaining stagnant nor trapped in the past.

Some lessons are harder to learn than others; by remaining open-minded and flexible, you allow your growth to evolve and blossom.

The goal isn't to always be right, but instead to adapt and learn from your setbacks and mistakes, to bring these lessons learned to your present and future.

Do you agree?

Work Lesson #158 — The individuals who plateau prematurely in their careers are incapable of adjusting from setbacks and learning new methods of executing their work.

The truth is, you generally learn more from your setbacks and mistakes than you do from easy successes.

Often when you have a setback, you didn't see it coming, either from lack of experience or from something out of your control.

To be able to move past the setback, you need to adjust and try a new method... This can lead to increased learning, which, in turn, can lead to success and greater confidence in your ability.

The individuals who cannot re-adjust and cannot learn from their mistakes will continue down the same path, potentially repeating mistakes and stunting their growth and learning in the process... this is the recipe to prematurely plateauing and not reaching your potential.

Do you believe our greatest lessons come from our mistakes?

Work Lesson #159 — Constant change is one of life's guarantees. Organizations, economies and technology evolve. The person that remains stagnant and doesn't try to re-adjust will become obsolete.

This is one of the harsher work lessons, but it needs to be stated.

If you cannot adapt and change when it's required... you may be left behind.

Just like technology evolves and becomes dated, if you allow your mind to become stagnant, your contributions can minimize over time, and this can lead to becoming obsolete.

I bought my first MacBook in 2012 when it crashed in 2018; the service representative at Apple told me, my computer can no longer be updated, as it's considered vintage.

Don't misunderstand what I'm saying; many experienced employees' mentor and contribute significantly to an organization; what I'm saying has nothing to do with age and everything to do with MINDESET.

If you're closed-minded and refuse to adapt to a changing work environment, you'll become the Nokia of the cellphone market, and just like Nokia losing their market share, you'll lose your perceived value to an organization.

An open mind remains adaptable and flexible, do you agree?

Work Lesson #160 – *If you become comfortable with the idea of constant change, it will become easier to adapt to a new position and remain flexible as opportunities present themselves.*

There is tremendous flexibility by being comfortable with change.

As discussed in the previous work lesson, constant change is one of life's guarantees.

Becoming comfortable in being uncomfortable will benefit your future, as you've trained your mindset to be open and, therefore, adaptable when change is needed or when unforeseen setbacks appear.

Many people waste critical time with their reaction to a problem than addressing the issue.

There will always be elements in your career and life that you cannot control, but the advantage you have is you can ALWAYS control your mindset and reaction.

If you can utilize your time to immediately address a changing environment instead of running away, delaying or being fearful, you'll be more successful.

Never be fearful of change; this is a losing battle.

How do you react to an unexpected change?

Work Lesson #161 – Accept that lifelong learning is part of a successful career. This will better prepare you for the unforeseen obstacles that will arise during your journey.

Careers are many things:

- A marathon – Some miles will be harder than others; finish the race.
- Bumpy roads – You may need to change the direction of the car, but you control the steering wheel; never stop and get out... re-adjust but keep driving.
- Poker - You cannot control the cards, but you can control how you strategize your wagers, calculate your risk versus reward, and gauge your audience.
- Chess – To get to checkmate, your moves must be in silence.

Just like you can't run a marathon without training, nor drive before learning nor gauge your competition correctly without practicing; careers are a set of learned skills.

Every journey has unpredictable variables in your equation for career success. You cannot control the order they appear, but you do control how they add and subject.

The common denominator in your career is YOU; put the time to train and practice while committing to lifelong learning. You'll have greater control in maneuvering and conquering the unforeseen obstacles that try to block your path.

Work Lesson #162 – *Part of successfully reaching your goals is to remain flexible when setbacks occur. Being able to look at mistakes objectively, learn from them, then re-adjust, will be a good formula for success.*

The learning process can have many variations and steps, but generally, a successful formula begins with a mindset, a constant adaptation to the lessons we learn.

Some of the steps to the Learning Process can include:

1. Surprise, setback, obstacle or unforeseen variable,
2. Reaction,
3. Assessment,
4. Re-adjustment,
5. Response,
6. Proceeding forward,
7. Re-assess,
8. Make additional adjustments if required,
9. Repeat the process.

The learning cycle never ends; there will always be something new to learn; this is why your career is a journey and not a destination.

Destinations change as your journey continues to proceed forward; goals grow and become more refined with experience.

Long-term career success will require dedication to lifelong learning; embrace change as knowledge is reduced when you remain stagnant.

What variables are in your learning formula?

Work Lesson #163 – *Always remain open to being advised and taught by others. Every career progression and level will have their challenges; never turn away help.*

You may decide not to proceed with the advice others have given you, but always listen.

If you make it a habit to remain open to being advised, you will indirectly be more open to receiving feedback.

No one can see all their weaknesses and strengths; sometimes we need to be shown and told.

If you turn away help, people will eventually stop trying to help you, and you may gain a reputation for not being open to feedback and being labelled as *'close-minded.'*

A label you desperately want to avoid. You always want to be mindful, how you make others feel and how your decisions impact them.

Ask yourself: When you offered to help someone and refused, how did it make you feel? Did you want to help them again?

Work Lesson #164 – People can PLATEAU; there may eventually be a level that your ability cannot surpass, but this should NEVER happen in the first 10 years of your career.

I have witnessed many individuals plateau in their careers, and no matter how many times I see this, it saddens me, as nearly all of them are preventable.

Your attitude and wanting always to learn, will assist you in navigating challenges and preventing you from prematurely plateauing.

The people I've seen plateau, nearly all of them were due to the same reason, and that was:

- Being Closed-Minded.

A close mind has a hard time learning and adapting to change.

Whether it's driven by ego, arrogance or narcissism, close-minded people have an expiry date on their learning curve, and it's often premature.

Closing the blinders when there is still light outside, is a poor way to tell the weather. Closing your mind means that you have chosen to live in darkness instead of embracing the outside climate.

What reasons have you seen people prematurely plateau?

Work Lesson #165 – If you're willing to expand, there are ways to increase your learning and challenge your mind:
- *Read*
- *Attend conferences*
- *Start a new hobby*
- *Ask more questions*

A curious mind is a gift that keeps on giving, that keeps on learning.

If you find yourself in a rut, find a way to get your mind unstuck.

Getting unstuck can simply mean doing a questioning exercise, where you question basic things like the status quo of a process, reading a new genre or attending a conference.

Learning can be found anywhere; you simply need to train your brain to look for it.

If you recognize your mind getting into a rut, try something new, which can help you branch out.

What technics do you do to get out of a rut and expand your mind?

Work Lesson #166 – A stagnant mind becomes a stagnant employee and eventually becomes a person incapable of learning new skills.

Continuous success is a result of highly driven individuals that have devoted their lives to the concept of lifelong learning.

It's certainly reasonable to rest to regain your energy and motivation.

There is a significant difference between resting and being stagnant.

Resting is clearing your mind and body so that you can reengage at your peak energy level—a temporary break.

By remaining stagnant, you're plugging away at the same thing each day, not improving and growing. And if you're not careful, you can remain stuck there permanently.

If you've dedicated yourself to lifelong learning, you won't be stuck in one place for very long, as you have trained your mind to continue to look for new ways to challenge yourself.

Have you dedicated yourself to lifelong learning?

Work Lesson #167 – The best job security is to be adaptable. Just like evolution, if you adapt, you are capable of changing along with any climate.

I may sound like a broken record, but constant change is one of life's guarantees.

Work environments are changing at a rapid pace; within 40 years, we have gone from using typewriters to computers to smartphones and tablets. Once relevant, vibrant, and booming companies are becoming dated and losing their market share.

Just like in Business, people need to adapt to a changing work environment continually; if they don't, they too may lose their market value.

If your skills are no longer required and you cannot learn and adapt to what is needed, you'll be replaced with people that possess the required qualifications; unfortunately, this is the reality of the work environment.

If you dedicate yourself to:

- Lifelong learning,
- Being open-minded and

- Adaptable when required.

You'll be able to retain your market value.

Do you agree?

Work Lesson #168 – *Wisdom, knowledge, and learning can come from all aspects of your life. Some of the most profound and meaningful learning will come from your own personal growth.*

Personal growth doesn't need to come from your career to have a significant impact on it.

Wisdom often comes from knowledge and experience, which can influence our mindset and perspective.

Embrace growth through all aspects of your life and learn the lessons you require to find your happiness and fulfillment.

Week 15 Theme: Know Your Company's Hierarchy

Learning your company's hierarchy means:

- You understand the hierarchy structure of your organization.
- You know the leading Organization Charts, including all business lines.
- You know the reporting configuration and who reports to whom.
- You know the face, name, title and responsibilities of all the key players within your organization.

Learning your organization's hierarchy is smart and will assist you in never being caught off guard; in case you accidentally bump into an influential person at your company.

Learn who's who and learn their general career history; therefore, when you have a chance to meet these people, you'll have a better idea of what subjects to strategically bring up in discussion.

Do you know your Company's Hierarchy Structure?

Work Lesson #169 – *Learn your Company's Hierarchy structure before your interview. What structure do they operate under? How does your role fit into it?*

Learning your future employer's hierarchy structure before your interview is wise and helpful.

It can assist you in asking better prepared questions, such as learning the reporting structure you're expected to follow.

The most common Hierarchy Structures are:

- Traditional
- Functional
- Divisional
- Matrix
- Holacratic

If you're ignorant of your company's hierarchy structure, this can hurt you, as you may misread a situation and make an accidental blunder. Such as approaching a higher up, when this is frowned upon by your organization.

Learn the company's hierarchy structure before your interview, so you can assess whether this structure will offer you the freedom you require to meet your career development needs.

Do you agree?

Work Lesson #170 – *Learning your Company's Hierarchy will assist in understanding your company culture.*

Company hierarchy influences company culture.

An open-door policy that is genuinely in effect allows access to company officials. This policy helps significantly in building an influential network.

Of course, you need to establish your credibility and build your reputation before you truly have access to the higher-ups in your company, but an open-door policy does assist in building a network quicker.

If your company has an old hierarchy structure (meaning Top Down), they may not have a true open-door policy, and therefore, it's frowned upon to approach company officials.

If you don't know your company's hierarchy structure, you may make some significant blunders, therefore, learn it and learn it quickly.

If your company is old-school, it may suffer from being too conservative and too rigid, which can highly influence company culture.

An out-of-box thinker may not dwell to well in an old hierarchy structure, and the sooner they realize this, the quicker they can make informed decisions that are best suited for their future.

What are your thoughts on Company Hierarchy influencing Company Culture?

Work Lesson #171 – *Learning your company's hierarchy will assist in learning who's who within your organization. This can help you make a strong first impression.*

You have one chance to make a strong first impression; learning who people are in your organization can help you make an impressive one.

Being prepared is always a wise stance to take.

For Example:

You're new to an Organization and are attending your first company function. You're standing with a colleague when a man in a tailored suit approaches you. They introduce themselves,

"Hello, I'm John Doe."

In your head…. *"OMG, John Doe, the Vice President of Finance."*

Secretly, you have ambitious goals to be in their position one day. Now, imagine if this person introduced themselves, and you had no idea who they were.

I ask you what conversation do you think will go smoother? And what conversation would you be best to ask proper tailored questions?

By knowing who this person is, you can strategically bring up your career goals and ask them detailed career path questions to assist in your career development.

Learning who's who in your organization will help you put names to faces and titles, in case you bump into them.

Always be prepared with potential questions when you meet company' officials. If you're attending a company function, see if you can find out who will be attending ahead of time.

Work Lesson #172 – Knowing who's who in your company can benefit you. Only harm can come to you by not knowing it.

Hopefully, you don't need to walk on eggshells around the higher-ups in your company, but not all companies are created equal.

Sometimes, Senior officials should be avoided, and sometime, they shouldn't be, but you won't know the difference between these two options if you have no idea who is running the company.

Learning the backgrounds of the people who make critical decisions from your organization is wise.

When you're building your network, you'll want influencers and decision-makers to be members.

Since not all corporate leaders are true leaders, you'll need to learn their career history and what others say about their character. This information will help you develop a proper career development plan, where you're more likely to impress the true leaders and influencers within your organization and add them as members of your network.

Do you believe it is wise to learn the background and reputation of your company's officials?

Work Lesson #173 – Knowing the Major Players in your organization will assist you in recognizing situations and opportunities to impress them.

Careers don't become successful without proper preparation and help.

You'll need mentors and an effective Network to reach high-end positions within your organization.

Learn the people who can help you reach your career goals and go out and impress them.

Learn what values they look for in candidates and have these traits visible to them or their close network.

One way you can become visible:

Volunteer for a portfolio assignment, such as: Organize a charity event; lead a team of volunteers; this was how I gained my first leadership experience, and I made some excellent network contact.

Develop a plan that can assist in getting visibility. How have you gained visibility in your organization?

Work Lesson #174 – The Influencers and Decision Makers within your Organization are members you want to recruit for your network.

Below is a rough step by step plan of what you need to do, to recruit company officials into your network. Each step has been discussed throughout the week, but to recap:

Step One: Learn the major players, including responsibility and title.

Step Two: Learn their career history.

Step Three: Categorize them – The ones you want to impress and the ones you want to avoid.

Step Four: Learn some of their hobbies, e.g. Golf, scuba diving etc.

Step Five: Learn what impresses them and what they value, e.g. Leadership skills, Innovation, Out-of-Box thinker, kindness, charity work etc.

Step Six: Put a plan together that aligns with step five.

Step Seven: Ensure your plan will get you visibility to the Major Players.

Step Eight: Execute your plan.

Step Nine: Readjust when required.

Use your network and social media to assist in learning information regarding the people you have chosen to impress.

Building influential networks take time. Start early and dedicate the proper amount of time to ensure you recruit people you can learn, evolve and grow from.

How have you built your network?

Work Lesson #175 – Knowing your Company's hierarchy will allow you to know who you need on your side to support moving forward an idea or strategy.

Pitching a novel idea to your organization can help build your reputation as a person who brings solutions to difficult problems.

Part of ensuring your pitch moves to implementation requires influential people on your side.

Learning who the influencers are within your organization is critical, and having them think highly of you will assist in getting them to help you.

For example:

Which of these two scenarios will have a pitch approved for implementation?

Scenario One:
You pitch your idea and strategy to a group of Decision Makers at your organization that are hearing it for the first time and don't have prior knowledge of the concept.

Or...

Scenario Two:
For two months before your pitch, you've discussed your idea and strategy with your recruited influencers. These influencers have spoken to the Decision Makers and got critical feedback regarding your idea. You listened and adjusted your pitch before attending your meeting.

Be strategic, be smart and never surprise Decision Makers. Get their feedback before entering that meeting room. This is how you sell an idea before you pitch it.

Week 16 Theme: Know Your Company's Culture

Company culture will be the environment you work in every day; because of this, it's critical to find your proper fit.

Finding an organization that can nurture your growth, allowing you to blossom to your potential will be imperative for your career.

If you're with an organization that doesn't allow you the freedom you need to blossom, you may not be happy, not fulfilled, and your place at this company will likely be temporary.

Throughout the week, I'll be discussing how company culture is established and how to find your proper fit.

Are you happy with your Company Culture?

Work Lesson #176 – *The definition of Company Culture is simple; it's the personality of your organization. It should be obvious.*

As Simon Sinek states:

Culture = Values x Behaviour

"Only when we take our values off the wall and actually live them, can we say we have a strong corporate culture." – Simon Sinek

Company culture isn't something you need to dig deep to find and, more importantly, to feel.

The root of your company culture may be hidden, but your work environment will have a distinct, clear and obvious personality.

To reach your career goals, you'll need to work within an environment that encourages your development.

How would you define Company Culture?

Work Lesson #177 – *The Leadership Team establishes company culture. When Leadership is poor, often, the Company culture suffers as a result.*

Leadership sets the tone for company culture; such as:

- How do they hire... On attitude, on credentials?
- How do they promote and recognize talent?
- Does the company's behaviour align with its vision and mission statements?
- What are their core values? And do they live by them?
- Do their actions match the standards they're preaching?

If your organization's Leadership Team isn't strong and aligned, mixed messages can be communicated through the Corporate chain resulting in gaps, miscommunication and poor company culture.

If Leadership's behaviour doesn't align with the company's core values, the culture will suffer as a result.

Building your career through the environment, you work in will influence the steps and goals you set; therefore, ensure the company culture allows for this growth.

Remember, *"There are only two ways to influence human behavior: you can manipulate it, or you can inspire it (- Simon Sinek)."* You want to be at a company that executes the latter.

When you need to force or manipulate company culture, you're not operating in truth, and therefore, this will be a temporary fix (the Band-aid solution).

When you're in an environment that encourages progress through honesty and transparency, you inspire adaptation and growth.

Do you agree?

Work Lesson #178 – *If you make the choice to fight company's culture and aren't in a position of influence. Ensure you're ready for the battle, as the war may not be able to be won.*

Company culture is established by company leadership. By choosing to fight your company culture, you've indirectly decided to go up against the Leadership Team; this means:

- You'll be sailing, both against the wind and against the current.

Before you make this decision, ensure you understand what you're doing and what you may lose as a result.

Fighting an uphill battle, cannot always be won, you must be fully aware of this before you engage. The larger the organization, the harder the climb will be.

I want to be clear; I'm not stating, not to fight a poor company culture, you may be in the right, but if you aren't in a position of influence, you may torpedo your reputation and be blacklisted as a result.

When deciding to go against the company current, NEVER be naïve.

Poor company culture is often a result of poor company leadership and a broken system of command.

Ensure you're investing your time wisely; if the probability of success is extremely low, you may be better finding an organization that values the abilities you offer, then trying to force someone's hand.

What are your thoughts about fighting to change Company Culture?

Work Lesson #179 – *Understanding your Company Culture is important to ensure you find a proper fit that matches your values and career needs.*

Priorities evolve and change as you mature into your career. Values rarely change.

For example, if teamwork is a core value of yours, best to find a company that shares this belief, instead of trying to change and adapt to an environment that doesn't fit you.

Core values cannot be compromised nor be forced; they are who you are. The authentic you!

To find a proper fit, you'll need alignment.

You'll rarely find a company that fits all of your career wants, but ensure they align with your values and provide your essential career needs.

What has been your experience trying to adapt to company values that don't align with your own? Was it a losing battle?

Work Lesson #180 – *Analyze the Company Culture during your Interview. You should be interviewing the company to ensure it's the proper fit for you and your career goals.*

Interviews go both ways—a reciprocation of giving and taking.

An interviewer will be interviewing you to ensure you're a proper fit for the role; therefore, you should be doing the same.

You want a win-win scenario after completing an interview. You have something to offer the company, and the company can provide you with an environment where you can flourish to your potential.

Therefore, you should be interviewing the company before you accept a position. Analyze your goals and ensure the company and position can, at a minimum, be a stepping stone to get there.

To help assess the Company culture during your interview, ask prepared questions to the interviewer, such as:

- Can you explain to me the company culture? Or

- What do you enjoy about the company culture? Or maybe something more discreet...
- What makes you proud to be working here?
- Is there anything you would change about the company?
- How does the company support talent growth and career development?

What questions do you like to ask an Interviewer to help assess the company culture?

Work Lesson #181 – *A Company with a strong culture, retains and attracts better talent.*

You'll learn more within an organization that values its people and encourages mentorship, through teaching and sharing.

To learn at an exponential rate, you want to surround yourself with intelligent, interesting and ambitious people.

Companies that have a great culture that encourages teamwork, transparency, and growth allow their best talent to flourish.

If you're an aspiring professional with ambitious goals, you'll want to be at an organization that nurtures your growth.

You're the seed, the company is the water, and the company culture is the green pasture.

Work Lesson #182 – *Company Culture cannot be forced. It's not set in stone, but rather like a large ship trying to change course, it takes time for the rudder to influence the ship's direction.*

The larger the organization, then the larger the ship; the slower the change.

There are a few exceptions for organizations, such as Corporate takeovers or coming back from the brink of bankruptcy, where company culture can change rapidly, but generally, this takes time and cannot be forced.

The Captain and his crew control the rudder of the ship. In Corporate terminology, the CEO and their direct reports make up the Corporate Leadership Team (CLT).

The team members are critical in establishing company culture, as they decide the company's strategic direction. They develop the values and behaviour the company operates under.

If the CLT is compromised, meaning they're self-serving, lack vision, send mixed messages, promote the wrong 'types' of people into crucial leadership positions, the system the company operates under, is broken.

If you sit in lower management and don't have an effective Network of influencers, you'll be hard press to change or impact your company culture.

If the system, in which company culture has been established, is broken... The Company Culture will suffer as a result, and you may struggle to find your proper fit within this company.

When choosing a company to invest in, choose a company that offers you the environment where your career goals can be achieved.

Week 17 Theme: Know What You're Selling

Regardless of the organization, you work for: You're ALWAYS selling yourself.

If you want to create career opportunities, you'll need to sell your abilities and reputation to secure them.

This week I'll be discussing effective selling, whether it's building a sellable name for yourself or entering a negotiation with a Client; selling is a critical part of the business world.

How important do you think selling is, in the business world?

Work Lesson #183 – *Selling is the foundation of the business world; you cannot escape it.*

There are guarantees in the business world, and one of them is selling.

Regardless if you're selling:

- A product;
- An idea;
- A brand;
- A reputation / Your name; or
- A business.

You'll need to learn to sell; accept this as a fact. There is no escaping selling in business.

The entire concept behind the business world is to earn a profit, which requires selling. Even most governments need selling, whether it's a new bill, law, grant or election. Selling is part of the game.

If you try to avoid selling, your career will be limited.

You can, of course, work behind the scenes and behind a team, but you'll still need to sell your skills and build your reputation to secure career opportunities.

Part of building a successful career will require you to sell. Do you agree?

Work Lesson #184 – *Regardless of your field or industry, never forget, you are ALWAYS selling yourself.*

Whether, it's:

- Your credentials;
- Your qualifications;
- Your name;
- Your brand; or
- Your reputation.

How you present yourself is what people see, and how they'll form an opinion of you, this can include:

- Your appearance;
- Your body language;
- Your words;
- Your tone of voice; and
- Your actions.

Understanding how you present yourself will assist in selling your credentials and reputation.

- Appearance = Overall presentation (clothing, looks - pick clothes appropriate for your industry; ensure they're always clean and wrinkle-free).

- Body language = Head held high, eye contact, firm handshake; be confident.

- Words and tone = Use strong words such as pioneered, created, delivered, committed. Convey the correct tone with the message you want to provide, such as confidence, concern etc.

- Actions = Back your words with the correct actions. Always show kindness and generosity. Be humble.

Remember, YOU are ALWAYS selling yourself. People are ALWAYS watching. Do you agree?

Work Lesson #185 – *The best job security is making yourself a 'Self-Bet.'*

Your credibility will be established based on your character, personality and ability.

This will directly feed your reputation, which will help build a sellable name.

Once you have established your credibility by delivering on your commitments while producing high-quality results, your reputation will grow to be a sellable name and, eventually, be given the label of *'Safe bet.'*

Safe Bet means:

- Guaranteed investment = Low Risk / High Reward

When you have become a *'Safe bet,'* influential people will invest in you and not only will you have job security, you'll be given career growth opportunities.

How have you built your reputation and sellable name?

Work Lesson #186 – *To increase your market value, you must offer something the market demands.*

The business world is often based on supply and demand.
To guarantee career success, you must be in demand and develop your skills, so you have something to supply.

The highest 'in-demand' skills based on a report published by the World Economic Forum[1] are:

1. Complex problem-solving.
2. Critical thinking.
3. Creativity.
4. People management.
5. Coordinating with others.
6. Emotional intelligence.
7. Judgement and decision making.
8. Service orientation.
9. Negotiation.
10. Cognitive flexibility.

These are all soft skill-based; therefore, with practice, experience and developing your mindset, you can learn them all.

Build your skills to create a track record that makes you a known product and, therefore, in demand.

How have you maintained your skill level? And how do you continue to learn new skills?

---

[1] https://www.weforum.org/agenda/2016/01/the-10-skills-you-need-to-thrive-in-the-fourth-industrial-revolution/

Work Lesson #187 – *Don't waste your time selling what people don't want. Learn your audience and learn when to walk away.*

Learning your audience and understanding when to walk away can benefit both your professional and personal relationships. Understand:

- If someone cannot see what value you bring to the table, whether it's your ability, a product or a business; and
- You have tried multiple times to show them using different methods; then, they miss the value you can bring; therefore, you should move on.

Not all relationships are meant to work out or expected to last your entire career. In fact, most won't.

As you proceed through your career, your time will become more valuable; you won't be able to spend as much time with as many people as you did in your early career.

Teach yourself at the beginning of your career to gauge your audience and gauge people's character; this can be a learned skill, it takes practice and trial and error, but you can learn. This skill will save you time.

The sooner you gauge a person's integrity and the time you're willing to invest in them, the better off you'll be. Keep it simple and ALWAYS recognize who's buying and willing to spend.

This goes into the secret of effective selling and establishing the correct strategy for a sale.

Gauge your audience, learn what they need versus what they want, understand their budget and create a win-win scenario.

If a win-win scenario cannot be established, walk away.

Do you agree?

Work Lesson #188 – *When you're talking, you aren't learning. Ask questions and listen; gain as much information as you can.*

To better serve your clients and customers, you must understand what they need.

Sometimes your clients won't understand what they need. They may not know the difference between a want and a need.

If they have strict budget restraints, only sell them what they need. This will assist in building trust and establishing a long-term relationship and, most likely, repeat business.

Understanding what your client truly needs, understanding what they are willing to pay and then selling them on what you can offer, is what takes talent...

...You won't be able to truly learn all this information if you're the one doing all the talking.

Listen to your clients, ask questions and clarify when you don't fully understand something.

What do you believe makes a strong, lasting relationship with your clients?

Work Lesson #189 – *Learn your bottom line and never compromise on it. To secure a successful negotiation, a win-win scenario is required.*

You must know your bottom line, the invisible line you cannot surpass.

It may be:

- A financial amount, or
- Core values.

The critical point is that you're aware of your bottom line and don't compromise on it.

A bottom line is something you cannot compromise, and because of this, if you're in a negotiation, you never start with your bottom-line offer, as you rarely walk out the door with your initial ask.

A negotiation is a give and take where both sides compromise. This is why you must understand your bottom line so that a win-win scenario can be accomplished.

If it's a true bottom line and you compromise, you may feel cheated or used. And generally, you don't repeat business with people, if you feel cheated.

Do you feel a win-win scenario is required to be deemed a successful negotiation?

Week 18 Theme: Know Your Clients Priorities

The business world is supply and demand, an endless circle of exchange.

Regardless if you're a business selling a product to a customer, a nurse treating a patient, an elected official coming up for re-election, or a CEO speaking to their shareholders, someone is providing the supply, and someone is receiving the demand.

When you enter the business world, to truly understand your organization's business drivers, you'll need to understand what drives your clients' businesses. This will include their:

- Values;
- Priorities; and
- Bottom line.

To ensure you can best serve your clients, you must understand and align with their expectations.

This week's theme is dedicated to learning how to best serve your clients.

Work Lesson #190 – *One of the best recommendations you can receive; can come from a Client / Customer.*

A general rule in the business world is *'Please your Client.'*

Your organization, regardless of what they do, will want to please their end-user; this is how you receive repeat business and often, how you stay in business.

If a client has recommended you, then there is a greater chance they have been pleased.

Ask yourself: If a Client has given you a recommendation to your employer, what are the odds, you'll be working again with this client?

Some of the best job security can come from your clients, as you have become an asset to your company and can now better secure continuous work with this client.

Who are the best people to get recommendations from?

Work Lesson #191 — *It will be hard for your company to deny a Client request, therefore, build strong relationships with your Clients.*

If your client requests you on a project or an account, it will be hard for your company to deny this request.

Make it a goal to build strong client relationships; this will assist in making a name for yourself and help you be in high demand.

One way to increase job security, even a potential stretch assignment or promotion, is to have your client recommend or request you.

You want to build an influential and diverse network, and this must include your clients.

As I grew into my career, many of my peers moved onto client organizations. When you build an effective network, eventually these relationships span vast distances, as people move onto different companies and career paths.

Regardless of your role, and seniority, ALWAYS make it a goal to build strong relationships; you never know when these relationships can assist you. Do you agree?

Work Lesson #192 — *In many Industries, it's the client who pays your salary, not your employer. Ensure you understand their values, priorities and bottom line.*

Part of building a sellable name and becoming a safe bet is by delivering consistent, high-quality results.

If you don't understand what drives your clients' business, which keeps your employer in business, you'll have a hard time delivering the desired and correct results.

If you don't understand your client business drivers, you'll be steering the car, but in what direction?

Never rely on luck in your career... timing can undoubtedly play a role, but relying on luck gives away your control. If you don't understand what drives your organization and, therefore, their clients' businesses, you won't truly understand how your role fits into the bigger picture.

To deliver consistent, high-quality results, ensure you learn what drives both your organization and client businesses. Do you agree?

Work Lesson #193 – *The better you understand your clients, the better you can serve and deliver to their needs.*

As Bob Hooey elegantly states, *"if you are not taking care of your customer, your competitor will."*

Your job is to keep your clients satisfied, and this requires you to know what they need before they do.

Don't misunderstand me; you don't need to be a mind reader, and you don't need to say *"Yes"* to every request. Sometimes doing your job effectively is saying, *"No."*

But before you can give any response to your clients, you must understand their needs, wants, and what they can pay for.

I've stated this before; many clients want GOLD for the price of BRONZ. To build a healthy long-term relationship means you create a win-win scenario, and no one feels cheated. To accomplish this, you NEED alignment.

You get alignment through transparent communication and understanding your client.

When you're working with clients, ALWAYS play the long game. Trust is built over time. This requires you to listen, learn and ask questions.

What has helped you understand your clients needs more effectively?

Work Lesson #194 – *A Client saying YES, is a powerful word.*

They can provide a recommendation or a new account; whatever it is, a client agreeing to move forward, often begins the process of satisfying your client's needs.

It's not that the client is always right, and saying *"No"* can hurt you.

Sometimes you must say *"No"* to the client to save them from a poor decision... It's HOW you say *"No"* that makes your reply effective.

Strong, trusting relationships take time and to build them requires honesty.

NEVER lie to your client, or over-promise what you know you can't deliver. If you do this, you won't establish trust, and you'll reduce the chance of repeat business.

When building trust with the client, you must deliver on your promises, and you must be transparent with them when things don't work out.

Align with your client at the beginning of a project, on how they want to handle communication when issues arise.

Every project has its hiccups. Often, a speedy response will assist in mitigation; therefore, align with your client on how they want to handle potential hiccups long before one appears.

Do you believe alignment in communication protocol is essential for a trusting relationship with clients?

Work Lesson #195 – *To satisfy your client, you must meet their expectations and exceed them. Alignment is critical.*

Align with your client at the beginning of a project on their definition of success.

- What is their ideal result (include: schedule, budget and any other critical item)?
- How do they want to handle communication on the project (especially bad news as discussed in the previous Work Lesson)?
- How involved do they want to be?
- What keeps them up at night?
- What aren't they telling you?

You must know the answers to these questions, at a minimum, to be able to deliver their desired results.

Remember, there are often things the client won't tell you, potentially their exact bottom line or what internal politics is going on within their organization that can impact the project. You must learn this from asking the right questions and observing. How have you learned this information?

Work Lesson #196 – *You won't have a STRONG relationship with your client if you haven't built trust. Trust leads to respect, which leads to the foundation of a strong relationship.*

Having strong relationships with your clients can become a significant differentiator between you and your peers.

Endorsements and recommendations don't come from clients that don't trust you.

Build your relationships with trust and strength; there aren't many negatives that can come from having strong client relationships.

Learn and understand your clients. Know their values, priorities and bottom line. Understand their business drivers as if they were your own organization.

Treat your client's money like you would treat your own, and trust will gradually be built.

Do you agree?

Week 19 Theme: Ask Powerful Questions

The Why? The Why Not? The What if? Why won't this work? What's wrong with it?

Revisit, rethink, the willingness to keep on asking, and discovering the right questions are always present within a curious mind.

A curious mind keeps on learning and improves as it gains experience and knowledge.

This week's theme will discuss the power in asking questions.

Questioning is often the first step in solving difficult problems; never underestimate the power of examination, especially questioning the status quo or what has always been.

Is questioning your first step in understanding a problem?

Work Lesson #197 – *The curious mind is a gift that keeps on giving.*

The curious mind never stops learning and, therefore, never stops growing.

The mind is like any muscle; the more you use it, the stronger it becomes.

If you find yourself becoming stagnant and unsure how to get unstuck, begin to question more.

Even if they're simple questions, the more you train yourself to question the obvious, the things that have always been, the more you may see something new, which can help you get unstuck and moving forward.

Ask the powerful five W questions (with the how):

- Who,
- What,
- When,
- Where,

- Why, and the bonus,
- How.

What questions do you ask to help get yourself unstuck?

Work Lesson #198 – *If you don't know the answer, it's not a stupid question.*

Many people never ask a question, due to the fear of asking what appears to be a stupid question.

I've been to many open discussions, meetings, conferences, forums etc. I've heard nearly every type of question, and the general rules I have concluded are:

- If you don't know the answer, then it's not a stupid question.
- If you have listened intently during an entire presentation/speech, and the question wasn't asked previously or addressed in the presentation, it's safe to ask.
- The only stupid questions I have witnessed are:
  - Repeat questions (meaning you weren't listening);
  - Aggressive/argumentative/Bigoted questions (you don't need to agree with everything you hear, but you must remain professional. Phrase your questions respectively); and
  - Topics that aren't related to the topic being discussed.

If asking questions makes you nervous, prepare questions in advance and practice addressing them in front of a mirror.

Asking questions can be learned, therefore, practice.

How do you practice addressing questions? Do you prepare questions in advance before attending an event?

Work Lesson #199 – *To find the right solution, you must first ask the right questions.*

Finding the real root of a problem can take time.

Many people solve the symptoms of a problem instead of the root cause. This is because, many times, the root cause of a problem is hidden amongst numerous symptoms.

Depending on how large the problem is, a thorough investigation may unleash what is causing the true problem. This may require you to:

- Go through the leaves,
- Then the branches,
- Down the trunk,
- Through the dirt,
- To the roots.

Many times, roots are covered from years of watering the surface but never breaking ground to expose the truth.

When you have been given a difficult problem to solve, ensure you find its true roots... don't develop a 'band-aid' solution... as these are temporary at best.

Question everything regarding the problem, even the obvious.

What technics do you use to discover the root cause of a problem?

Work Lesson #200 – *Asking questions is one of the simplest, yet effective ways of acquiring information.*

Acquiring information is the first step in acquiring knowledge.

Add some experience with your exponential learning curve, and you will begin to build your knowledge base.

If you don't know the answer, then you should ask the question. Asking questions is a simple way to gather information.

Add effective mentors and an influential network into the mix, and accessing critical information will become easier and faster.

Career success occurs when multiple variables align to create a powerful and efficient equation.

Work Lesson #201 – *Status quo flourishes in environments deprived of questions. Unless you question it, it will never change.*

Never get comfortable in what has always worked in the past.

Environments are continually adapting and changing.

The employee that is incapable of changing and adapting will eventually become obsolete and be left behind.

Train your brain to question, to learn and, therefore, to adapt and grow continuously.

A stagnant brain eventually stops learning and may plateau prematurely, as a result.

If you're stuck, one way to get unstuck is to train your brain to question your surroundings.

Do you agree?

Work Lesson #202 – *Curiosity, the lifeline to innovation... don't let it flatline. Keep it alive with your questions.*

I have believed that curiosity is the lifeline to innovation for a long time and that it drives progress in all innovators and the organizations they lead.

The reality is, that before anyone can do anything innovative or original, there has to be:

- A sense of wonder,
- An open curiosity,
- A spark of interest, and
- A whole bunch of questions.

The thirst to gain knowledge and to discover answers is always present within an innovator...

...Curiosity, the lifeline to innovation... don't let it flatline. Keep it alive with your questions.

Do you believe curiosity is the lifeline to innovation?

Work Lesson #203 – Train your brain to question. This will assist in igniting your creativity and help see an issue from a fresh angle.

Questioning leads to more questions and more thorough, detailed questions, which can often lead to ideas and original solutions.

Questions build off of questions... as you acquire more information, your brain will process this and begin to ask additional questions. This is how you get the momentum you need to solve difficult problems.

An idea can be the start of:

- A career game-changer,
- An invention, and
- An original idea.

Questions and ideas build off each other. Start the momentum in your favour by observing and questioning your surroundings and environment. Get your brain curious.

Do you question your surroundings and environment to trigger new ideas?

Week 20 Theme: Keeping UP Appearances

This is a simple work theme, yet, often missed, especially by inexperienced employees.

Acting like a Professional and keeping up appearances is often a part of the game; this means at a minimum:

- You dress appropriately for your industry;
- You monitor what you share on social media;
- You don't talk poorly about colleagues or your organization in public;
- You look your best during work hours; and
- You professionally conduct yourself at all times

If you're unsure of what is considered professional, ask yourself: if what you're doing, is caught on camera, how would it look? What would my boss say?

How you present yourself in public, whether you're at work or not, can impact how others see you, do you agree?

Work Lesson #204 – Your appearance is the first thing people see, and therefore, a major variable in making a strong first impression.

Part of keeping up appearances, is you're always selling yourself as a professional...

...Part of this is, dressing appropriately for your industry.

I remember a colleague telling me about an important Executive visiting a construction site, in a full WHITE suit.

For those who are unfamiliar with construction.... Construction sites are dirty...

Not only are their strict protection protocols to follow, such as appropriate gear and clothing to wear; you ALWAYS dress in clothing that can get dirty, and wearing white isn't a smart choice.

Before this person even stepped out in the field, everyone had judged them as someone that didn't belong and didn't have a clue regarding construction. This person made a MAJOR blunder in not dressing appropriately for the situation...

...Regardless of what this person said after this initial judgement was likely not heard.

Making a strong first impression, often requires you to dress appropriately for your industry, do you agree?

Work Lesson #205 – Your appearance is often the language not spoken.

For many people, their first sense is by observing... before they can smell, hear, taste or touch; they can see.

As soon as a person can see something, they begin their initial response and start processing this response with thought... this can happen in seconds.

Before a person can even realize they have assessed a person or situation, they have made a judgement based on what they've seen... You want that initial response to be positive.

Understanding how people process their responses and thoughts from what they see... is what I mean by the language not spoken.

People often judge, especially professionals, on their appearance, this judgement can be controlled to some degree, by always acting professional and dressing appropriately for your industry.

If you can't keep up your appearance, people may begin to believe you can't keep it together, and this may include their perception that you can't do your job effectively.

Dressing appropriately and presenting yourself in a positive light will assist in making a strong first impression.

Do you believe keeping up your appearance will assist in making a strong first impression?

Work Lesson #206 – *The way you carry yourself can feed your reputation and how you're perceived; this includes how you dress, body language and tone of voice.*

If you dress disorderly (e.g. wrinkle clothes, messy hair), don't be surprised if people perceive you as unorganized.

How you appear, often gets you labelled, whether it's favourably or not.... And this can feed your reputation.

The truth is, it's easier to observe than to investigate. Investigation takes time. Busy people don't have a lot of time.

If you fail to make a strong first impression, people may not give you their time, and they won't get to know you...

...Just like in a resume, if your Executive Summary doesn't capture a recruiter, they won't spend the time reading the rest of your resume. It will be tossed.

Your appearance is the first thing people observe; don't discourage them from getting to know you, by not appearing your best.

To help keep up your appearance:

- Dress well for your industry (look orderly);
- Stand straight, shoulders wide (appear confident); and
- Speak clearly and at an appropriate speed.

Would you give your time to someone who appears disorderly?

Work Lesson #207 – *Never underestimate the power of perception. What you believe of yourself and your capabilities, may not be what others see and think.*

Learning someone's capabilities requires a person to get to know you.

Often what you think of yourself may not be what others distinguish. How people perceive your ability as a professional may not be your truth.

Perception can be labelled the truth about your capabilities; just ensure what is being said, matches what you want.

Perception of your work and capabilities is essential, as this can feed your reputation.

If you're producing excellent work, but no one knows about it, you may not be given the proper recognition you deserve.

Part of keeping up appearances is playing a role; this can include your appearance, body language and tone of voice.

When presenting yourself, be well-groomed and confident. Confidence can come from your body language, tone and handshake.

If you can keep up appearances, while delivering excellent results, you can appear to be the full package to your organization.

Salesmanship comes from appearing confidently, and selling your capabilities effectively, do you agree?

Work Lesson #208 – Social Media can assist in building your reputation and personal brand. This can be a gift; use it effectively to be a strength and not a deterrent.

As a professional, you need to maintain a certain standard of professionalism, and this includes what you post on social media.

When I'm preparing for a critical meeting or an interview, and I know the names of the people attending, I ALWAYS and I repeat, ALWAYS do an internet search. This includes:

- A Facebook and Instagram search (including other social media, Twitter, YouTube etc.);
- A LinkedIn search, including looking at their recent activity and posts they have written or shared; what types of comments they make to other professionals; and
- A google search.

If the posts you have shared over social media are highly inappropriate and argumentative; this can hurt your reputation.

A recruiter won't choose to interview a candidate:

- That appears to be argumentative with other professionals on LinkedIn;
- Who brags about how much they party and drink on Facebook; and
- Who posts highly inappropriate photos on Instagram.

I ALWAYS do an Internet search, because you can learn a great deal about someone you've never met.

For example, say I'm going to attend a meeting with a client, and on my LinkedIn search, I see they appear to always be argumentative with others through their posted comments. This can help me prepare for a difficult meeting with someone who appears to enjoy arguing. This can help give me an advantage.

What you choose to post on social media can impact your reputation. A recruiter or hiring professional may never tell you the real reason you were overlooked for a position; just ensure what you post on the internet is something you don't mind having your future employer witness.

Work Lesson #209 – You can often hear the company culture speaking, by how employees conduct themselves. Ensure you observe this during your interview.

Use your senses when assessing a future employer.

As I mentioned earlier in the week, appearances are often the language not spoken.

A job interview goes both ways, a give and take. The organization is interviewing you and your interviewing them.

Observe as you walk through the office during your interview, how do people appear:

- How are they dressed? What's the dress code?
- Are they laid back, worried or uptight?
- Is the office noisy through collaboration or silent?
- Are doors closed or open?

You can learn a lot based on what you observe walking through an office. What is the company's true identity? What is your first impression of your potential future employer?

Have you used an interview to observe the internal operation of a company?

Work Lesson #210 – You're ALWAYS representing yourself, but remember, you're also representing your organization. Ensure the two are aligned so that you can create balance.

A balanced life can mean all things vital to you, are aligned.

A job can simply be a job, a paycheck, if that is all you want it to be.

If you want your career to contribute to your balanced lifestyle while being happy and fulfilled, you'll need your work and life to align.

For example, if you're a free spirit, then maybe, you shouldn't be building your career at a rigid conservative Company.

Of course, you can have differences at home versus work. I like structure and to be in charge at work, while I want to be laid back and follow at home.

Home is where I rest, and work is where I strategize... this is what works for me. I'm in alignment between work and home.

When you aren't at work, you still represent the organization you work for...

...What you do outside of work, can impact your work... just like what you do at work, can affect what you do at home. A stressful work situation can impact your health and family life.

A work/life balance fluctuates, just ensure your values and priorities align on significant items to reach fulfillment.

How have you handled work/life balance?

Week 21 Theme: The Unwritten Rules of the Workplace

Every organization has Unwritten Rules.

The tricky part with unwritten rules is they aren't publicized, and they aren't spoken.

You learn of their existence, through observing and analyzing:

- Contradictions,
- Actions and
- Avoidances...

...you witness your organization do, or not do.

Some examples of unwritten rules could be:

- The true open-door policy, a company, can preach that everyone is available to you, but this simply isn't true.
- Who you should CC in an email, no need to tell the world.
- How you should approach people's time. Managers and company leaders are busy people, be prepared, and don't waste their time.
- The top priority of the company is their employees.... maybe not, maybe it's the shareholders.
- We don't have a rumour mill... does internal office gossip reign supreme?

This week, I'll be discussing the Unwritten Rules of the Workplace, how to learn and how to avoid breaking them.

What are some of the classic Unwritten Rules, you've witnessed?

Work Lesson #211 – Unwritten rules are not advertised; you will need to learn these on your own or through your trusted inner circle.

There are unwritten rules, wherever you go, both at work and home...

- When you borrow a friend's car, you're expected to fill the tank;

- You're expected to eat with your mouth close; and
- Leave a urinal gap between you and another.

Most people won't tell you unwritten rules; you're simply expected to know them. Unwritten rules aren't advertised. They require you to observe and pay attention.

When you enter a new organization, make it a habit to observe and see if there are taboo topics people shy away from discussing; if there is, you may have found an unwritten rule.

Unwritten rules of an organization take time to learn, be patient and never assume you know them all. Often new rules get established as time moves forward, and leadership changes.

What tips do you have to assist in learning the unwritten rules of an Organization?

Work Lesson #212 – Don't be naïve; every organization has unwritten rules. Learn them quickly, and don't break them.

Every organization has Unwritten Rules...

Rules that you're best not to break.

Breaking unwritten rules, generally, always have repercussions.

Most organizations have taboo topics you should avoid discussing at work. The obvious ones are:

- Salary;
- Religion;
- Sex Life;
- Medical history (giving too much information);
- Politics etc.

But what about the not so obvious topics such as:

- Open door policy;
- Dress code, appearances and overall presentation; and
- Unconscious bias of your organization (e.g. gender gaps, pay gaps).

The potential repercussions of breaking unwritten rules can be:

- Being blacklisted, potentially losing:
  - Promotions,
  - Career growth opportunities, and
  - The label of *'high potential.'*
- Gaining a poor reputation, being labelled:
  - Difficult;
  - A loose cannon;
  - Can't be trusted; and
  - Lacks common sense.

The consequences of breaking unwritten rules can be severe; therefore, be mindful when choosing sides and taking unfavourable risks (e.g. picking a battle against an influential key player).

If you decide to break an Unwritten rule, do it by making an informed decision, meaning you understand the potential consequences.

What repercussions have you witnessed when people broke unwritten rules?

Work Lesson #213 – *What a Company preaches, is not always what they practice.*

When trying to discover your organization's unwritten rules, ask yourself:

- What do they preach?
- What actions do they take?
- Do they walk the talk?
- What do they sweep under the rug?
- What don't they want the public to know?
- What image are they trying to sell the public?

- Does the image represent the internal workings of the organization?

When you learn what your organization is hiding, you're beginning to discover their hidden rules.

Many Organizations operate differently than the image they sell their clients and the public.

For example:

An organization in North America that doesn't support gender and minority equality would be condemned in the media, and the organization's reputation would be damaged. Therefore, every image they post on their website has both men and women, and several visible minorities, but ask yourself, does your organization promote with equality in mind, or does your organization have a glass ceiling?

Unwritten rules can often be labelled as the internal politics of your organization. Learn what your organization sells the public and analyze if they use the same principles in operating the company. If there are differences... you may have found some unwritten rules.

Do you agree?

Work Lesson #214 – Company Culture often stems from the Unwritten Rules of an Organization. If you don't know where to start to learn these rules; start with analyzing the company culture.

As discussed in an earlier theme, company culture is the personality of an organization, and it should be obvious.

Company culture isn't something you need to dig deep to find and, more importantly, to feel.

The root of company culture may be hidden, but its environment will have a very distinct, clear and obvious personality.

If you don't know where to learn your organization's unwritten rules, start with company culture and work backwards. Company culture begins at its roots; these hidden roots are often where many unwritten rules lie.

To work backwards, work your way through:

- The leaves
- Then the branches,
- Down the trunk,
- Through the dirt,
- To the roots.

What other tips are there that can assist in discovering an organization's unwritten rules?

Work Lesson #215 – *Classic Unwritten Rule #1: Your ACTIONS reveal your TRUTH, and you will be judge by others on how you treat people.*

For the last three Work Lessons of this theme, let's discuss some classic unwritten rules.

The first one, your ACTIONS, reveals your TRUTH, and regardless of what you think, you'll be judge based on these actions.

The classic action is how you treat people.

Nothing screams louder than a 'faker' and a 'taker' than someone who says one thing then does another. People who care about people, generally, do the following:

- Stand when you're introduced to someone. Have a firm handshake.
- Always bring something with you, if you're invited to dinner.
- If you haven't seen someone in a while, always ask them how they are and how their families are? And listen to their response.
- Remember people's birthdays.
- Always give credit to those who've earned it.
- Say please and thank you.

A classic <u>example</u> of a disrespectful person:

Reeving up their engine in a heavy traffic area... and listening to their music blasting with the windows down... yes, you should be judged... as you're an asshole. We're sharing the world... it's not all about you.

What classic examples have you seen that reveal someone's true character?

Work Lesson #216 – *Classic Unwritten Rule #2: Invest in Your Appearance.*

You must always dress for your industry... your appearance will be the first thing people see; therefore, let's not discourage them from getting to know you.

Part of keeping up appearances is playing a role; this can include your appearance, body language and tone of voice.

Some tips:

- Dress well for your industry (look orderly), invest in proper clothing if needed;
- Stand straight, shoulders wide (appear confident); and
- Speak clearly and at an appropriate speed.

When presenting yourself, be well-groomed and confident. Confidence can come from your body language, tone and handshake.

If someone appears not groomed; people may assume the worst and, therefore, not make an effort in getting to know them; don't allow this to be the case with you.

Invest in your appearance; pay for the appropriate clothing, and use a department store stylist to help you choose clothes that will compliment your body type.

What are your thoughts when someone appears disorderly?

Work Lesson #217 *— Classic Unwritten Rule #3: Don't go to battle against an Unwritten rule.*

Next week's theme is, Choose Your Battles Wisely, where I'll go into detail on how to choose a battle wisely and when to walk away.

Today, I'll provide a sneak peek with our Classic Unwritten Rule #3.

Unwritten Rules aren't advertised; they're often what an organization wants to keep hidden depending on how dark their truth is...

...Because of this, don't go to battle against an unwritten rule. If you're not in a position of influence, you'll most likely not have enough authority to win this battle, and it can hurt you.

Unwritten rules are hard to change and influence, just like company culture... they can change, but it takes time and generally, the shift needs to be started from company leadership.

If you engage in a battle against an unwritten rule, be prepared for a long climb up a mountain, where you may not be able to summit.

If there is no chance of winning the war, never engage in the battle. Do you agree?

Week 22 Theme: Choose Your Battles Wisely

To proceed forward in your career, you must be able to work well with others. Teamwork is a standard core value of numerous organizations.

You'll come across different people throughout your career; they'll range from wonderful to terrible.

The professional who can learn to adapt to their environment will generally build a reputation as reliable and easy to work with.

The one standard variable, irrespective of the team, will be you and how you can work well with anyone. This week's theme is dedicated to, Choosing Your Battles Wisely, I'll discuss:

- When to go to battle and engage,
- Recognize when the war cannot be won, and
- When to walk away.

Learning the battles to engage in and the ones to walk away from, takes experience and wisdom, let's discuss!

Work Lesson #218 – Never underestimate the power of walking away.

There can be a great strength in walking away.

Walking away can sometimes be viewed as a weakness, but this isn't always the case. If you have made an informed decision, supported by facts and merit, then walking away can be wise, as sometimes, you should cut your losses.

Not all battles can be won. If a battle is hopeless, and you're up against a person that regardless of how wrong they are, will stick to their stubborn and inefficient ways, then maybe you're best to leave the situation.

Situations to walk away from:

- There is no benefit by staying to argue;

- The stress of continuing the battle is too excessive and will impact your health; and
- When the battle infringes on your core values, boundaries and limits, certain things shouldn't be compromised.

Learning when to walk away and cut your losses, can save you time throughout your career.

Remember, admitting a battle cannot be won and walking away can make you the winner. Do you agree?

Work Lesson #219 – *Some battles you just can't win; you must learn to recognize these before you engage. Evaluate the consequences of engaging in the battle.*

When deciding to enter a battle or to walk away, ask yourself the following:

- Can a win-win scenario be established by engaging?
- What's on the line? Is it critical to engage? Will engagement hurt you? (e.g. Reputation, Credibility, Core Value etc.)
- Will your opponent fight fair?
- What are the consequences if you lose?
- Will you alienate your team/someone by engaging?
- Does it matter? Will this be important tomorrow or in a week?

If you're unsure whether to engage in a battle, remember, Warren Buffets, quote:

> *"It takes 20 years to build a reputation and five minutes to ruin it. If you think about that, you'll do things differently."*

Sometimes engaging in a battle can reflect poorly on your character and reputation. Have you shown your immaturity, because you haven't been able to move on from a topic gracefully?

When deciding to engage in a battle, ensure that it matters, meaning it's essential, and the result will impact your future... a future that will last longer than a month.

Short term gain for long term repercussion is not choosing wisely. Do you agree?

Work Lesson #220 – *The high road can be how you win the war. Refusing to play the game, can make you the winner.*

Engaging in too many battles can prevent you from winning the war.

If you engage in unimportant matters, engage in too much office politics and gossip, this can hurt your reputation. You may become known as someone who cannot be trusted.

Engaging in stupid battles will PREVENT you from winning the war.

If you don't follow what I'm saying, go read, The Art of War by Sun Tzu, you will not regret it.

As Sun Tzu summarizes,

> *"The one who knows the enemy and knows himself will not be endangered in a hundred engagements."*

Instead, they're:

> *"The one who knows when he can fight, and when he cannot fight, will be victorious."*

Refusing to play the game and engaging in a pointless confrontation/battle can be a strategy that makes you victorious... it's hard to lose when you aren't playing.

> *"Subjugating the enemy's army without fighting is the true pinnacle of excellence."*

What are your thoughts? Can you win the war, by not going to battle?

Work Lesson #221 – *Learn to save your breath, when dealing with people who severely lack self-awareness or need to stroke their own ego.*

There's a reason people believe, *"Ignorance is bliss,"* because the ignorant don't know they're ignorant; therefore, they may not know the difference between a battle won and a battle lost.

There are three types of people to avoid going to battle with:

- The ignorant;
- Low Emotional Intelligence; and
- The Ego-driven / Narcissist.

Don't go into battle with the ignorant... they're too stupid, reckless and senseless to realize they lost... and may just keep going, relying on pure stubbornness to win.

Avoid going into battle with low emotional intelligence (EQ) types. Low EQ is similar to ignorant people, meaning they may not understand the real issue at hand, especially in situations where their capabilities are in question. People who severely lack self-awareness, often have inflated and a false sense of their abilities and generally don't handle constructive feedback well. Your words can be lost on low EQ types.

The Ego-driven / Narcissistic type rarely fight fair and can lack integrity; they may simply be willing to take the battle to a level you can't follow. Winning at all cost is what matters to them, and there will be very little chance of a win-win scenario. They can lack empathy and a basic understanding of emotions. Avoid going to battle against someone that needs to win to feed their ego. They're normally trenched in insecurity, and therefore, don't play fair.

Avoid battles with these three types; if you engage, you'll be wasting your time. Proper communication requires both parties to compromise.

What types of people do you avoid going to battle against?

Work Lesson #222 – *Learn what is important and what you can influence. Be mindful of what you're heard discussing.*

Understanding what you can influence is critical in gauging whether you should enter a battle.

If you don't have influence over a situation, engaging in a battle may look like complaining and wasting your time on something that won't change.

People that bring a solution mindset don't complain; they may vent behind closed doors to clear their chest and then move on and take action over what they can influence.

If they have deemed something important, they will put together a plan to gain influence so they can change.

If you settle for complaining, you've already lost the battle, as complaining solves nothing. You'll most likely be complaining about the same thing a year down the road.

If you've deemed something important, learn what you need to do to gain influence to change it, never settle for an undesirable situation. Do you agree?

Work Lesson #223 – *Never engage in an argument when you are emotionally compromised.*

You must always remain level-headed, calm, and in control, if you're engaging in a confrontation.

Emotionally compromised individuals often make poor, misinformed decisions. They can unnecessarily offend others, as well as alienate people.

An emotionally compromised individual often build a reputation of being unpredictable and a loose cannon... you don't want to send someone who can be emotionally compromised into critical meetings, where things can get heated.

If you feel you're beginning to lose control of your emotions, take a break from the discussion. Go for a walk to clear your head or do whatever it takes to calm down.

If something has caught you off-guard, don't react immediately, take a pause and evaluate. Don't continue a conversation if you're emotionally compromised.

What technics do you use to calm down, when you're beginning to become emotionally compromised?

Work Lesson #224 – *Trying to avoid a confrontation is wise, but not always possible. Sometimes avoidance creates a greater issue.*

There is a reason why passive-aggressive people are often considered poor communicators... not all confrontations can be avoided, nor should they be.

Sometimes, you must be the bearer of bad news, that someone must-hear.

If you're leading a team, part of your responsibility will be to provide feedback to your team members, and this could mean constructive feedback.

If you have a team member who is disturbing other members with poor behaviour, you'll need to interject. If you choose not to, the situation will get worse, not better, and you may lose valuable team members.

You cannot ignore poor working situations and hope they'll improve on their own... this is rarely the case. You'll need to interject if you want the situation to improve.

When providing constructive feedback:

- Timing is critical, pick the right time and have the conversation in private;
- Watch your tone of voice; be apologetic, but firm.

- Reach an agreement together on what the individual needs to improve on; help set targeted goals.
- Revisit the conversation a few months down the road to gauge progress (interject earlier if required).

You can't always escape a confrontation, especially if it's impacting others. These situations should never be avoided.

You must deal with them if you want to see improvements, do you agree?

12 Lessons of Life

"Embrace your struggles, reflect on your growth, share your lessons and above all, enjoy the journey."

To round out the 2019-year, Work Lessons 101 will be posting special content targeting other vital lessons.

For the past 22 weeks, I've been posting work lessons centred around a specific weekly theme, but for the next two weeks, I'll share the number one lesson I've learned in each of the below 12 categories.

1. Destiny
2. Health
3. Friendship
4. Knowledge
5. Parenting
6. Fun
7. Education
8. Love
9. Financial
10. Sports
11. Marriage
12. Leadership

Work Lessons 101 is passionate about sharing lessons and knowledge with the community. Since work is only one aspect of our lives, I thought it would be fun to share new experiences.

This is my version of the *'12 days of Christmas,'* except this version is called *'12 Lessons of Life.'*

Destiny Lesson – *The hands you hold can either raise you up or hold you down.*

Life isn't fair... we don't always get the parents we deserve, the promotion we have earned, or the luck we dream of.

Your destiny isn't written in stone; if you're willing to put in the effort to change and learn, you can become the person you desire.

If you aren't living the life you want, you must make the change.

Dreams become a reality when you decide to pursue them. This takes strength, confidence, ability, hard work, preparation and help.

Strength, because you may need to pursue this dream alone if your family and friends don't support it.

Confidence, because you'll need to get back up every time you fall. Build off of your mistakes and learn.

Ability, because you'll need to leave your comfort zone to develop new skills.

Hard work, because often dreams are built after your 40 hours of work are done.

Preparation, because you'll need a plan and strategy to execute. Luck happens when people have developed their ability and have prepared thoroughly.

Help, because if you aren't born with a support system around you, you'll need to build one. Build relationships that will assist you in developing into the best version of yourself.

Start today!

Health Lesson – *You're no good to anyone sick, including yourself.*

In your busy day to day life, you can often compromise your health and not realize the long-term detriment you're doing to yourself. You tell yourself:

- Just grab a quick lunch to go...
- I'll work-out tomorrow...
- I'll catch up on sleep on the weekend...

Even though what you're doing today, may seem more important than eating a home cook meal or skipping out on the gym... if you continue to compromise, our bodies will begin to show the neglect.

- Does it take longer for you to get over a cold?
- Do you continue to work through a cold?
- Do you get sick more often?

Don't ignore the signs your body is trying to tell you when you need to slow down and concentrate on both your physical and mental health.

If your health is compromised and you get sick, you cannot provide for your family, and you can't provide for yourself... therefore, your health is nearly always a number one priority and shouldn't be compromised.

Everyone reacts differently to life's pressures and stresses; the secret is to learn these reactions and put protocols in place to cope with these stresses before they take an undesired impact on your body.

How do you cope with stress?

Friendship Lesson – *Friends are the family you choose.*

Some of the most impactful and life-changing relationships will happen from your friendships.

As the German writer, Goethe said, *"We are shaped and fashioned by what we love."*

This saying applies to all aspect of your life, from the music you choose to listen to, to the books you read... to the friendships you make.

If you're born into a family that doesn't encourage you to be the best version of yourself, you can build the family you desire.

A family doesn't need to be blood-related to be considered a family. Family is love... and you love, what you choose to.

Have you embraced friends into your family?

Knowledge Lesson – *Knowledge is the source of unlocking the hidden path to success.*

Knowledge is the ultimate reward for leaving your comfort zone.

Throughout your career, you'll be overlooked for promotions you deserve; you'll be dealt setbacks and obstacles. Organizations can often hold the key to your career success in the form of salary, promotions, or stretch assignments, but they can never take your credibility, skillsets and, therefore, your knowledge.

In my opinion, knowledge is the best job security you can have... as you can bring it to every corner of your life.

If your organization cannot see what you bring to the table, find an organization that can.

If you build your knowledge by collecting skills, information and gaining experiences, you'll have far more control over which direction your career goes.

This is why knowledge is powerful... it allows you to pave your own path.

What do you think offers you the best job security?

Parenting Lesson – *The actions of a parent often stem from two things, that of love... and that of fear.*

I've been a parent for all of 8 months, and it has been one of my greatest lessons. And one I feel compelled to share.

I've learned a whole new meaning to the definition of love, of Selflessness.... And of Fear.

When you love someone more than you love yourself... It can drive fear in you that you never knew existed. If you aren't aware of it, it can drive and control your choices and decisions, for better and for worst.

I think this fear stems from the fact that you, under all circumstances, want to protect your child from pain.

But the truth is, you can't always protect them... a person needs a certain amount of resilience to be happy and successful in life... Life isn't fair, and you don't get everything you want; this resilience, which is only built through difficulty, will protect your child from allowing those difficulties to get the best of them.

It's our resilience that gets us up after we fall.

So, as a new parent, I'm met with fear... I worry about how much he's eating that he doesn't get sick (you always have SIDS in the back of your head)... future worries like when he starts school, whether he'll get bullied... the fear, the worry, just continues...

You cannot always be in control; if you allow this fear to get the best of you, your decisions will be highly compromised.

"No, you can't," can often be the words of a parent living in fear...

I'm learning to cope with these new fears by talking to parents and being aware of when these fears creep into my decisions.

Fun Lesson – *You should spend the needed time preparing for your future, but not always at the cost of today or the cost of your youth.*

Not everyone gets to grow old.

I have sadly buried six friends by the age of 28. Not everyone has a tomorrow, and not everyone gets to live out their bright future.

I learned from these losses never to postpone fun, never to postpone working towards your dream.

- Take that trip you always wanted.
- Say I love you when you feel it.
- Write the book you imagined.

Stop postponing doing something that can make you happy, in sacrifice for what you think you should be doing today.

I believe life is truly a gift; therefore, you should spend the needed time preparing for your future but not always at the cost of today or the cost of your youth. Do you agree?

Education Lesson – *The best students never stop learning; they're entrepreneurs for life.*

Continuous success is a result of highly driven individuals that have devoted their lives to the concept of lifelong learning.

The thirst to gain knowledge and learn far exceeds any other form of education, whether it's through formal methods, discovery, reading, listening or all of the above, wanting to learn is critical to personal growth and development.

Dedication to lifelong learning takes discipline, motivation, hard work and time...

...But the reward for continuous learning is continuous improvement. This is the simplest method to reach the best version of yourself.

What are your thoughts?

Love Lesson – *Love can be the cause of our greatest pain and fears. But it's in this fear that our deepest values and priorities become clear.*

I cannot define love... because for me, it's merely life... the meaning of my life.

The power of love has brought me my greatest happiness, my greatest fear and my greatest pain.

Whether you've fallen in love, have a fear of losing someone, or have lost a loved one... it's all part of love and the risk of loving someone.

Loving someone doesn't mean you're happy and joyful all the time.

My childhood best friend told me, *"Sometimes loving someone may mean you watch them die."* She told me this at her father's funeral after a lengthy illness. She stood by his side, watching him slowly slip away from her.

This conversation was life-changing... it gave me an entirely new perspective on love. Love can sometimes mean you're helpless and deeply uncomfortable, but regardless of what you're feeling, you stay by their side because you love them.

Love has caused me my greatest pain and fear, but when these pains become evident and alive, it has allowed me to understand my priorities much clearer, I've learned my core values and what I truly need in my life to be fulfilled, and because of this, love is truly a gift.

Financial Lesson – *Before you go into debt, ensure you know it's worth it.*

Debt should concern you because it can turn into a painful trap, making it hard for you to escape.

You'll likely not be able to avoid debt throughout your life completely, but you should, at a minimum, weigh the pros and cons of a purchase before you decide to commit... education... house... expensive luxury items etc.

Yes, education and childcare costs are on the rise, and because of this, you need to be organized and understand where all your money is going. What is coming in and what you have leftover to invest.

If you want a comfortable retirement, you must start your financial education early and begin to save and invest.

I started saving for my retirement two years after I graduated from university. Now that I'm in my mid-thirties, these investments are finally providing me with some security and freedom.

I know many people are avoiding college because of the high cost and debt... this may or may not be a wise decision, but just remember, many businesses cost money to start.... Trademarks and patents aren't cheap, and securing Venture Capitalists requires some form of investment, time and likely some money.

Choose the path that best suits your goals, priorities and lifestyle. Just ensure you're making an informed decision before you commit to large long-term debt. Do you agree?

Sports Lessons – *A team player means you care more about the name on the front of your jersey than the back.*

During my hockey days, we often spoke about the players who cared more about the name on the back of the jersey, versus the front.

Without question, it's always the front name that matters more; be the player that represents the team.

A team needs all types of roles to be complete.

It's possible to have too much talent on a team. In sports, many times, the teams that are the best on paper don't always win the championship; if this were true, then the New York Yankees would win the World Series more often.

Supporting members of a team can be as crucial to winning, as the superstars.

Many people believe they need a team full of superstars, the 'A' players. A capable team needs their 'A' players, the 'superstars,' but it also needs support, the labelled 'B' players who do most of the work; the players that will sacrifice for the greater good; and the ones who don't care who gets the credit.

Team sports have changed my life; I've learned that it's an honour to be a part of a team and that sometimes you must fill the role the team needs versus the position you want. If you can remain adaptable, there will always be a team in need of you.

How has team sports changed your life?

Marriage Lesson – *Respect is the glue that strengthens and binds a happy marriage.*

Love, Friendship, Parenting... so many variables enter into a marriage at one point. They may be there at the beginning or may come at a later date.

I've been with my husband for nearly 12 years... and I've learned many things about him and many things about myself. This partnership has been the most rewarding relationship of my life.

But the most surprising thing I've learned is that love isn't the most important variable of a happy marriage; instead, it's respect.

Love can be the reason you enter into a marriage, but respect is often what keeps it intact.

Respect is what strengthens and binds your foundation to build a long and happy marriage... the strength of marriage comes from the establishment of respect.

- It's respect that prevents us from choosing words we will later regret in an argument.
- It's respect that prevents us from speaking poorly or belittling a person when they aren't around; and
- It's respect that drives our behaviour... behaviour that our children observe.

Marriage is a dish with many ingredients, but remove respect, and it simply won't taste right.

What ingredients do you believe goes into a happy marriage?

Leadership Lesson – *True leaders are rare because they're aware of what they're putting aside, which is themselves.*

The definition of leadership can be a simple statement, or it can be a complex one.

The traits that build a leader tend to be complicated, as numerous situations can amplify a leader's capabilities, yet from my experience, picking one out of the crowd is simple and straight forward.

There is a selflessness in being a great leader... they don't desire power or legacy... they want to serve their teams.

Their actions support the greater good, even if it doesn't truly benefit them self.

A True Leader's clear action is they take all the blame in failure and share all the rewards in success. It takes true integrity to take full responsibility for failure and to share success in times of triumph.

Leaders live in truth; they don't deny their weaknesses; they often recruit others who carry the strengths they lack; they build the best team while learning from their team.

True leaders never allow their egos to blind them... even during great success, they remain humble and continue to strive to be better versions of themselves.

These are the actions of a true leader.

Have you had the opportunity to work with or for a true leader?

Week 23 Theme: Work Bootcamp

I'm not a big supporter of New Year's resolutions, as I feel they can create additional pressure that's not helpful. Withstanding that, I'm a supporter of setting goals to improve yourself; so, given it's the New Year, I felt this week's theme could provide some helpful work tips and exercises to re-energize yourself.

This week I'll discuss how to get ourselves back in work shape... yes, we exercise to stay healthy, but how many of us do work exercises to keep our brain active and skills relevant?

The purpose of Work Bootcamp is to assist in getting you into career shape, whether you're in a slump, burned out, unemployed or simply need a change, stay tuned for our work lesson exercises and tips that can help keep you on top of your game.

What habits have you developed to keep yourself re-energized?

Work Lesson #225 – Becoming comfortable being uncomfortable, requires you to embrace change and be adaptable. Small steps can add up to a leap.

Today's Work Exercise Tip: Step out of Your Comfort Zone

If you want to continue to grow, and improve, you must be willing to learn, either by trying something new or becoming better at something you've done... this can require you to branch out of your comfort zone.

Step 1: Choose something you want to develop and improve; that also scares you (e.g. Public Speaking).

Step 2: After you choose something, develop a 30-day plan on how to improve it.

Step 3: For the next 30 days, practice and work on it for 30min each day.

Step 4: After a month, begin to slowly branch out with this new skill by either practicing in front of others or testing it in some manner.

Step 5: As you build your confidence and improve, branch out further.

Example: If you want to become a strong public speaker, practice in front of a mirror for 30 minutes a day for 30 days. Pick any topic to practice speaking and change this up throughout the month. Then, slowly start speaking in public, maybe ask a question in a meeting or at a conference, build up the skill till you can present a 30-minute presentation without getting nervous.

The purpose of this exercise is to branch out of your comfort zone, learn to embrace change, adapt, and put a plan together to develop new skills even if it scares you.

What technics do you use to branch out of your comfort zone?

Work Lesson #226 – Being prepared for the unexpected, requires you to be overprepared.

Today's Work Exercise Tip: Update Your Resume

Your resume captures what you have accomplished in your career. If you don't update this regularly, you risk forgetting something that could help sell yourself to a future employer.

Step 1: Update your bible resume 2 to 3 times a year, so your accomplishments get recorded before you forget them. If you don't have a bible resume, start one.

Your bible resume has all your academic, work and volunteer experience, including all your accomplishments and achievements you have gained throughout your entire academic and professional career. It holds everything. The purpose of your bible resume is to take bits and pieces from it to tailor your resume (the one you send employers) specifically for a position. Never send your bible resume to an employer; as you gain experience, it becomes a large document (mine is over 10 pages).

Step 2: Ensure that you have an updated 2-page resume highlighting your most relevant accomplishments and career history. Your short resume should be your highlight reel.

Step 3: Make it a habit when you feel lost, or stuck, to read your bible resume, front to back. This can show you how far you've come since you began your career.

Remember, without an effectively written resume, you may not get the position you desire. You must sell yourself through your resume to help secure an interview. Once you have the position, your career development plan will be your strategy to reach your career goals.

How do you prepare for unexpected opportunities?

Work Lesson #227 – Goals are the map, but you steer the vehicle.

Today's Work Exercise Tip: Goal setting through your Career Development Plan (CDP)

Goals assist you in positioning your efforts to hit correct targets, ensuring you spend your time productively to reach each career milestone. If you start your career without goals:

- How will you measure your progress?
- How will you know if you're on the correct path?

Goals can help gauge where you are in your career and show you that you're going in the direction you desire. A CDP captures the plan you'll execute to reach your career goals.

Step 1: Your CDP will address the who, what, when, where, why and how, you'll achieve your career goals. Ensure your CDP addresses the following:

- Where do you want to be in 1 year, 2 years, 5 years, 10 years?
- Why do you want to be there?
- What motivates you about these career goals?

- What skills and knowledge gaps will you need to develop to reach your desired position?
- How will you gain the skills, knowledge and experience to reach your goals?
- Who are the people that you need on your side to help get you there?
- What relationship do you need to build?
- When do you need to develop these relationships by? What's your timeframe?

Step 2: Update your CDP once a year. A good time to do this is one month before your performance appraisal, so you're prepared to have a proper discussion with your boss on your career progression and the support you need.

The path to accomplishing your goals can take many routes. Deviate and pivot when required; goals mature and develop as you progress through your career as priorities change.

Do you set check-in targets when assessing the path to your goals?

Work Lesson #228 – An active brain trains itself to see what's missing. Bringing a solution mindset to every problem means you first bring the right questions.

Today's Work Exercise Tip: Brain Cardio through Questioning

Asking questions is one of the simplest yet effective ways of acquiring information.

Step 1: Pick something, anything, a process, a product, an object etc.

Step 2: Put 30 minutes aside to focus solely on what you picked.

Steps 3: Then, question absolutely everything about it. Its colour? Its shape? What's its purpose? What don't you like about it? Can you improve it? Is it needed? Is it redundant? Can it be updated? Questions, Question, then question some more... do this for 30 minutes.

Step 4: Do this exercise weekly, each week with something new.

Questions often build off of questions... the first few times you do this exercise, it may be difficult, but as you continue, it will become easier.

This exercise aims to train your brain to question pass the obvious, pass the status quo, and develop a process for yourself to become a better solution provider. Individuals who can solve difficult problems are rare, become this person. Bring a solution mindset to every problem you're given.

By training your brain to question, you're igniting your creativity, which can help you see an issue from a fresh angle.

What cardio do you give your brain?

Work Lesson #229 – If you recognize your mind getting into a rut, try something new to help you branch out of your comfort zone.

Today's Work Exercise Tip: Learn Something New

Learning can be found anywhere; you simply need to train your brain to look for it.

Step 1: Choose something new: a skill you want to develop, a new genre of book you want to read, a new hobby you want to start, take online courses, attend a conference etc.

Step 2: Pick a timeline you want to dedicate to this new 'something.' For example, if you pick pottery, ensure you take enough classes to give it a real try and to learn the skill. Generally, you need to dedicate a minimum of 3 months to something before you can honestly say you tried.

Step 3: If you don't end up liking your choice, give it a few tries... some things take time to truly experience.

Step 4: Do this exercise annually to bi-annually, depending on what you choose.

The purpose of this exercise is to get you out of your comfort zone and to assist you in your continued learning.

Highly successful people have dedicated themselves to lifelong learning. If you find yourself in a rut, get your mind unstuck by trying something new. If you have committed yourself to lifelong learning, you won't be stuck in one place for very long, as you have trained your mind to continue to look for new ways to challenge yourself.

What technics do you do to get out of a rut and to expand your mind?

Work Lesson #230 – You can be the best at what you do, but you can't be everywhere, to truly open big doors, you'll need help opening them.

Today's Work Exercise Tip: Grow Your Network

Many times, career success comes from who you know, therefore, make networking a priority. This exercise can help you build a strong network without missing gaps.

Step 1: Review your network, isolate any missing gaps (level, age etc.).

Step 2: Every month, set a goal of how many new contacts you want to make and what type of relationship you want (make missing gaps in your network a priority).

Step 3: Put a plan together to meet these people (through work, social media, conference etc.).

Step 4: Mix it up each month and slowly build your network to span large distances through multiple companies and industries.

Understanding the type of relationship you want with your new contact will assist in approaching the recruitment process. I caution you by chasing a title and numbers. Think strategically on who you'll need in your network to help make you successful, such as influencers, mentors, trusted colleagues etc.

The purpose of this exercise is to grow your network, as you never know who can open unforeseen doors; therefore, always put time aside throughout your career to network. A strong network has all levels and generations accounted for; ensure you have no missing gaps.

Don't rush building your relationships, as trust takes time to earn. When building an effective network, it's quality that matters, not quantity.

What's the best method you use to network?

Work Lesson #231 – Sometimes, to understand where you're going, you need to reflect on where you've come from.

Today's Work Exercise Tip: Reflection Practise

There can be significant growth and learning from reflecting on the past.

Step 1: For a month, write in a journal. You can write anything, your thoughts, quotes you like, things that happened to you, lessons you've learned.

Steps 2: After the month, don't read what you wrote for another 30 days.

Steps 3: Pick up your journal on Day 31 and read what you wrote. What have you forgotten about? A random insightful thought? Do you see anything from a different perspective?

Reflection exercises can provide a new perspective on an old thought; you can see it through new eyes. Time can help us see things differently.

When I started my career back in 2006, I had a personal journal. I wrote in it for years, then moved 1000 km away, and my old journals went into a box. Four years later, I reread them... and I was shocked at how accurately I recorded the first few years of my career... and voilà... the birth of Work Lessons 101... you never know what you think today; what you write today may turn into tomorrow.

Remember, you must move on from the past but not before you've learned from it. Take the time and reflect, ensure you learn your lessons.

Have you learned from reflecting on the past?

Week 24 Theme: Career Myths Versus Career Reality

This past year, I have had countless discussions on the path to building successful careers, and it has surprised me how much incorrect information is out there.

What worked for your friend may not work for you. Each career has a unique formula to reach the success you desire. Yes, there are common variables, but don't be discouraged if something that has worked for others appears to be failing for you.

Many common career beliefs are indeed incorrect.... Yes... Of course, you can apply for a position if you don't meet all the criteria, and No, it's never too late to change careers.

This week's theme focuses on debunking career myths and discussing the reality of building successful careers.

What's the biggest career myth you've heard?

Work Lesson #232 – Career Myth: Put your head down, work hard and you'll be promoted. Career Reality: You get rewarded by delivering consistent, high-quality results that are visible to your Organization.

A great work ethic will benefit you through your career, but only if you use it to work productively and improve.

Throwing hours at a problem doesn't mean you solve it.

If you're not able to:

- Learn from your past mistakes,
- Understand what went wrong and didn't work; then
- Readjust and try again.

Your hard work is primarily for nothing because you haven't improved nor solved the problem... you mostly have nothing to show for your hard work.

Many people tell young professionals to work hard, keep your nose to the grindstone and you'll be promoted... this may work, but if hard work were the real secret variable to career success, there would be far more successful people.

I know many of us like to think our boss has great plans for us and recognizes our work, but in many cases, this simply isn't true.

- If you're working long hours at the office and no one sees it, did it happen?
- If you're working long hours and have nothing to show for it, did it happen?

You get rewarded for what you're seen doing and for delivering consistent results; therefore, ensure your work is visible to your boss, the team, and the boss's boss.

Get results, be visible then, to guarantee you're recognized and promoted, be likeable and network.

What do you believe gets you promoted?

Work Lesson #233 – *Career Myth*: *You'll know what you want to do with your life once you graduate. Career Reality: It's OK not to know what you want. Careers grow and change as you mature, remain open-minded and flexible.*

Finding the right career can be a journey, and many times you find it through trial and error.

Don't stop yourself from accepting a good job because you aren't sure. You must take the first step to build towards a second.

Learning what you don't want to do can be as valuable as learning what you want to do; therefore, don't be scared if the first job you take doesn't end up being permanent.

There may never be an exact scenario or situation that is ideal, but you need to start somewhere. Never be afraid to start... You'll be making a few new starts throughout your career, as priorities and needs change as you progress and mature.

Being flexible can be one of your greatest assets. You don't need to know it all or have it all fingered out, especially at the start of your career.

If you remain flexible and open-minded, you can adjust when opportunities present themselves.

Who is still trying to figure out what they want to do with their life?

Work Lesson #234 – Career Myth: It's too late to change careers. Career Reality: It's never too late; if you're alive, able, then develop a plan to move careers.

Life's too short to be unfulfilled in your career.

If you're not happy nor fulfilled, you'll need to make some form of a change.

You don't always need to entirely change careers but make a pivot in a new direction. Many skills are transferable, and therefore, you can build on what you have already established.

Some steps to assist in making a career change:

1. Target an industry and position you're interested in.
2. Learn what skills are required to execute this new role.
3. Assess what skills you have that can be transferred to the new position.
4. Develop the skills your missing; while you're doing this, network with people that can help you move into your new career with your potential employer.
5. Sell your qualification to a new employer.

Remember, it takes courage to make a career change. Be brave and put together a plan, then execute the heck out of it!

What steps do you recommend in making a career change?

Work Lesson #235 – <u>Career Myth</u>: Working for yourself will provide you with freedom. <u>Career Reality</u>: Yes, the freedom to work 60+ hour weeks.

Working for yourself may provide you freedom at some point, but when you're starting, you'll be working around the clock, and you can say goodbye to 40-hour weeks.

I work a minimum of 60 hours a week, and I can't call in sick when I'm not feeling well, because, if I don't do the work, it doesn't get done.

Many business owners are always on call; if a staff member calls in sick and can't find a replacement, guess who gets to cancel their plans and replace them?

When you work for yourself, it takes a great deal of self-motivation and discipline, because there is no one there to pick up the slack. If you don't work, then it doesn't get done.

Working for yourself is hard, yet, it can be truly rewarding, but it takes a strong, driven, smart and entrepreneurial person to succeed.

Which path do you think is more laborious, working for yourself or working for an employer?

Work Lesson #236 – _Career Myth_: *A degree will provide me with a high paying salary and job security. _Career Reality_: Being great at your job, adaptable and keeping your skills relevant will offer you better job security.*

When you graduate with your degree, it may be an incredible personal achievement, but you'll generally be untrained and have little experience. You have yet, to bring value to your employer...

...Therefore, don't expect to start at a 6-finger salary right out of school. And don't think your degree will offer you job security. Some advanced degrees provide extra security, but generally, a degree will simply get you in the door, along with every other new graduate. It won't differentiate you.

In today's rapidly changing world, there isn't much job security; therefore, never be naïve in thinking a degree that is theoretically based will help you create job security in a world that requires you to be practical.

If you want to make yourself hard to replace, then deliver results... consistent, high-quality results that solve difficult problems.

People who can provide solutions to difficult problems are the rarest type of employee; be this person.

What skills do you think provides the best job security?

Work Lesson #237 – _Career Myth_: *Being unavailable will lose me opportunities. _Career Reality_: People need to earn your time and availability.*

Being too accessible doesn't mean people value and respect you. Sometimes, this can get you perceived as a doormat and taken advantage of.

If you're always saying yes and making yourself available, people won't prioritize you, as they will think they can come to you and exploit your time based on their convenience.

Even though I firmly believe you should say Yes at the beginning of your career. You need to ensure you can handle the request.

If you say yes to every request, including the ones that have zero benefits to yourself, you risk taking on too much, risk burning out, and risk disappointing people by not following through on your commitments... this is what will lose you opportunities and hurt your reputation.

Understanding and creating your boundaries and what you're willing to do will help you make you more productive.

Have you made yourself available to your colleagues? Did people take advantage of this?

Work Lesson #238 – *Career Myth*: *I won't get the job without experience.* *Career Reality*: *It's your job to sell your qualification and capabilities to an employer.*

Another remarkably similar career myth, I must have all the qualifications before I apply.

Most people don't have all the qualifications an employer is looking for. Personally, if I met 50% of the requirements, I apply.

As for not finding a job due to little work experience, well, this requires you to be a bit creative.

Most candidates graduating from University have some experience; you simply need to know how to sell it.

, say the job application is asking for leadership experience:

- Was captain of the University Varsity baseball team, led the team to the State Championship. Mentored and developed new teammates etc. or

- Was a camp counsellor accountable and responsible for program development of over 100 children.

Do you have volunteer experience? Such as: running a charity campaign, spending time at an elderly home, camp counsellor etc. Many of these roles have leadership and time management experience.

Do you have extracurricular experience that is relevant? Sports, write a blog, Social Media business... social media businesses have experience in branding, marketing, and content development. YouTube channels require writing, storyboarding, film editing etc.

It's your responsibility to sell your qualification to an employer.

You do this by linking the skills you have to what the employer is looking for. This may require you to think out of the box and use your sports or volunteer experience to help sell your capabilities.

How did you land your first job?

Week 25 Theme: Acing the Interview

Most people are nervous about entering a job interview, and this doesn't always lessen as you gain experience.

Interviews can be nerve-racking, but they don't have to be. Some methods can highly reduce your nerves during the interview process.

Remember, it's your job to turn your interview into a job offer. You do this by showing you'll be a suitable candidate for their organization; that you have the right attitude and motivation to fit their company culture.

This week, I'll be discussing techniques that can help reduce your nerves and prepare you to ace your interview.

Learning how to stand out through your responses, telling your story and how to prepare for an interview properly will assist you in getting an offer of employment.

Work Lesson #239 – When answering a question, respond in a way that can amplify many skills without stating them.

You want to show an interviewer that you're a leader, team player, strong communicator, analytical and a skilled problem-solver, without sounding too preachy and overusing these words.

Open-ended questions are a gift because they allow you to tell a story that not only answers their question but can answer multiple queries at the same time while highlighting your qualifications.

The reason you don't want to call yourself a leader, is because leaders are labelled leaders based on their actions and results, therefore, tell a story that amplifies the characteristics of a leader without stating it.

For example, your interviewer asks you, *"tell us a story of how you solved a difficult problem?"* or *"Tell us a story of how you helped someone?"*

- This is a great time to tell a story of how you came late to a project that was falling behind, and you came up with an idea to get it back on track; or
- How you mentored a protégée that got to the next level in their career and how it made you feel; or
- Tell the story of how you needed to change roles on a team to fill in a gap by learning a new way of thinking, this was able to get the team back on track.

I love this question because you can tell them a real example that genuinely showcases your value and the value you'll soon bring their organization.

Do you tell stories during interviews?

Work Lesson #240 – One way to stand out during an interview is to have unique responses to standard interview questions.

One of the most common interview questions is, *"Tell us about yourself?"* And many people don't prepare properly for it.

Since this is usually the first question, the interviewer asks you, prepare for it. This is a way of starting the interview off right and build your confidence.

Some pointers on how to address this question:

- Don't give them your entire life nor career story.
- You want to keep your response clear, concise and captivating. This is your elevator speech.
- Tell them a little bit about your career history, why you took certain positions and what you gained and learned from them and have this story lead to how you got to your current job (fit in a significant accomplishment in your story).
- The most important part of your elevator pitch is to make it relevant to the position you're interviewing for.

When you're asked standard interview questions such as:

- Why do you want to work here?
- How did you hear about the position?
- What are your weaknesses and strengths?

Never and I repeat, never, give a standard typical response. Standard interview questions are an excellent way for you to stand out during an interview from other candidates; therefore, provide unique and energetic answers.

Do you agree?

Work Lesson #241 – The goal of an interviewer is to determine if a candidate will be a reliable employee and right for the position. Your job is to convince them of this; therefore, prepare your response to likely questions.

Most interview questions will involve a combination of resume-based, position-based and behavioural-based questions. Some potential questions you can expect to receive during an interview:

- Why do you think you're the correct candidate for this position?
    - o You completed a very similar project with a similar team; or have performed a similar role;
    - o Restate critical achievements from your career that are relevant to the position;
    - o Summarize your background that is relevant (office, site, volunteer etc.); and
    - o State your attitude to new challenges and how you enjoy stepping up and getting results. Give an example of how you've done this in the past, without exclusively stating a standard response, tell your story.
- What do you believe are the critical factors for success for this position?
    - o Strong communication with the team and client. Provide an example of this success on a previous project.

- Alignment with the employer and client vision, expectations and core values;
- Alignment and ongoing communication;
- Timely decision making.
- Are you available?
  - Yes. Yes, should be the only answer you provide here unless there is a necessary reason your start date must be delayed, such as: finishing your degree, giving your current employer due notice.
- How familiar are you with what this company does?
  - Since you prepared, you've researched the company extensively. State a brief description of your understanding of the company, including:
    - Company's core values and vision statement;
    - Business lines (e.g. Finance, Infrastructure, Technology);
    - How big the company is (e.g. 18 offices globally, 40,000 employees); and
    - Speak to how you align with the company's core values and vision (show them that you fit their company culture).
  - This would be a good time to ask a prepared question regarding the organization.

How do you prepare for interview questions?

Work Lesson #242 – The best candidate doesn't always secure a job. The candidate who sold themselves the best gets the job offer.

There are at least eight steps in preparing for an interview; they are:

1. Research the company extensively
2. Practice potential questions and responses
3. Prepare questions for the interviewer
4. Research salary expectations in advance
5. Perfect your verbal and non-verbal communication

6. Dress appropriately for your Industry
7. Bring supporting material with you
8. Send post-interview thank you

If you follow these eight steps, your confidence will increase, and your nerves will reduce during the interview.

You've prepared for likely questions, and you know how you'll answer them. You know your elevator speech and how you'll deliver it.

You'll provide individual responses that showcase your qualifications and character.

All this preparation will assist you in standing out from less-prepared candidates. Remember, no runner enters a race without warming up ahead of time, and neither should you; therefore, practice.

How do you prepare for an Interview?

Work Lesson #243 – The type of questions the interviewer asks you, can reveal the kind of employer they are.

Companies who truly value company culture ask more character and scenario-based questions during the interview process.

They do this because they want to ensure you'll fit in with the company; that you can solve difficult problems; and that you'll be an asset to the company

Smart companies understand that they can train you, your resume speaks to your qualifications, but it often doesn't speak to how teachable you are.

Below are a few examples of some interesting questions from world-famous companies.[2]

---

[2] www.eliteworldhotels.com.tr/blog-en/15-interesting-questions-asked-by-world-famous-companies-during-job-interviews.3378.aspx

- Tesla Motor – Communication question: *"How would you explain dynamometer to an 8-year-old?"*

- Goldman Sachs – Problem Solving question: *"There are an infinite number of black and white dots on a plane. How would you prove that the distance between a black and white dot is one unit?"*

- Google – Creativity question: *"If you had a box of pencils, what would be the 10 creative things you would do with them?"*

Many of these questions won't have an answer that is repeated... your answer will be unique.

Observe, listen and reply to these types of questions in a way that amplifies your value and character. Yes, you want the job, but you also want to find a company that can offer an environment for you to develop and flourish in.

What's the weirdest interview question you got?

Work Lesson #244 – Interviews are a two-way street. They go both ways—a reciprocation of give and take.

An interviewer will be interviewing you to ensure you're a proper fit for the role and company; therefore, you should be doing the same.

You want a win-win scenario after completing an interview, where you have something to offer the company, and the company can provide you with the environment where you can flourish to your potential.

Therefore, you should be interviewing the company before you accept a position. Analyze your goals and ensure the company and position can, at a minimum, be a stepping stone to get there.

Below are some tips to help assess the company during your interview:

- Do they offer to show you around? A company proud of their culture may offer a tour, especially if they were pleased with your interview.

- During the tour of the office, observe how employees are dressed? Casual, formal, business casual? Is the office quiet or loud? Do people appear to be collaborating? Are there open areas for group discussions? How have the employees personalized their desks?

- How were you received? Were you warmly welcomed, and given a handshake? Analyze your first impression of the company. Often our instincts tell us what we've may have missed.

- Ask the interviewer how they would describe the company culture and environment? Is their response sincere and unique? Or do they provide a textbook response?

You can learn a lot about a company by simply observing, analyzing and evaluating your interview.

How have you assessed a company during an interview? What do you look for?

Work Lesson #245 – Interviewer: "Do you have any questions for us?" Me: You better have a question!

If the interviewer asks you if you have any questions... your response should never be, *"No."*

Always, and I repeat always, have questions prepared in advance to ask your interviewer. If you don't and you don't ask one, the interviewer may think you don't care or that you didn't prepare.

This is such a simple thing for you to prepare in advance. When you're researching the company, and you're not sure about something, make a note, this could be a great potential question to ask the interviewer.

If your struggling to think of a question to ask, below are a few to get you started:

- What are the next steps in the hiring process?
- What do you enjoy about the Company Culture?

- What makes you proud to be working here?
- Is there anything you would change about the company?
- How does the company support talent growth and career development?

What is a question you like to ask an interviewer?

Week 26 Theme: Important Career Statistics

From understanding the importance of a sellable and effective resume to learning how to be happy at work, from learning how recognition can inspire your team to the likelihood of having a poor boss during your career.

This week's theme will discuss critical and, at times, shocking career statistics that you need to be aware of. Let's learn the facts, examine them, and adjust accordingly.

What's the weirdest career statistic you've heard?

Work Lesson #246 – On average, every corporate job opening attracts 250 resumes, but only 4 to 6 of these people will be called for an interview, and only 1 of those will be offered a job.[3] Lesson: Have an effective resume that highlights your accomplishments and qualifications.

Having an effective resume will assist you in securing a job interview.

Compelling and sellable resumes highlight your accomplishments, not merely your responsibilities and duties.

Accomplishments can vary from personal to professional.

A personal accomplishment or achievement could be a prestigious award you won, such as a scholarship or sporting trophy.

A professional accomplishment can be quantitative results you delivered, such as: Led the project under budget and saved your Client 2 million dollars.

You want your resume to be full of accomplishments; this is your highlight reel; the interview can dive more into the movie.

---

[3] www.inc.com/peter-economy/19-interesting-hiring-statistics-you-should-know.html

Learn to highlight the right qualifications to differentiate yourself from your competition.

List your accomplishments throughout your entire resume, especially in your Executive Summary. This is not a time to be humble. Ensure you put something to grab their attention and then lay out all the accomplishments you've earned in each position.

By doing this, an employer will begin to see a common theme: by having you on the team, you'll bring value to their company. Do you agree?

Work Lesson #247 – *A study by CareerBuilder shows that 58 percent of managers said they didn't receive any management training.[4] Lesson: If you're able, help others. Many people haven't been given the right tools to succeed.*

I needed to let this statistic sink in. It indicates that the majority of managers haven't been trained to be a manager.

Most people get promoted based on excelling in a previous role... these skills may or may not be transferable to managerial and leadership roles.

Management is primarily soft skill-based, requiring you to be a strong communicator. Therefore, if you got your promotion based on being excellent in a predominant hard skill position, there is no guarantee that you'll be right in a managerial role.

I shared this statistic for two main reasons:

- **First**, if leaders of departments and teams are aware of this, they can try to secure proper training for their managers and assist in providing them with the tools to help them succeed; and

- **Second**, for the employees that have a manager who is struggling. Most of us will have a poor boss during our career, but some are poor not because of a lack of trying; but because they haven't been

[4] www.forbes.com/sites/davidsturt/2018/03/08/10-shocking-workplace-stats-you-need-to-know/#649e500ef3af

given the correct support. If this is the case, help them be successful and share in the success.

Does your Organization offer Management training?

Work Lesson #248 – *A Harvard Business Review survey reveals 58 percent of people say they trust strangers more than their boss.*[5] *Lesson: Bad bosses aren't that uncommon.*

Yesterday's statistic was 58 percent of managers said they didn't receive any management training... and today' statistic reveals 58 percent of people say they trust strangers more than their own boss.

These statistics are alarming and can nearly guarantee that you'll have a poor boss during your career.

You can't control who your boss is, but you can control how you allow them to impact you, and you shouldn't settle for a work environment that won't assist you in reaching your goals and potential.

If you don't trust your boss, this is concerning, as they may be the person in control of your next promotion. People will come and go throughout your career, which you don't like, don't trust and don't respect; at times, you may need to work with them.

Regardless of the situation, always act professional and mature. Be a respectable profession as you develop a detailed plan to escape this undesirable situation; you're not a hostage to your current circumstances. As long as you have a plan you're executing; you're in control.

If you know you aren't happy with your current work situation, you're the one that needs to take action to improve this. Do you agree?

---

[5] www.forbes.com/sites/davidsturt/2018/03/08/10-shocking-workplace-stats-you-need-to-know/#649e500ef3af

Work Lesson #249 – *The Conference Board reports that 53 percent of Americans are currently unhappy at work.[6] Lesson: Be the minority.*

You can spend over 70,000 hours of your life at work. If given a choice, wouldn't you rather enjoy those hours and have them contribute to your happiness?

Your happiness is no one else's responsibility but your own. If you're unhappy and not sure what to do, ask yourself these questions:

- What do you want to be thinking about the day you retire?
- What will you value on that day?
- What do you want to accomplish over the course of your career?
- What will you want to leave behind when you are gone?

Learn what you value then pursue it!

By thinking of what you want to be and what you want to accomplish by the end of your career, you can help you choose wisely today.

Working backwards can be an effective way of understanding what you value and what you ultimately want to accomplish over your career. And what will make you happy.

How have you made a career change?

Work Lesson #250 – *Recognition is the number one thing employees say their manager could give them to inspire them to produce great work.[7] Lesson: Recognition is powerful.*

Global studies prove that when it comes to inspiring people to be their best at work, nothing else comes close—not even higher pay, promotion, autonomy or training.

---

[6] www.forbes.com/sites/davidsturt/2018/03/08/10-shocking-workplace-stats-you-need-to-know/#649e500ef3af
[7] www.forbes.com/sites/davidsturt/2018/03/08/10-shocking-workplace-stats-you-need-to-know/#649e500ef3af

Loyalty comes from trust and respect. When you're recognized for your effort and results, you feel inspired and motivated to continue striving to reach a higher level. You've been ignited as someone believes in you.

As Mary Kay Ash states, *"Everyone wants to be appreciated, so if you appreciate someone, don't keep it a secret."*

If you see someone doing a good job, tell them. Make it a goal to give recognition daily.

If you want recognition, make it a goal to recognize others as it takes a team to succeed. No one makes it to the top by themselves; we have all had help.

How often do you recognize others? I challenge you to make this a daily goal.

Work Lesson #251 – *Approximately 80% of available jobs are never advertised.*[8] *Lesson: Network, Network and Network.*

Well-connected people have access to information that isn't normally advertised.

Many opportunities, such as new positions, aren't advertised. You hear about them through your network of contacts.

If you want to hear about these opportunities before the general public, build an influential and diverse network.

A strong network will increase your business reach and increase your chances of hearing about these hidden opportunities.

When I was in my last year of University, my professor helped me secure an interview for an unadvertised position at a major corporation. Over the course of my degree, I impressed this person, and when he saw a proper fit for my personality and qualifications, he put my name forward... this is how

[8] www.collingwoodsearch.co.uk/our-insights/recruiting-retaining-talent/15-interesting-recruitment-facts/

I got my first position in the corporate world and started my career journey.

This was all possible because I built a network with an influential reach.

How are you securing these opportunities?

Work Lesson #252 – *Sixty-five percent of children entering primary school will hold jobs that currently don't exist.[9] Lesson: You can't predict the future, teach skills that will always be relevant.*

This statistic isn't too surprising given how technology has changed over the past two decades. Simply think of the people born in the 1980's, and all the website designers and IT positions there are today. These didn't exist a few decades earlier.

The reason I shared this statistic is that I see many parents worry about their children's schooling. If this statistic is accurate, what your children are learning in school today outside of the fundamentals, may not be relevant.

Maybe it's more important to teach children to be confident and resilient. To teach cognitive and analytical skills... skills that are needed to be successful in life. A statistic that supports this way of thought:

"Demand for higher cognitive skills, such as creativity, critical thinking, decision making, and complex information processing, will also grow through 2030—by 19% in the United States and by 14% in Europe, from already sizable bases. The same research predicts the fastest rise in the need for advanced IT and programming skills, which could grow as much as 90% between 2016 and 2030."[10]

The world is changing, and one of the essential skills to teach and learn is adaptability and flexibility. If you're capable of changing, you're capable of learning new skills and new skills allow you to stay relevant in a changing world. People incapable of learning new skills become stagnant employees.

---

[9] http://reports.weforum.org/future-of-jobs-2016/chapter-1-the-future-of-jobs-and-skills/
[10] www.mckinsey.com/featured-insights/future-of-work/skill-shift-automation-and-the-future-of-the-workforce

What skills do you believe will be critical in the future?

Week 27 Theme: Job Security

In today's rapidly changing work environment, there isn't a lot of job security. Once vibrant companies are losing their market share and making cuts, while new companies are coming in and taking over.

How businesses gain and lose their market share isn't different from how employees gain and lose their market value.

To remain in high demand, there are things you can do to help secure your position. This week, I'll discuss the best forms of job security and what you can do to ensure you maintain your market share in a rapidly changing world.

What do you think offers the best job security?

Work Lesson #253 – Knowledge is powerful... it allows you to pave your own path.

Knowledge, which is gained from experience and information... It has the power to transform into wisdom and can be the ultimate reward from learning and branching out of your comfort zone.

When you become knowledgeable, it builds your level of competency. Once knowledge is gained, it can't be taken away... this is why knowledge is powerful, as it strengthens your market value and can be a significant differentiator between you and other candidates.

Over the course of your career, you'll be overlooked for promotions you deserve; you'll be dealt setbacks and obstacles. Organizations can often hold the key to your career success in the form of salary, promotions, or stretch assignments, but they can never take away your credibility, skillsets and, therefore, your knowledge.

Knowledge can be the best job security you can have, as it becomes a part of who you are and what you can bring with you to any role.

Knowledge can often be the source of unlocking the hidden path to success. If you build your knowledge by developing skills, gaining information and experiences, you'll have far more control over which direction your career goes. The power of the steering wheel will remain in your hands.

Do you think knowledgeable people have better job security?

Work Lesson #254 – *Safe Bet means: Guaranteed investment = Low Risk / High reward; therefore, become a Safe Bet.*

Your credibility will be established based on your character, personality and ability. This will directly feed your reputation, which will help you build a sellable name.

You establish credibility by delivering on your commitments (keep your word), producing high-quality results and being a person of integrity. When your reputation is attached to being labelled a high performer that consistently brings high-quality results, your name has become sellable and will eventually be given the label of *'Safe Bet.'*

When you've become a *'Safe Bet,'* influential people will be more likely to invest in you, as you're a guarantee with low risk and high rewards. When people invest in you, this will increase your job security; and you'll be given more significant career growth opportunities.

What has helped you get labelled a Safe Bet?

Work Lesson #255 – *To be in demand, you must be requested—secure recommendations from influential people.*

The best recommendations come from:

- A Client / Customer;
- A Supervisor / Boss;
- An Influencer; or
- A significant Decision Marker.

General rules in the business world are:

- 'Please your Client;'
- 'Build a strong reputation;' and
- 'Build a strong influential and diverse network.'

During your career, regardless of what you do:

- You'll want to please your clients; this is how you receive repeat business and often, how you stay in business.
- You'll want to build a sellable name with a bulletproof reputation; and
- You'll want to build a strong network with an extensive business reach.

If you can do these three things, you'll likely be in constant demand. When you're in constant need, your name often comes up during conversations, and this is how you get put forward for stretch assignments and career growth opportunities.

Some of the best job security can come from being recommended by the right people. Build your relationships with respect and trust, deliver consistent, high-quality results, and witness your name getting recommended.

Who are the best people to get recommendations from?

Work Lesson #256 – Bring solutions to difficult problems.

When obstacles rear their ugly head, be the solution, not the problem.

Instead of complaining, question why the problem keeps appearing. Complaining solves nothing.

The world is full of people that can discuss and complain about a problem; there are far fewer who can solve it, be the latter.

If you're a person who can solve difficult problems and deliver high-quality results, you'll always be in high demand.

People in high demand have greater job security and get career growth opportunities presented to them. Do you agree?

Work Lesson #257 – A strong and influential Network can provide you with job security and shield you from external defamation.

When you're building momentum in your career, you'll attract all types of attention. Influencers and decision-makers will begin to pay attention to you; they may even put your name forward for new challenges and stretch assignments.

When this starts to happen, you'll attract both positive and negative attention. When high performers begin to gain momentum up the corporate ladder, it gets noticed, and it can often create jealousy amongst their peers.

One of the big reasons I preach to build a strong and influential network is yes, it can open many doors for you, but it can also protect you.

The more well-known you are, the more connected you are, the more people that think highly of you... offers a significant layer of protection to you. If your network can span a large distance with reinforcement, people will think twice before they try to defame your name, as they don't know who you know and who will protect and stick up for you when you're not around.

Having a strong network behind you offers additional support and reinforces your security in your reputation and protects you from people that may want to discredit your hard work.

Has your network protected you and offered you additional security?

Work Lesson #258 – *A person who can change, who can fill in the missing gap on a team, is the chameleon that can switch and become any variable regardless of the equation.*

Like evolution, if you adapt, you're capable of changing along with any climate; this can make you highly valuable.

Since constant change is one of life's guarantees, training yourself to be adaptable and flexible is wise. Be the person, that regardless of the role, can bring value to any team.

Part of maintaining your adaptability requires you to be open-minded and willing to learn continuously. By doing this, you'll continually develop and refine your skills and grow as your environment changes.

Instead of being uncomfortable with change, you've trained yourself to embrace it and learn from it. If you can remain adaptable, there will always be a team in need of you.

How have you trained yourself to embrace change and be adaptable?

Work Lesson #259 – *To maintain and increase your market value, you must have something the market demands.*

Work environments are changing at a rapid pace; within 40 years, we've gone from using typewriters to computers to smartphones and tablets. Once relevant, vibrant, and booming companies are becoming dated and losing their market share.

You don't want to be a professional who becomes dated, stagnant and incapable of changing with progress, if you do, you too, may lose your market value.

If your skills are no longer required and you cannot learn and adapt to what is needed, you'll be replaced with people that possess the required skills. You'll be replaced, just like blockbuster was.

If you can't bring:

- An open mind;
- Dedicate yourself to lifelong learning and
- Be adaptable when required.

You won't be able to retain nor increase your market value over the course of your career.

How have you maintained and increased your market value?

Week 28 Theme: The Elephant in the Room

Since the dawn of the caveman, there have been topics people naturally shy away from discussing.

Whether it's the employee that never wears deodorant or the person who spits on you when they speak, some topics are hard to discuss... even when EVERYONE is aware of it.

This week's theme focuses on discussing the topics we avoid; the classic Elephants in the room.

Let's discuss the issues sitting in the middle of the room, blocking your television, yet most people pretend they don't exist.

From mental illness in the workplace to pregnancy impacting women's careers, to questioning poor leadership... the elephant in the room is always present; so, let's destroy the stigmas and discuss.

What's the biggest elephant you've seen avoided?

Work Lesson #260 – *A leader who cannot handle constructive feedback, is no leader.*

Are you allowed to question the effectiveness of your leadership team? If you do, do you risk hurting your reputation and career progression?

Some fake leaders can't handle criticism, and they create an environment that isn't engrained with free speech, shutting down anyone who disagrees with them.

Remember, influential leaders, allow you to question their decisions.

There are entire books written on leadership, but I'm going to summarize simply.

Leaders don't make you:

- Walk on eggshells,
- Feel inferior, and
- Feel you're in the wrong.

Leaders are:

- Strong Listeners,
- Self-aware, and
- Confident in their ability but aware of their weakness.

If a team leader doesn't allow free thought and speech within their team, then they haven't established trust, and when there is no trust, then the leader is only getting a portion of the information the team has access too.

Strong teams can go to their boss with any information, including concerns, mistakes they made and questioning a decision.

Leaders embrace constructive feedback as they want their teams to trust them. It's a sign of a poor leader if they cannot allow their ego to listen to feedback on their performance.

What are the signs of a poor leader?

Work Lesson #261 – There is power in asking for help; seeing a therapist can be for your brain what exercise is for your body.

Why do we need to consider mental health when developing our careers?

Having good mental health and understanding your needs allows you to put your best self forward.

Productivity is one of the most significant impacts poor mental health can have on a person and company. Costing them both to lose money, as well as potentially damaging their career prospects.

Mental ill-health can impact your concentration and motivation, which can hold you back from sounding enthusiastic about your work, bringing your 'A' game to an interview and maintaining consistency in your work.

How can you look after your mental wellbeing?

- Learn your needs, boundaries, and communicate them effectively.
- Make time to sit and consider where you are mentally. How is your stress level looking? etc.
- Listen. You need to know your team and their boundaries to be an effective team player and leader.

This is a broad topic, but these pointers are a start. Let's talk about mental health. If it isn't an everyday conversation, the stigma will stay.

Thank you, Hannah from Engineer Your Mind for writing this post.

Work Lesson #262 – Office dating can be a gamble; as you haven't been dealt all the cards, yet, you still must make a wager. Operate in silence and BE DISCREET.

Many topics should be discussed in silence at work, and one of the biggest ones is dating a colleague.

Dating at work can be a complicated topic, but it doesn't need to be. If your organization allows it, then this must simply be done professionally and kept private.

These are the unwritten rules of office dating:

1. Check if your company allows this; if yes, move to #2.
2. Align on keeping this private between the both of you. BE QUIET.
3. Start slow and test the water. Is there something here?
4. Align together on when to tell people.
5. Don't advertise your relationship, be low key.
6. Keep all private matters outside of work; never expose your dirty laundry.

When dating a co-worker, you can't afford to be naïve. Office dating is a gossip-worthy topic, as it's juicy, therefore, be quiet and discreet.

The 3 Big No-Nos:

- Dating a direct report is always a NO, and most employers will have a policy on this.
- A major gap in reporting level. Be careful in how this appears, especially if you're within similar departments. A senior vice president dating an intern or junior employee may be highly frowned upon.
- If it breaks company policy, you can be fired over this.

When you're in the figuring out stage, it's imperative to do this discreetly. If this is going to stop after a few dates, then there is no reason to let others know.

When the relationship gets serious, you can often be more open about your commitment to each other.

Have you dated a co-worker? Would you recommend it?

Work Lesson #263 – *Diversity in the workforce means an organization protects its most vulnerable employees.*

Does your organization honestly believe in diversity? Do they have policies in place and actions that amplify fairness? Meaning there is no glass ceiling and no favouritism. Let's talk about a significant elephant that many women face at some point in their careers.

Does maternity leave hurt women's career progression?

- How often does a pregnant woman get a promotion?
- How many times does a pregnant woman get asked, how long will their maternity leave be?
- How often is a woman questioned about her loyalty to her career after becoming a mother?

From HBR – *"Evidence from a variety of countries reveals that the longer new mothers are away from paid work, the less likely they are to be promoted, move into management, or receive a pay raise once their leave is over. They are also at greater risk of being fired or demoted. Length of leave can be a factor in the perceptions of co-workers as well – women who take longer leaves are often seen as less committed to their jobs than women who take much shorter leaves. This trade-off undercuts a major goal of legislating national parental leave policies: ensuring that women don't have to choose between motherhood and career success."[11]*

As a new mother, these studies worry me, because I'm a driven professional. Many women have written to me with these concerns, and based on statistics; their worries are justified.

Work Lesson #264 – *Classic unwritten rule: Don't make enemies with the* 'off-limit' *people.*

Many organizations have favourites, people that regardless of their performance, seem to be able to do no wrong.

It doesn't make any primer reason:

- Why are they a favourite?
- How did they get such a prominent role?

Many times, this will remain a mystery. If you're aware of an individual that appears to do no wrong even when they are in the wrong, you probably found an *'off-limit'* person.

Off-limit people get away with more... and no failure seems to stain their white shirt.

Because of this, these people can be dangerous. You're best not to call them out because clearly, they have connections that you most likely don't have. Going after them, even if you're in the right, will likely result in you losing the battle.

If you choose to call out an *'off-limit'* person, ensure you're making an informed decision and not a naïve one.

What's your experience with *'off-limit'* people?

---

[11] https://hbr.org/2018/09/do-longer-maternity-leaves-hurt-womens-careers

Work Lesson #265 – *When talking about sensitive topics at work, remember, your inside voice. Don't overshare, as this can hurt your reputation and, therefore, career.*

Over-sharing can hurt an employee. This can happen both at work and on social media. What you share on the internet can potentially be there forever, so think before you post, especially if you're emotionally compromised.

There are sensitive topics that you should avoid speaking about at work, such as:

- Your Sex Life,
- Religious and pollical beliefs,
- Too much medical information,
- Too much of your personal life, and
- Confidential career information.

Avoid opinions of controversy and oversharing too much information... as this can alienate people and make them feel uncomfortable. It can anger people and potentially get you labelled as careless, a loose cannon, and a person who lacks judgement.

Somethings are private matters (e.g. sex life), and when you discuss them openly, people may question your sense, your integrity, and whether you're trustworthy, as you clearly aren't showing discretion.

Do you agree?

Work Lesson #266 – *When Leaders pick favourites, they indirectly prioritize/rank their team, and each member is no longer equal.*

Leaders should never have favourites... corrections, if a Leader has a favourite, it shouldn't be known to the team.

We're all human, and there'll be people we work better with than others. There will be people that we get on better with than others, and people we simply have better chemistry with... this is all perfectly normal...

...but when you get promoted into a managerial or leadership role, you need to keep who your favourites are, to yourself. You can't be seen to have favourites, as it can create jealousy on your team and demotivate and uninspired the members who haven't made this little elite group.

It can cause unnecessary and unproductive behaviour that won't benefit the team as a whole.

When you're leading a team, you're responsible for each member. Be mindful of how you treat each member and ensure you don't have visual favourites.

Have you had a leader that had favourites? How did this make you feel?

Week 29 Theme: Critical Career Variables

Countless variables go into making a successful career; the equation can resemble many variations.

This week, I'll be discussing that regardless of the equation, there are variables that will be an integral part of building a long and successful career full of opportunities.

I'll be discussing the importance of:

- Establishing your professional Credibility;
- Developing a strong Reputation;
- Building an influential Network;
- Creating Resilience in your Character;
- Being Teachable and dedicating yourself to lifelong learning;
- Remaining Adaptable and flexible; and
- Becoming a Driven professional who motivates and inspires themselves.

The height of your career skyscraper will be based on how strong you build your foundation.

What variables go into a long successful career?

Work Lesson #267 – *Without integrity, you're a boat without a sail, a body without a heart, talent without a team. You can't build a skyscraper when your foundation is missing its rebar. A successful career starts with integrity.*

Your integrity is a significant variable in establishing your credibility as a professional. It's your foundation in which you can build a long successful career.

Credibility is your capabilities as a professional; it's your ability and talent. There are three main ingredients to establishing your credibility: character, personality, and ability.

- **Character** – Your integrity and accountability build your character; without it, your reputation will be susceptible to defamation. Always keep your word and deliver on your promises.

- **Personality** – Remain humble as your success gains momentum. Be kind and fair to everyone you meet. Be generous and help others when you can.

- **Ability** – Develop your skills and increase the talent you bring to every role. Bring consistent, high-quality results for every challenge and obstacle given to you.

When building successful careers, start with establishing your credibility, as this will feed your reputation as a high performer who has integrity and can solve difficult problems.

Where would you start to build a long successful career?

Work Lesson #268 – Your reputation is your identity as a professional. Build it strong with reinforcement.

There are hundreds of variables that go into a successful career, and they're all critical. Still, nothing is as important from a career perspective than your reputation, and because of this, you must protect it under all circumstances.

You tarnish your reputation; you'll have a hard time getting rid of the mark, and may miss out on opportunities because of this.

YOU feed your reputation from your words and actions. If you establish your credibility and deliver, you'll be accountable, and your integrity and strength of character will be strong.

If you become someone that people want to work with, you'll begin to acquire a large fan club, and this will assist in building and protecting your reputation. When others respect you and enjoy working with you, they tend to tell others (if they do not like working with you, they tend to tell others); so, let's ensure that when you're discussed, it's only positive.

How have you secured a strong reputation?

Work Lesson #269 – *Build your network with all levels and ranks of the organization accounted for. Properly developed networks don't have gaps. The simple truth to a truly effective network is that every member matters.*

To build an effective network full of credible, diverse, reliable, loyal and influential people that you can trust and who want to help you; will be easier if you've first built a solid foundation through establishing your credibility.

Starting your career by establishing your credibility will directly feed your reputation, which will, in turn, creates trust in your character. With the trust of character, you'll allow yourself to build strong, trusting relationships.

Once you have access to trusted individuals, you can start to build an impressive network with a far business reach.

Your network will be built by:

- How you gain peoples trust,
- How others enjoy working with you,
- How you deliver high performing results,
- How you can influence, and persuade; and
- How to be the team player that everyone wants to work with.

How have you built your network?

Work Lesson #270 – *The more resilient you become, the more your mindset will be determined to succeed. This is often the hidden variable in strong leaders.*

Resilience is a trait that will play a critical role in both your life and career.

I have learned this, many times over. From being diagnosed with severe dyslexia at the age of six, from not being able to read till I was nearly nine, to becoming a writer; from being put on academic probation, to graduating with honours... this was all to make me strong, to make me resilient and to persevere.

You'll have obstacles and setbacks in your career; you'll have the proverbial road bumps trying to block you from reaching your goals and destination; work through these. Because as Thomas J. Watson elegantly stated, *"success is often found on the far side of failure."*

Resilience teaches you to get back up and keep trying. You don't fall if you keep getting up, it's merely a stumble. Successful people make mistakes, but they learn and try again. They've learned that failure is only permanent when they stop trying, so don't stop.

How has resilience impacted your career?

Work Lesson #271 – *An open-mind has no rules.*

An open-minded person is teachable, as they:

- Listen before forming an opinion.
- Question when they don't understand.
- Don't assume they're right.
- Analyze the information presented to them in a logical sequence.
- Discuss ideas with different types of people.
- Respect differences of opinion.

An open-minded person continues to learn and grow because they allow themselves to remain vulnerable, understanding that they may be the person in the wrong and therefore, they're the one that needs to make a change.

Being teachable and remaining open-minded as you gain success in your career is critical. Many people allow their ego to inflate their perceived importance, which can hamper their growth and prematurely plateau as a result.
As you gain traction in your career, remain humble, open-minded and dedicate yourself to lifelong learning. The person who closes off their mind stops learning and, therefore, stops progressing.

Do you agree?

Work Lesson #272 – Being able to always provide value, requires you to be willing to adapt and change.

There is tremendous flexibility when you're comfortable with change, as change is one of life's guarantees.

If you can remain calm and open-minded when unforeseen events appear, you can react immediately and adapt quickly to the obstacle.

- Many people waste critical time with their reaction to a problem than addressing the issue. Wishing something to go away, doesn't change anything except losing time, you'll never get back.

- If you can utilize your time to immediately address a challenge instead of running away, delaying or being fearful, you'll be more successful over the course of your career.

- There will always be elements in your career that you cannot control, but you can ALWAYS control mindset and actions.

Being fearful of change is a losing battle, as it's natural for things to change. Remaining adaptable when things change will allow you to provide value when everyone else is panicking.

How do you remain calm in a stressful situation?

Work Lesson #273 – It's not about having all the answers and never failing. Successful people simply find a way to motivate and inspire themselves during their darkest days.

It's easy to be driven on your good days and after major successes and breakthroughs. It can be an entirely different story to remain motivated after you've failed or experienced a significant setback.

When you have dedicated yourself to your goals, you understand that a setback is simply part of the journey.

Failure is a part of success... when you have ambitious goals, you'll enter areas that you lack experience, and therefore, you'll make mistakes by default... this is the reality of the game.

Since mistakes are a part of learning, you cannot rely on others to provide you with the motivation and inspiration for your success. You must find a way to tap into your own motivation and learn to inspire your own actions, especially in times of failure.

Remember, continuous success is a result of highly driven individuals that have devoted their lives to the concept of lifelong learning. When you can find a way to motivate and inspire yourself on your darkest day, you're on the path to success.

How do you remain motivated through setbacks?

Week 30 Theme: The Importance of Emotional Intelligence

When you work in an industry of educated people, education doesn't differentiate you from your peer group. It rarely gets you recognized. Many of the Work Lessons I discuss have an underlining theme engrained in them.

I have spent that last 15 years observing and recording all angles of the corporate environment, and I'll tell you, the person with the highest IQ rarely leads... many times, you wouldn't even know what their IQ is... because when you're under a strict schedule and tight budget... yes, you need smart people, generally just smart enough is needed... but what you do need and what becomes rare in stressful circumstances, is someone who can read the situation, react accordingly, and then solve the problem.

This requires someone to be emotionally intelligent. This week, I'll be discussing the five components of emotional intelligence (EQ) extensively and their home within the workplace. They are:

- Self-Awareness.
- Self-Regulation.
- Motivation.
- Empathy.
- Social Skills.

Let's discuss the underlining importance of EQ within our work and how it's a critical factor in being victorious over the course of your career.

How has EQ impacted your work?

Work Lesson #274 – When you know who you are and are proud of this person, you don't need the approval of others. Self-worth comes from within; set your price.

Emotional Intelligence Component #1 – Self-Awareness

Self-aware people are aware of their emotions and understand why they feel them, what they mean and where they originate. They know how their feelings and actions impact others.

Many variables stem from self-awareness, such as self-worth and confidence. Insecurity and arrogance often stem from a lack of self-awareness.

Arrogance is bred from the feeling of superiority; self-aware leaders know this isn't how to motivate a team and, therefore, remain confident but humble.

Insecurities can allow the approval of others to weigh to costly, preventing you from making necessary moves to further your career.

Without self-awareness, your understanding of yourself, how you perceive others, and others' actions won't be adequately understood. A lack of self-awareness will make breaking bad habits nearly impossible to overcome as you may be ignorant of their existence.

To continue to grow and improve over the course of your career requires you to understand your capabilities and work on your real weaknesses.

Do you agree?

Work Lesson #275 – If you allow yourself to react to everything said to you, you have permitted other people to control your strings. Never be a puppet to people's words. Learn to control your emotions.

Emotional Intelligence Component #2 – Self-Regulation

If you want to be successful over the course of your career, you'll need to learn to choose your battles wisely, and when you do engage in a confrontation, always remain level-headed, calm and in control of your emotions.

Emotionally compromised individuals often make poor, misinformed decisions. They can overreact, unnecessarily offend, and alienate people.

People who cannot control their emotions build a reputation of being unpredictable and a loose cannon... you don't want to send someone who can't control their feelings into critical meetings, where things can get heated.

If you feel you're beginning to lose control of your emotions, take a break from the discussion. Go for a walk to clear your head or do whatever it takes to calm down.

If something has caught you off-guard, don't react immediately, take a pause and evaluate.

The goal isn't to ignore your emotions but instead to find your balance.

How do you practice self-regulation?

Work Lesson #276 – The main ingredient of self-motivation is discipline. Relying on motivation to get things done often results in missed opportunities. Learn to motivate yourself through discipline.

Emotional Intelligence Component #3 – Motivation

Highly motivated people set goals and encourage themselves to reach them.

When I decided to write my book, it took 11 months to write the first draft. I wrote nearly every weekend for a year. If I had waited to be motivated to write... I would have completed 5 chapters of 101.

I was rarely motivated to write; therefore, I just did it. I learned to trust the process and hoped that my motivation would creep in after I started, which it usually did. But on some days, it didn't, and I still kept writing. My book got written because I was disciplined.

Set goals and find methods to motivate yourself without external support. Strong leaders cannot afford to rely on others to drive them. To be consistent, you must learn the process and environment that produces your best work, then develop a schedule and stick to it.

Are you aware of the process and environment that produces your best work?

Work Lesson #277 – *To lead, you must understand what motivates, inspires and empowers your team. Without empathy, their truth will elude you.*

Emotional Intelligence Component #4 – Empathy

> *"Empathy is seeing with the eyes of another, listening with the ears of another and feeling with the heart of another."*
>
> *– Alfred Adler.*

Mr. Adler quote summarizes the elements of empathy perfectly. Empathy is seeing, hearing and feeling the emotions of others.

To be a leader, empathy is a critical part of your mindset. You must be able and willing to put yourself into someone else's shoes, understand their frame of mind, and where they're coming from. If you cannot relate to your team, you'll fail to motivate and empower them.

Empathy plays a vital role in understanding others, choosing your battles wisely, handling confrontation, seeing the bigger picture, motivating your team, and communicating effectively.

How has a leader motivated you?

Work Lesson #278 – *You can have a magnificent vision that can change the world... If you can't communicate it to others, for them to see its greatness, you have a problem.*

Emotional Intelligence Component #5 – Social Skills

Leaders who possess social skills are strong communicators.

They are strong communicators because they possess the two fundamentals of communication:

- First, they can translate ideas to their team; and

- Second, they listen to their wants and needs of their team.

Part of motivating your team is understanding their needs and creating an environment where they can flourish and reach their goals. You learn this information by observing, asking the right questions and listening.

Strong communicators are good at recognizing problems, building trust with their teams and encourage an open-door policy. They want to hear from their team regardless of the news. The sooner you're aware of a problem, the sooner you can solve it. With this built trust, their team will go to them with any problem and solve it as a team.

Leaders recognize their team members' contributions and provide constructive feedback when required. Communication is most potent when there is an establishment of trust.

Do you agree?

Work Lesson #279 – "In Whoville they say – that the Grinch's small heart grew three sizes that day." *(– Dr. Seuss) Emotional intelligence isn't set in stone; it can improve, grow and flourish, you simply must work at it... allow your heart to grow.*

Emotional intelligence isn't set in stone; it can be improved; you simply must work at it. The grass is greener where you water it.

Each component of Emotion Intelligence is critical to creating an emotionally intelligent person; therefore, you must isolate what areas you need to improve. The five components are:

- Self-Awareness.
- Self-Regulation.
- Motivation.
- Empathy.
- Social Skills.

Go the link[12] to conduct a simple 15 question EQ test to see what areas you need to improve.

Once you take the test, you'll understand at a high-level what areas of EQ are your strengths and which ones you need to improve. The first step to improvement is acknowledging, the second is to develop a plan to make improvements, whether this is placing mental checks to become a better listener or exercises to practice empathy.

Create your plan to improve your targeted areas and put goals in place to work on them.

What areas have you had to target to improve to become a more emotionally intelligent person?

Work Lesson #280 – *Higher EQ Leaders are effective because they don't focus on leading; instead, they get people to want to follow.*

A leader operating under the five components of emotional intelligence has brought the real power of knowledge to their team, and they're effective as a result.

They're aware of their emotions and understand why they feel them, what they mean and where they originate. They know how their feelings and actions impact their team.

They practice self-regulation and always remain level-headed, calm and in control of their emotions during all confrontation and stressful situations.

They're highly motivated people who set goals and encourage themselves and their teams to reach them. They target goals that will inspire their team.

They practice empathy and can put themselves into someone else's shoes.

They're strong communicators. They can translate ideas to their team; and listen to their wants and needs.

---

[12] www.mindtools.com/pages/article/ei-quiz.htm

Lower EQ Leaders are usually concerned with leading and getting their desired results. Higher EQ leaders are effective because they don't focus on leading, instead, they get people to want to follow. High EQ Leaders bring a solution mindset to every problem.

Do you agree?

Week 31 Theme: The Art of the Resume

A resume can be your first impression for a future employer. Make it a strong and lasting one. Never underestimate the power and lasting impact of a first impression.

Most employers and recruiters don't know you; your resume can be the first thing they see regarding who you are and what you can offer; therefore, list your accomplishments and credentials, highlighting why you're the best candidate for the position.

The best candidate doesn't always get the interview; the candidate who sold them self effectively gets the interview.

This week, I'll be discussing how to write an effective resume and cover letter, how to sell yourself to an employer through your resume, and how to ensure your resume passes the ATS software.

How would you define an effective resume?

Work Lesson #281 – There are new rules to resume writing, ensure your resume template passes the ATS screening software.

Depending on the study, at least 2/3 of all Fortune 500 companies use an ATS (Applicant Tracking Software) to sort and score resumes, meaning a human being doesn't read around 75% of all resumes.

Many large and middle-size companies use ATS. You must pass this software to ensure your resume is read; therefore, the first step in writing an effective resume is to ensure it passes the ATS screening software.

Tips to pass the ATS:

- Don't use tables, columns, headers and footers. Most ATS cannot screen them accurately; nearly guaranteeing your information won't be processed correctly. Unless you know the software being used, stick to a word document with pure text.

- Don't use a fancy resume template; many ATS cannot process the information correctly; therefore, keep section headings simple (e.g. Work Experience), use consistent formatting for your work experience and dates. Use a traditional resume font (Georgie, Garamond, Times New Roman).

- Use keywords from the Ad within your resume; nearly all ATS do keyword searches, then provide a score to the recruiter on its matches. Utilize key skills and job titles from the Ad; this will optimize the ATS search.

- Save file in .docx

- Never try to trick the ATS by whiting out keywords to be invisible throughout your resume. You may pass the ATS, but you won't pass the recruiter's review, as your ATS score won't match your credentials, giving it away that you cheated.

Will your resume pass ATS software? If not, change your template.

Work Lesson #282 – *An effective resume amplifies the value you brought to your previous roles and organizations. Highlight this value through your accomplishments.*

I've reviewed over 1,000 resumes, and nearly all of them failed to highlight their accomplishments. Effective and sellable resumes highlight your achievements, not your responsibilities and duties.

Responsibilities and duties are daily tasks that nearly everyone does.

Accomplishments can vary from personal to professional and amplify your value.

A personal accomplishment or achievement could be a prestigious award, such as a scholarship or sporting trophy.

A professional accomplishment can be a quantitative result you delivered, such as leading the project under budget and saving the Client $2 million.

Responsibilities need to be within your resume as they're standard practise, but to stand out, ensure your accomplishments are there, this will help differentiate you from other applicants.

Does your resume highlight your accomplishments?

Work Lesson #283 — You must differentiate yourself from other candidates and sell yourself effectively through your resume.

Differentiating yourself from your competition will first start with your resume. Learn to highlight the right qualifications to differentiate yourself from your competition.

<u>For example</u>, you were a waiter during college and think you don't have any accomplishments, think again. Which one sold themselves more effectively?

1. Waited tables for 4 years at *'NO Name'* Restaurant; or
2. Worked from hostess to Head Waiter in 2 years. Spent the following 2 years serving patrons from over 50 nationalities. From observing when a glass needed to be refilled, to learning when a table didn't want to be interrupted, I delivered top customer service. Waiting tables has taught me to serve, listen, and adapt to my customer needs, providing me with vast experience in managing people.

List your accomplishments throughout your entire resume, especially in your Executive Summary. Many recruiters won't read past your Executing Summary if it doesn't have anything unique. Put something to grab their attention and then lay out all the accomplishments you have earned in each position.

The more accomplishments you list throughout your resume, the employer will begin to see a common theme: you'll bring value to their company by having you on the team.

What's your common theme?

Work Lesson #284 *– The top and most qualified candidate may not get an interview. The candidate who sold them self effectively secures the interview.*

If you want to be the candidate that secures an interview, you must sell yourself to a recruiter. You do this by telling them what they want to hear. You NEVER want a recruiter to say, *"So What?"* after glancing at your resume.

They want to read:

- How you align with the company culture and how you're a proper fit for their organization. Therefore, use the employer's own words from the Ad and sprinkle in their core values, vision and mission statements into your resume. Tailor your resume to match the position and organization.

You do this by showing them that you'll be a suitable candidate for their organization and have the right attitude and motivation to fit their company culture.

For example, if you're applying for a position at Disney, they discuss within their core values, Leadership, Engagement and Service, to ensure you use these terms within your accomplishments. (e.g. Developed a new method to track customer engagement).

You can sell yourself by highlighting your accomplishments using the employer's own words. If they use *'Servant Leadership,'* ensure you use this term to describe your management style.

How have you utilized keywords in your resume?

Work Lesson #285 – Each part of a resume serves a specific purpose: Executive Summary – The Hook and Elevator Speech, Work Experience – Your Story Told through Accomplishments, Education / Skills / Activities and Interest - The support to round out your credentials.

Each section of your resume serves a purpose.

1) Executive Summary – This is your highlight reel that has the most relevant information for the position. Executive summaries are tailored to each position. Include years of experience, leadership experience and industries you've worked in. Use keywords from the employer's Ad.

2) Work Experience - List all work experience starting with the most recent. Include all significant accomplishments, awards and recognitions you received in each role. When you list your accomplishments, give specific details such as quantities and percentages. Being specific allows others to quantify your results and understand the value you brought to your role. <u>For example</u>:

   - Wrote a weekly blog for three years, or
   - Wrote a weekly career development blog for three years that grew to have 1,200 hundred subscribers. Each blog entry got an average of 4,000 reads, 145 likes and 40 comments.

3) Education – List your degree and any significant registrations and certificates. If you've graduated from college, no need to list your high school.

4) Activities and Interest – Add well-rounded hobbies (e.g. one sport, one hobby, one volunteer – Play Basketball, write a career blog, and coach little league baseball). Let them learn about you. If you do high risks sports, you may want to leave this out.

Ensure your resume highlights the value you've brought to your career.

When reading a resume, what section do you read first?

Work Lesson #286 – "The resume focuses on you and the past. The cover letter focuses on the employer and the future. Tell the hiring professional what you can do to benefit the organization in the future." — *Joyce Lain Kennedy, Cover Letters for Dummies*

Your cover letter is your proposal to a future employer. When you're writing a proposal, it's not about you but rather what you can do for the organization. This will explain your worth; therefore, each cover letter is tailored to the role and organization.

Never use a generic cover letter, use your cover letter to voice your relevant career highlights to your future employer. Ensure your cover letter and resume match each other and have been tailored for the position.

You'll want to state your most relevant and impressive accomplishment within your cover letter and state how you'll bring the same results to their organization. Use your first paragraph to grab the employer's attention.

Cover letters are one page. Be concise and ensure you have answered the employer's question: *"Why should I hire this person?"*

If you've answered this question clearly, then they'll likely read your resume.

What's your biggest cover letter tip?

Work Lesson #287 – *A cover letter must be tailored to each position. There is no such thing as a generic cover letter.*

Each cover letter must be tailored to the position and company you're applying to. Below is a sample cover letter to assist in writing your own.

Dear [Ms. or Mr. LAST NAME – Never use Whom it May Concern and don't assume a woman is Mrs.]

I'm writing to express my interest in the position of [JOB TITLE] for [COMPANY NAME]. I have 5 years of experience in [FIELD/INDUSTRY] and have a proven track record of bringing high-quality results to my employer and clients. I believe my qualifications will be a strong fit for your organization and clients.

The value I'll bring to your organization will be a diverse skill set, including extensive leadership experience [MATCH SKILLS FROM THE AD, USE 3], strong communication, and timely decision making. I've contributed considerably to all aspects of project execution, leading multidiscipline teams, and teams with conflicting priorities [STATE 3 FROM YOUR EXPERIENCE] through my communication and teamwork abilities.

I have the cognitive and problem-solving ability [STATE SKILLS] required for the [JOB TITLE]. I bring an innovative, outgoing and openminded attitude [PICK 3] that wants to learn. I would welcome the opportunity of meeting you personally to discuss how my qualifications can add value to your organization. I can be reached at [NUMBER].

Thank you for your time and consideration.

Sincerely,

[YOUR SIGNATURE]

Week 32 Theme: The Rules of Trust

Trust is one of the founding variables in all strong relationships... remove it, and the relationship will typically crumble.

This week, I'll be discussing the rules of trust and addressing the following:

- How important is trust within your character?
- How to build trust?
- Which comes first, respect or trust in building relationships?
- Who you can and can't trust?
- Can you trust your instincts?
- Can you regain trust once it's broken?
- Can trust be bias?

Trust can be a simple character trait, or it can be a complicated one. Other emotions and attachments often accompany trust; therefore, it can reside in the white, the grey and the black zone. This week, I'll be dissecting the complexity behind trust and why it's critical to building long successful careers.

How important is trust to you?

Work Lesson #288 – Trust is the binding agent that holds your credibility and reputation intact. Without it, your foundation will show cracks.

The Rule of Trust #1 – Trust is critical to building a strong character; without it, your reputation is highly susceptible to defamation.

How close would you allow someone into your world that you don't trust?

Probably, not that far... the same goes for your own character. If you're not trustworthy, you'll have a hard time building strong, lasting relationships.

Your character is a significant variable in your professional credibility, which feeds your reputation; therefore, if your character is questioned, your credibility will be weakened, and result in a vulnerable reputation.

Credibility and reputation are your foundation to build your career skyscraper, without trust, you've removed your binding agent and risk your skyscraper collapsing due to faulty construction. When building your career, ensure your foundation is built strong, and this will require you to be trustworthy.

How do you behave around people you don't trust?

Work Lesson #289 – Without the establishment of trust, you cannot develop strong relationships; and without strong relationships, you cannot build an effective network.

The Rules of Trust #2 – Effective and influential networks are often built from strong trusting relationships.

When it comes to a network, think quality over quantity.

Large numbers don't always indicate effective and influential. When it comes to a robust network, you need it to be active and to work in your favour.

When people trust you, they usually respect you. With trust and respect, they have faith in your ability and, therefore, are much more likely to help you.

When you lack trust, you may have an extensive network, you may even be well known, but generally, a mistrusting reputation is also well known. This extensive network doesn't mean you have a strong inner circle of people that will use their influence to open doors for you.

Effective networks are built from the inside out, from your inner circle and expand outwards. If you're not trustworthy and it becomes known, the tarnish against your name will be hard to clean, and your network will suffer as a result.

How strong is your inner circle?

Work Lesson #290 – *Respect and trust go hand and hand. They bind together to create loyalty.*

The Rules of Trust #3 - Respect is your left hand, and trust is your right hand; when they come together, they create loyalty.

Loyalty is a powerful element in an effective network. Loyalty protects you and opens doors to opportunities you may not be unaware of.

When you create loyalty within a group of people, they feel compelled to help you. This can come in the form of mentors, friends, partners, and strong supporters. All effective networks have these members.

Strong inner circles of a network are embedded with loyalty. They'll drop what they're doing to help you, and you would do the same.

When you lack either respect or trust in your character, you'll have a hard time building a loyal network, and without loyalty, you'll be trekking through a good portion of your career alone. A team of one can only go so far. We all need help opening doors from time to time.

Do you believe Respect + trust = Loyalty?

Work Lesson #291 – *Words can shield the truth; actions begin to expose the truth.... And results are the truth.*

The Rules of Trust #4 - Results are the truth of your capabilities and your credibility as a professional.

Words can come easy and without responsibility for some people. In simple terms, they lie, to you, to themselves and to their organization.

If you want to learn whom you can trust, watch their actions.

- Do they deliver on their commitments?
- Do they overpromise and under deliver?
- Do they blame others when things go wrong?
- Do they always have an excuse as to why something wasn't done?

- Do they communicate when they're going to be late?

Strong credible professionals communicate and deliver on their promises. Even if they're going to miss a deadline, they don't wait until the last minute to announce it, they communicate, ask for help and do whatever they can to meet their commitments. These are the actions of a trustworthy person.

When you deliver consistent, high-quality results, people begin to trust your capabilities as you've become a safe bet, and safe bets often get chosen first for the team, as they know exactly what they're getting with their draft pick.

What are the classic actions of untrustworthy people?

Work Lesson #292 – *Instinct often sees what our brains miss. Trust your intuition.*

The Rules of Trust #5 – Don't ignore your instincts. Your intuition may be trying to speak to you.

There are many variables to making an informed decision, but when all other methods fail to produce a clear choice, or when time is in the form of urgency, instincts and intuition can be a valuable tool.

I remember early in my career I was working with a senior leader; he was kind, polite, seemed encouraging of my career goals, but there was always something a little off about him... and no one else seemed to see it. I don't even know if I saw it, but I certainly felt it. I ignored this gut feeling. I worked hard for them, long hours, even weekends, and when it came time to put my name forward for a promotion, they disappeared. It stung, not because I was overlooked, but because my instincts told me this was going to happen a year before it did, and I ignored it.

Sometimes there is no apparent reason to feel what your instincts are trying to tell you. Our logical brain wants to discredit what doesn't make sense. My advice is, don't ignore it. You may not change your decision based on your instincts; just never ignore them; force yourself to reflect on why you feel what you are.

Should instincts be trusted?

Work Lesson #293 – *The loss of trust can be like a capsized ship; it may stay afloat, but it will never resemble its original form again.*

The Rules of Trust #6 – Never Lie.

This is a simple work lesson; don't lie. Don't lie to others, and don't lie to yourself. If you can't disclose the information a person is requesting, tell them this. Don't create a lie; be honest.

The problem when you lie and when you lie often, is you need to remember the lie and who you told. If your memory isn't great, then it will simply be a matter of time until you're caught in a lie.

When you're caught in a lie, people will question your ethics, integrity, and whether they can trust you again. These aren't questions you want people asking of your character.

Being caught in a lie can have severe and potentially permanent repercussions, depending on the severity of the lie; therefore, use extreme digression when you contemplate lying. It can sink your reputation, and you can lose close relationships.

To close, remember, Warren Buffett's quote, *"It takes 20 years to build a reputation and five minutes to ruin it. If you think about that, you'll do things differently."*

When you summarize it that way, is lying worth it?

Work Lesson #294 – *Trust must be earned, don't allow the halo effect to cloud your judgement.*

The Rules of Trust #7 - Trust can be prejudiced, don't fall victim of the halo effect.

'Who's Jim?'
'He's good friends with Dan.'
'Oh cool, he must be a good guy then.'

During your career and life, you get labelled by association ('guilty by association'). This can be good or bad, depending on the person doing the association. You can't control what others believe, but you can control your own assumptions and, therefore, don't make them.

Allow people to earn your trust and respect, don't give these out blindly, and the same goes, for thinking poorly of people, because they hang out with someone you don't like.

Part of learning who to trust requires self-awareness of your prejudice, preferences and beliefs. Be aware of your own bias, and don't allow these to interfere with your assessment of people. For example, if you believe in a religion, this doesn't mean everyone who shares your beliefs is a good person.

Sometimes, we can categorize people into what we subconsciously believe, and we must be aware of these prejudices, so we can give people a fair chance to earn our trust.

Do you believe trust and respect should be earned?

Week 33 Theme: The Power of Time

"Time can bring you down, time can bend your knees.
Time can break your heart, have you begging please."

— Tears in Heaven by Eric Clapton

Time can be our most significant and precious asset. Eric Clapton's words always bring tears to my eyes when he sings that line from Tears in Heaven, knowing they were about losing his son. For me, the line carries the reality of time to the forefront and reminds me of how precious it truly is that your life can forever change in a moment.

This week, I'll be discussing the power of time.

- From time management,
- To making time for your priorities,
- To not overacting to an urgent matter,
- To recognizing time stealers.

Managing your time is critical to reduce stress and to be your most productive, so let's discuss how we can improve our time management.

What's your best time management hack?

Work Lesson #295 — Understanding when you need to get into the weeds and when you need to water the grass is critical to managing your time.

The proper judgement allows us to gauge the time required to complete a task, assignment or project.

Without this judgement, you can spend too much time on the wrong tasks, missing critical details that require your attention.

Managers who micro-manage are notorious for getting into the weeds when they should focus on watering the grass. As a manager, their primary responsibilities are their team and client's overall well-being. By micro-managing, they spend most of their time focusing on the responsibilities of others, which can disengage and demotivate their team, while potentially neglecting their client's needs.

Micro-managers need to learn to delegate, train their team better and begin leading instead of interfering.

Learning to recognize the tasks that require a deeper dive and those that don't will help immensely when managing your time. When completing a task, record the time it takes to complete it and see if it matches the time you thought it would take. Practice and improve as you learn better ways to achieve your responsibilities.

Do you record the time it takes to complete your tasks?

Work Lesson #296 – There are important matters and there are urgent matters; don't confuse them. Finding your balance requires you to make time for important matters.

When I was conducting interviews for my book, I interviewed dozens of Vice President, and the final question I asked in every interview was, *"What's your greatest regret?"*

100% of the answers were linked to some form of poor time management and understanding of their true priorities.

Not one answer was, *"I wished I worked more,"* or *"I wished I took that promotion."*

All replies were something they missed, that they had wished they hadn't.

"I wish I saw my daughter graduate."
"I wish I say my son hit a grand slam.
"I wish I spent more time at home, more time with my spouse."

So many of their answers had, *"I wish I spent more time..."*

Urgent matters don't necessarily constitute important matters. Many times, it's the urgent matters that take us away from the important matters.

If you're continually not making time for something you believe is an important matter, then you need to ask yourself whether it's a priority?

True priorities get scheduled and don't continually get overlooked. If they do, this will likely end in future regret.

If you've deemed something a priority, ensure you make time for it and not merely do it when you have free time.

Do you make time for your priorities?

Work Lesson #297 – *Time can be your most precious asset and your biggest investment. Once it's lost, you can't get it back.*

Don't be too quick to move into the future.

We see it so regularly with children, can't wait to be adults, then as adults, we recognize how precious our childhood was.

If your fortunate, your story will be told over many decades. Be proud of your past, learn from it, be present with it, then leverage it for your future, just be mindful, that you don't spend too much time reliving your past or planning too much for your future.

Your past is over, if it no longer serves you, release it and move on.

Your future is a question mark and not guaranteed to have an answer... therefore, ensure you do enjoy your present and where you are in life.

Being able to embrace the present and be happy without dwelling on the past or too focused on the future can be a blessing.

You never really know how much time you get, as tomorrow isn't promised, so please ensure your happiness isn't dependent on your future. There is no better time to be happy than right now.

Do you agree?

Work Lesson #298 – Careers span decades. It takes time for your actions and results to reveal your truth. Be Patient.

Careers take time to build. Credibility isn't gained overnight. And your reputation requires momentum to get rolling.

These all require time. To sustain long-term career success, you must deliver consistent, high-quality results that are visible to your organization.

Solving difficult problems requires time. When you do solve them, and they're visible, you begin to establish your credibility as a professional, and your reputation starts to gain momentum.

Results are the truth of your capabilities and essentially your credibility as a professional. To build your skillsets and ability will require dedication, hard work and time. Be patient when your building your career.

The highest skyscrapers take longer to construct. To lay their foundation take times as they're deeper, larger and have greater reinforcement to optimize their strength.

When building your career, you want the Empire State building, not a two-story house.

When building your career, think long-term, do you agree?

Work Lesson #299 – Be mindful in benchmarking yourself against others... their sprint may not be your marathon.

People progress at different speeds. Just because someone is ahead of you today doesn't mean they will be in 5 years; stick to your plan.

Worrying about what others are doing, takes away your attention and focus from yourself and your plan. It wastes your precious time. Time that you'll never get back.

There won't be anyone that cares more about your career than yourself. When you focus on what others are doing, you've taken your greatest asset away, which is your focus, drive and energy.

Understanding the timeline for career progression within your organization is useful information to have. Still, it can be dangerous if you try to benchmark yourself against people who appear to be the exceptions rather than the standard rule.

If the standard labour grade promotion is every 3 years within your company, and your peer did it in 2. Don't feel that you failed when you did it in 3 years, as you'll never know all the variables that went into their promotion.

Stick to your plan. I've been in the corporate environment for a long time, and have seen double, triple promotions occur... don't concern yourself with other's career progression... run your marathon; you may catch a second wind at mile 14 when someone crashes at mile 16.

Careers span decades, you're in the middle of your story. By focusing on what you can control will assist in your story having a happy ending.

Do you think it's dangerous to compare your success to others?

Work Lesson #300 – You control your schedule... create the balance you need for a healthy life.

As you progress forward in your career, your time management skills will need to improve, as you'll gain more and more responsibilities. Not only in your career but likely at home as well.

From becoming a first-time lead to a spouse, to a parent, as you progress forward in your life and career, your responsibilities will increase, and your time will become more valuable.

Think of it this way, you have an empty plate, and as you progress, more and more food gets added and eventually, it becomes overcrowded. When this happens, you risk some of it slipping off and falling onto the ground.

This is why time management skills become critical as you progress. Skills like delegation and managing stress become essential to learn. Unmanaged stress and burnout can cause illness, hampering both your career and family life.

If you find yourself always struggling to complete your responsibilities, you need to focus on your schedule and learn what's not working.

- Do you simply have too much on the go? Is there anything you can remove, or delegate away?
- Are you focusing on the wrong things?
- Are you a perfectionist, when good enough is all that's required?

Find out what's stopping you from being productive, remove it and take control of your schedule!

How have you taken control of your schedule?

Work Lesson #301 – Be aware of the Time stealers. They interfere and prevent you from being productive.

Time stealers can be many things, such as people, poor habits, and unmanaged impulses.

Working hard isn't necessarily working smart.

What worked for your five years ago may not be working for you now as a manager.

If you find there is never enough time in a day to finish your tasks and responsibilities, you'll need to make a change. Working late hours and always compromising isn't sustainable.

If you can't find time to finish your daily responsibilities, you'll need to isolate the reasons and make the necessary changes.

An excellent place to start is finding out what and who is stealing your time? Do you have too many unplanned visitors? Are emails and phone calls interrupting your workflow?

Once you isolate what is killing your productivity, you can put protocols in place to prevent it from interfering.

For example, if emails and phone calls interrupt your productivity, place time allotment for addressing emails, 30 minutes in the morning and 30 minutes in the afternoon. Send phone calls to voicemail when you're completing important tasks.

When you address what's stealing your time and put protocols in place to prevent interference, you will begin to take back your time.

What protocols have you put in place to address time stealers?

Week 34 Theme: The Rules of Talent

Talent is the ability and skills you bring to the table. And in most circumstances, you control what you bring to the table.

One of the great qualities of talent is that it can be exponential, never reaching a plateau. Your mindset is how you choose to approach developing your weaknesses, which can help gain new skills and abilities—reaching higher levels as a result.

This week, I'll be addressing the following:

- How to pick talent?
- How to grow and nurture talent?
- When talent isn't enough?
- What holds back talent from developing?
- How to prevent plateauing?
- How to cope with success?
- How to pick a well-rounded team?

Talent is often accompanied by other traits, such as work ethic, discipline, attitude and character (all within your control). Talent can be grown based on circumstance or forced out of its shell. This week, I'll be dissecting the complexity behind talent and why it's critical to building long successful careers.

How important is talent for career success?

Work Lesson #302 – True 'A' Players want to be surrounded by other 'A' players.

Talent wants to be around talent. As they're aware, if they're to develop into their best version, they must be around people that drive this out.

The more you're around greatness, the more it rubs off on you.

Insecure people chose *'yes'* people and the 'B' and 'C' players. The true 'A' players want to be around the best, so they can continue to improve and grow.

Insecurities can get the best of people and take over their rational side of their brain. If you're the leader of a team, you should want the best people on your team, as this will reflect on how effective you are as a leader, yet, somehow, insecurity can creep in, and they feel threatened; driving away the 'A' players with micro-managing or poor behaviour. If you witness this, this is a sure sign of an ineffective and insecure leader. Avoid working for them.

The Rules of Talent #1 - You can be highly influenced by who you surround yourself with; therefore, choose to be around intelligent, ambitious, kind and interesting people.

Who do you choose to surround yourself with?

Work Lesson #303 – When it comes to predicting talent... observe their attitude both in times of major success and major defeat. This often reveals the answer.

Being talented and developing your ability is a great start... but never forget, it's what you do with the talent that truly defines its effectiveness.

Regardless of how talented you are, you'll make mistakes; this is a guarantee and often reveals your real character and personality.

You can often learn someone's real character and personality during two extremes: one during extreme success and the other during a severe setback.

With major success, have they allowed themselves to be arrogant? Have they let their ego get the best of them?

When dealt a setback, do they retreat? Runaway? Blame others? Or step up to fix the mistake?

If you need to predict talent, observe the candidate's attitude during times of extreme stress. Are they resilient? Do they persevere regardless of the challenge? Or do they give up?

The Rules of Talent #2 – If a candidate can only utilize their talent during times of comfort... then they aren't truly effective, as difficult problems and challenges rarely appear during times of convenience.

What do you look for when assessing talent?

Work Lesson #304 – *To cultivate talent, help them recognize their potential, through developing their skillsets and growing their ability.*

A mentor will guide, support and help you through difficult career obstacles.

As you progress through your career, you'll need effective mentors to assist in your learning. An effective mentor will teach and share their experience, skillsets and knowledge with their protegees. This will help you grow and nature your talent.

Many aspiring professionals can lack confidence or be blind to their weaknesses. They may have all the right intentions but are putting their efforts into the wrong areas. This is why we all need a helping hand to guide us, as we can all have our blind spots.

The Rules of Talent #3 - Effective mentors will tell you what you NEED to hear, not what you WANT to hear. Weaknesses can hold you back from reaching your potential, therefore, you want mentors that will tell you the truth, even if it hurts your feelings.

How do you cultivate talent?

Work Lesson #305 – *The employees and entrepreneurs who don't 'play nice' with others, have limited career paths.*

You can be an extremely talented person, but if you can't get along with others, your career choices will be limited.

There aren't many positions that don't require teamwork, leadership and communication skills.

Talent is a great start, but it isn't enough on its own. You must be able to work well with others and be a contributing member of a team. This requires you to:

- Listen to others; don't interrupt or assume you know what they're going to say.
- Being open-minded and understand you may be the one that needs to change.
- Know the difference between when you need to lead and when you must follow.

There will be times during your career when there is someone else that should lead a team, even if you're capable. It means there is a better choice or a greater need.

The Rules of Talent #4 – A leader who chooses to follow, knowing they're capable of leading, is a sign of a true leader.

What traits are more important than talent?

Work Lesson #306 – *Your dedication towards lifelong learning, will assist you in navigating challenges and prevent you from prematurely plateauing.*

Your mindset can be a powerful tool.

Your mindset influences your perception. Your perception influences your attitude, which, in turn, influences your behaviour.

Your behaviour creates habits (good or bad).

The habit of discipline can be highly effective and keep you motivated during difficult career setbacks.

Bad habits can damage your career prospects, such as poor listening, negative thinking and being closed-minded.

Close-minded people have shut off part of their brain from learning, and when you're not learning, you're not improving and growing. This is often when an employee becomes stagnant and plateaus as a result. Often prematurely.

Professionals who have dedicated themselves to lifelong learning continue to grow and improve. They have trained themselves to be disciplined by creating good habits that contribute to their education, such as remaining open-minded, bringing a solution mindset to every challenge and persevering through difficult problems.

The Rules of Talent #5 – Creating good habits contributes to your career success by producing the environment your talent can flourish within.

What holds back talent from reaching their potential?

Work Lesson #307 – A mind driven by EGO, has an expiry date on learning.

Never allow your success to go to your head.

Your early supporters are the people who got the momentum going in your favour... your success can very well be linked to this support. When you begin to be highly successful, this isn't the time to change the formula that got you there.

Never forget where you came from... your story can inspire others to reach for the sky, just like you did. When people are inspired, they'll go to extreme lengths to support and help you... you have their loyalty.

Allowing your ego and arrogance to take over... will slash the inspiration and motivation you've created with your team and supporters. It can be the quickest way to lose their support, and the fastest way to stunt your growth and learning. People who allow their ego to get the best of them generally close their minds to receiving constructive feedback preventing them from developing new skills and overcoming bad habits.

To learn at an exponential right, you must remain humble and put your energy into important matters... don't waste time feeding your ego; it won't get you anywhere

The Rules of Talent #6 - Stay humble.

Do you find humble leaders inspirational?

Work Lesson #308 – If you want to continue to progress forward in your career, be ready for the climb. Build the right habits and train yourself to develop formidable skills.

> *"I don't count my sit-ups; I only start counting when it starts hurting because they're the only ones that count."*
>
> *– Muhammad Ali*

Continually developing new skills is hard work. The further you progress in your career, the habits to develop new skills will get easier, but gaining the skills will get harder.

The further you go, the more you're entering new terrain, and the smaller the group will become. There may be less competition in the form of numbers, but the talent pool will be tight. To remain agile and ahead of the game, you'll need to dig deeper than you have previously.

Just like Muhammad Ali demonstrates in his quote, when things get hard, or when things begin to hurt, how you react then and there, can be the difference in building the necessary skills in making you successful and continually reaching the next level.

When pursuing ambitious goals, ensure you have created the right habits and trained yourself to work through the pain. You don't summit Mount Everest with good intentions; you must put in the time and train.

The Rules of Talent #7 – The air is harder to breathe the higher you climb. Ensure you've trained accordingly for the tough climb.

Do you believe the competition is harder, the farther you climb up the corporate ladder?

Work Lesson #309 – *The truth in your talent is revealed in how you can bring talent out of others.*

A sign of true leadership is how they can develop talent in their teams and get average performers to become star performers.

Strong Leaders will tell you what you NEED to hear, not what you WANT to hear.

- An effective Leader doesn't feed your ego; they help keep you grounded and working on self-improvement.

- You want leaders that will tell you the truth, even if it hurts your feelings as weaknesses can hold you back from reaching your potential.

The Rules of Talent #8 – Strong leaders are rare; therefore, if you find yourself working for a great leader, ensure you listen to them and learn as much as possible.

Do you agree?

Week 35 Theme: Embracing Change

One of life's guarantees is change. As we've witnessed these past few weeks, change can happen rapidly and leave us feeling uncertain.

This week, I'll be addressing change and how you can embrace it and plan for the unexpected. From making a career change, to returning to the workforce, let's discuss how you can better prepare for change and live with the uncertainty.

Just as the seasons' change and winter rain bring Spring flowers, when you're in the middle of a significant change, the destination may not be known, and the journey can be blurry. Below are 5 steps to help embrace change.

1. Make a list of everything that creates discomfort in your life (e.g. financial uncertainty, health concerns, etc.)
2. Look for ways to lessen the discomfort, such as immediately cut out unnecessary expenses and strengthen your immune system by eating healthier.
3. Develop methods in managing the additional stress. (e.g. stretching, watching a movie, staying home).
4. Make an effort to self-assess your health and stress regularly, daily, if needed.
5. Don't be too hard on yourself.

How are you coping with the uncertainty?

Work Lesson #310 – Uncertainty can be scary. This is something you shouldn't deny, instead, accept your feelings and directly address your fear and understand where it stems from.

It's perfectly normal if you're scared of the uncertainty in the world at the moment. Being scared is nothing to be ashamed of; it indicates the humanity in you.

Your career is unknown, your health is unknown, and your finances may be unknown. Our future is blurry, and a clear picture has yet to reveal itself.

I'm reminded during times of uncertainty and change that yes, it's a time to focus on the positive and to try my best to practice gratitude, but in my darkest moments, fighting the darkness of my fear and thoughts seems to be battle I cannot win.

If this is where you are mentally, I don't think you should fight it. I think you should embrace it and learn where it stems from. <u>For example</u>, if you're worried about your finances, dive into your budget, immediately cut out what's not needed (e.g. Netflix) and put together a worst-case budget plan for the next 3 months. Begin addressing your fear and make preparations that will help control it.

By doing nothing, you allow the fear to grow and become a disease.

How are you preparing?

Work Lesson #311 – Career changes can be forced upon us at unlikely times, and we must adjust accordingly. Having a plan and strategy in place will assist in remaining calm and focused.

How to plan for a career change?

If you've been recently laid off or believe you may be laid off shortly, read below as an example to move forward.

You don't always need to change careers entirely but instead make a pivot. Many skills are transferable, and therefore, you can build on what you have already established (communication, leadership, software skills etc.).

Some steps to assist in making a change:

1. Target an industry, company and position you're interested in.
2. Learn what skills are required to execute this new role.
3. Assess what skills you have that can be transferred to the new position.
4. Develop the skills you're missing through online courses, while you're doing this, network with people on LinkedIn that can help you move into your new career with a potential employer.

5. Sell your qualification to the new employer through posting applicable content online that will be visible to the industry and employer you're targeting.

Remember, it takes courage to embrace change. Be brave and put together a plan, then execute the heck out of it!

Work Lesson #312 — Never forget that restarting your career after a long break takes patience, dedication and courage.

Never underestimate the power of a plan and the wiliness to execute it. It all starts with the first step.

If you've decided to rejoin the workforce after a long break (e.g. Illness or Mat Leave), I list a few things below that may help you get started.

1. Don't overcommit to early. Target a position you would like and begin developing the skills you lack through online courses and self-teaching. Develop your plan.
2. Be realistic with your plan, including the job you're targeting and the salary you want. Ensure you complete thorough market research.
3. Explain your absence from the workforce on your resume, but ensure you highlight the skills you gained (relevant to the position) during this time.
4. Take baby steps and build your confidence slowly. This may or may not be needed depending on your personality, but don't be discouraged if you're not getting interviews. Hire a career coach to review your resume and prepare you for interviews if needed.

Any other tips you want to add?

Work Lesson #313 – *Embracing change requires you to live in reality. This means shutting off the naysayers and planting your feet on the ground and taking a step.*

For many people, there has never been a more uncertain time in their career than right now. The world can feel a little surreal at the moment. Many people's ironclad plans have come unhinged.

Unfortunately, this is today's reality, but it may not be for tomorrow, especially for those who can adapt and change their plans to match the market.

Becoming comfortable being uncomfortable requires you to embrace change and be adaptable.

Remember, small steps can add up to a giant leap. To improve and grow often requires change.

Right now, giant steps may not be realistic, but small calculated steps could be. Therefore, put a plan together, turn away your self-doubt and begin.

How do you get rid of self-doubt?

Work Lesson #314 – *The world is changing, and one of the most important skills to teach and learn, is to be adaptable. If you're capable of changing, you're capable of learning new skills and new skills allow you to stay relevant in a changing world.*

People incapable of learning new skills become stagnant employees.

Like evolution, if you adapt, you're capable of changing along with any climate; this can make you highly valuable.

Since constant change is one of life's guarantees, training yourself to be adaptable and flexible is wise. Be the person, that regardless of the role, can bring value to any team.

Part of maintaining your adaptability requires you to be open-minded and willing to learn continuously. By dedicating yourself to lifelong learning, you'll continually develop and refine your skills and grow as your environment changes.

Instead of being uncomfortable with change, you've trained yourself to embrace it and learn from it. If you can remain adaptable, there will always be a team in need of you.

How do you embrace change?

Work Lesson #315 – Organizations that cannot embrace change will be left in the past. They will secure their spot in the history books as examples of what not to do.

Once relevant, vibrant, and booming companies are becoming dated and losing their market share.

As soon as you buy a cellphone, within weeks, it is outdated. At times, it can be overwhelming trying to keep up with the competition; yet Apple, Samsung and Google have found a way to compete, while Nokia and Blackberry didn't.

Finding new ways to be competitive has become a necessity in today's business world; the companies who cannot keep growing and evolving, are falling behind their competition.

Being able to adapt, grow and evolve as required to remain competitive and relevant in today's business world.

Watching a company lose its market share is not a pretty sight and best to observe from a distance.

A few classic signs of a failing company are:

- Their best employees leave,
- The Hierarchy system is ancient,
- The company lacks transparency,

- Status Quo reigns supreme, and
- Recycle instead of innovate.

What other classic signs are there?

Work Lesson #316 – *Wisdom can often be defined as a person who knows when to lead and when they must follow.*

Yes, the early bird gets the worm, but the second mouse gets the cheese.

Sometimes, people can be too quick to want a change and become impatient. They don't take the time to make an informed decision.

Most decisions have a level of risk to them. This is why we calculate the odds and then decide if the risk is acceptable. If we jump immediately into accepting a risk, this can often lead to problems.

Being first can certainly be a tactic, but it doesn't guarantee you'll win. Apple came late to the cellphone market and won. Of course, they did it by completing changing the market and essentially the game. But you get my point. Being first doesn't guarantee you can hold onto your market share. Sometimes, following and learning first can make you the winner later.

Understanding the difference of when being first is the correct tactic to choose, and when you're best to allow others to go first requires experience, judgment and wisdom.

Practice patience, discuss and listen to experienced leaders, who have had to make these difficult decisions and learn.

Patience can be a great teacher, do you agree?

Week 36 Theme: Know Your Manners

Good manners shouldn't be complicated, yet, I've witnessed, on many occasions, people who can't seem to understand its simplicity.

Good manners are but not limited to:

- Treating others how they want to be treated.
- Saying Hello and replying to a Hello.
- Saying Thank You when someone does something for you.
- Holding a door open for the person behind you.
- Offering a handshake when you meet someone new and when you're saying goodbye.
- Offering to help when someone is struggling.

This week, I'll be discussing good manners in the workplace to reduce alienating and offending others unnecessarily.

Sometimes a simple smile or a simple bite of the tongue can defuse an otherwise hostile situation. Good manners can be powerful.

How do you practice good workplace manners?

Work Lesson #317 – *Simple rule to live by: Be kind and fair to everyone.*

Being kind and fair to everyone is a great habit to accustom yourself with, as it takes little effort and generally has only positive results.

Kind and fair habits to develop:

- Smile often.
- Say hello to people and be friendly.
- Ask someone how their day is going and listen to their response.
- Make eye contact when you speak with people.
- Be positive.
- Allow people time to explain their actions.
- Never assume.

- Don't judge.
- Help if you're able.
- Say, thank you.
- Give recognition.

These are simple suggestions, which you have full control of implementing into your daily routine.

When you're kind and fair to everyone, you become a likeable person, and people learn what they can expect from you.

What kind and fair habits have you developed?

Work Lesson #318 – *Sometimes, you must accept people for who they are and who they aren't.*

There is freedom in acceptance.

Whether it's acceptance for yourself or others, when you practice acceptance, you eliminate your expectations.

Putting your expectations onto someone who isn't capable of living up to them isn't fair and will alienate them and disappoint you.

I'm discussing unfair and unrealistic expectations, for example, expecting a junior employee to fill in for a senior position. This isn't fair, and you shouldn't be putting this expectation on them without training and help. A reasonable expectation is expecting your staff to show up to work on time.

Living in reality and understanding people's limitations and boundaries is essential. Stop pushing your agenda onto people who don't want it. Just because an employee is talented enough to be a Lead, doesn't mean they want it. Many times, part of leading is accepting and respecting people's wishes and not forcing your expectations onto them.

Have you found freedom in acceptance?

Work Lesson #319 – *Practicing tolerance means you first try to understand a person's perspective before you disagree.*

The workforce is full of diversity, from gender, age, culture etc. We differ from each other in beliefs, values and behaviours.

And because of this, we will differ in opinions from time to time.

When operating in a team, there must be respect between all team members to work effectively. This means we must tolerate differences of opinion, as no one is always right. Sometimes, we are the one in the wrong, and sometimes we are in the right. How we choose to discuss differences of opinion can be the difference between a team that operates efficiently and a team that alienates each other.

When practicing tolerance, sometimes this may require you to remain silent but the majority of the time may simply need you to ask questions to gain additional information to understand where a person is coming from. Many disagreements on a team can happen respectfully, with everyone having time to explain their outlook and reach an agreement.

This will not happen if the team cannot practise tolerance and respect. You must be willing to listen, so everyone can have their chance to be heard.

How have you practiced tolerance on your team?

Work Lesson #320 – *Investing in your team can build loyalty faster than money can buy it.*

Money doesn't buy loyalty, and it isn't a guarantee your top employees are going to stay as the best employees don't need to settle for less than ideal work conditions.

Great employees generally have many options.

According to LinkedIn's 2019 Workforce Learning Report, 94 percent of employees say that they would stay at a company longer if it merely invested in helping them learn. This was the number one answer, not receiving a raise.

Candidates want development and learning, not empty sentiment. Continuous development and growth require a real investment in your team and staff. Loyalty is built over time and through caring actions.

A raise is a wonderful action, and an employee is thankful for it, but its impact will be short-lived if it isn't backed by other actions such as recognition, training and development.

Remember, investments can compound and grow, money once it's spent, is gone.

Do you agree?

Work Lesson #321 – *Showing gratitude to a colleague can be powerful, as you're grateful for what they have given and don't want anything more.*

Many employees feel their organizations take and take, rarely giving much in comparison to what they take.

One simple rule I live by, don't be a manager who takes.

If you can show gratitude to your team, this will help create a safe environment for them to work in, excel in, and relax within. If your people believe their best is never enough, you will, over time, get less and less from them as you risk them hitting burnout. And an employee who is fatigued, tired and burned out, will never produce their best work.

Practice gratitude with your team. Thank them for their contributions and reward them when they shine. Give clear and realistic expectations to your team and reward them when they meet these expectations. This can be a simple thank you, or a team lunch. Mix it up, depending on the tasks and their performance.

How do you practice gratitude?

Work Lesson #322 – *Before providing your opinion, ensure it has been requested.*

We are all human, and we all have our opinions. And sometimes, we may even feel compelled to state our opinions.

Before you do this, ask yourself these three questions:

1. Was my opinion asked for?
2. Does my opinion add value to the conversation?
3. Is the person willing to listen?

If the answers are "No," then it's best to remain quiet.

Stating your opinion when it isn't wanted, can alienate and unnecessarily offend people.

Sometimes remaining silent is the best course of action, as not everyone wants you to solve their problems, especially if they haven't asked you. Sometimes people just don't want to hear it. This is where your judgment comes in and handle case by case.

Obviously, if someone is in danger, you speak up, there are definite times when you must speak regardless if it offends just practice discretion when the times aren't distinct.

Do you believe you should remain silent when your opinion hasn't been requested?

Work Lesson #323 – *Be the employee that is the bright moment in someone's day.*

Sometimes all it takes is a smile to help someone have a better day.

Even the smallest task can improve someone's mood, such as:

- Ask people how they are? Make eye contact and listen to their reply. Ask a follow-up question if needed.

- Ask your colleague, who appears stressed if they need help with anything?
- Bring in treats to surprise your team.

Remember, offering your assistance may not always be accepted, but it will most likely be remembered.

Being sincere and willing to do a little extra may just turn out to be a positive moment in someone's day.

What do you do to be the bright moment in someone's day?

Week 37 Theme: Bullying in the Workplace

I believe we can all agree that bullying in the workplace is wrong, yet somehow, it still happens. For some people, bullying doesn't end in grade school.

Bullying in the workplace can resemble many different things from:

- Made to feel guilty for taking a sick or personal day.
- Making you believe you're going to lose your job.
- Creating unsafe workplaces through withholding employee rights.

Bullying in the workplace can be subtle to straight out blatant. This week, I'll be discussing bullying in the workplace, from how to recognize it, how to deal with it and how to make yourself less of a victim.

Have you ever had to deal with a bully at work?

Work Lesson #324 – *No one has the right to make you feel inferior.*

What is bullying in the workplace?

Sadly, bullying can be prevalent in the workplace.

Bullying in the workplace can be subtle, as the bully doesn't want others to recognize their poor behaviour; therefore, they do it quietly. Sometimes, they hide their real disgrace with fake kindness to get your guard down than they strike.

One of the telltale signs of bullying, is how a person makes you feel. Bullies often want you to feel inferior to them. This can be in the form of you feeling fear, fearful for your job, hopelessness, anger, lack of confidence in your ability, sadness, humiliation etc.

Generally, bullies want control over you and one way they can do this is through making you feel guilty.

Ask yourself:

- Does your boss make you feel guilty if you take a sick day?
- Do they tell you, you better make up the time?
- Do they imply you're lying and that you should come in?

These are all signs of an unhealthy work environment that is laced with subtle forms of bullying. If your boss is continually trying to make you feel guilty or have you feel inferior to them, you could be dealing with a bully.

Have you had a boss that has been a bully?

Work Lesson #325 – *If you're being bullied in the workplace. You'll have to address this difficult situation, as bullies rarely back off from a target that isn't sticking up for themselves.*

How to deal with bullying in the workplace?

Sadly, if a bully has targeted you, they'll generally won't back away, unless you give them a reason.

Depending on how they're bullying you, you'll decide on how you should approach the situation. The classic bully deflection is to stick up for yourself and to show strength as most bullies back down from strength. Bullies prey on easy targets that aren't capable of sticking up for themselves.

A step by step method in dealing with a bully in the workplace:

1. Look them in the eye when you're talking to them.
2. Be clear with what you're willing to tolerate from them.
3. Be clear in your direction and statements (e.g. I don't appreciate the language you're using).
4. Tell them *"No"* (e.g. I can't work late tonight as I have plans, had you told me earlier, I could have rearranged my schedule).
5. If it's ongoing, document the bully's actions. Secure proof through emails, record phone calls etc.
6. Escalate the behaviour to Human resources if required.

Any tips to add?

Work Lesson #326 – *When confronting a bully, you must be direct and transparent. This isn't a time to be subtle nor passive-aggressive.*

Dealing with confrontation can be uncomfortable; therefore, don't be too hard on yourself if it is painful. It's perfectly normal not to enjoy confrontation, you're not supposed to. Unfortunately, it may be required throughout your career.

There will be times during your career where it will be best to walk away, generally, this isn't the case with a bully. Bullying tends to continue till you deal with it, as it rarely disappears on its own, therefore, below are a few tips in confronting a bully.

- Mentally prepare for the confrontation. Your well-being is critical and therefore, prepare emotionally for the encounter.
- When they're bullying you, stop them, interrupt them if needed, and explain how their behaviour is impacting your work and present clear instructions on your future expectations. Make your boundaries clear. Potential wording, you can say, *"Please don't talk to be that way."*
- Remember, bullying is rarely about you. It feels incredibly personal, but it's rarely personal from the bully's perspective, therefore, confront them. No one has the right to make you feel inferior.
- If it continues, ensure you document the bully's actions and words, then report it to your higher-ups if required.

Any tips on confronting a work bully?

Work Lesson #327 – "A friend who bullies us is no longer a friend. And since bullies only respond to strength, from now onward, I will be prepared to be much stronger." – *Hugh Grant, Love Actually*

Several people have asked me, *"How to make yourself less likely to be bullied?"*

I'm going to address this question, but hope people comment their opinion and suggestions so that we can have an open discussion. This is an important topic that must be addressed, and people need help.

Many people have tried to bully me during my career, either by yelling at me, belittling me or discreetly threatening me. Each situation ended the same way, with me sticking up for myself. This often started with me turning the situation around on the bully by asking them a point-blank and direct question, such as:

- Why are you yelling at me?
- Why are you so angry?
- Why are you taking this out on me?
- If a bully is talking over you in a meeting and criticizing your work, turn it around and ask them to make a recommendation. Anyone can be a critic, put them on the spot to come up with a suggestion. Put an end to their complaints.

Always look a bully straight in the eyes and use a firm tone of voice when you speak to them. You're not here to play games. This will assist in you not being a target again in the future.

To get rid of a bully, you must be strong. Strength isn't an easy target, and many bullies want an easy target.

Any additional tips?

Work Lesson #328 – You can't pick out a bully by their appearance. You pick them out based on their words and actions.

Once you know what to look for, a bully is rather easy to pick out of a crowd, as they often resemble the same traits as a taker.

Words of a bully:

- They speak in absolutes, *"No one likes you,"* or *"We all think you're underperforming."*
- Makes things personal, *"You're horrible at your job,"* *"You're hard to like,"* or *"You have a weird way of doing things."*
- Ask inappropriate questions, *"Why are you wearing that?"* or *"Are you gonna cry now?"*

Actions of a bully:

- Verbal attacks through criticism, inappropriate jokes, and harsh language.
- Try to intimidate others.
- Manipulate, blame and sabotage others.

Traits of a bully:
- Insecure, often trying to mask their insecurity with acquiring power and control.
- Selfish, their needs are a priority.
- Impulsive and have a hard time managing their emotions and, therefore, can have anger issues.
- Lacks empathy and respect for authority.

What traits have you seen in a bully?

Work Lesson #329 – *Bullying in the workplace should never be tolerated. If you witness an employee being bullied, you must take action.*

Bullying should never be tolerated. It creates a poor work environment, as people may fear coming to work or stating their opinion.

To bring the best out of your team, to retain great talent, people must feel safe and, in an environment where bullying is tolerated, is not secure. If you witness an employee being bullied, you must take action.

Sometimes, you'll need to interject immediately and stop the bullying from occurring; this will most likely require you to interrupt, ask the individuals what's going on. Ensure you maintain full eye contact with the bully. Generally, the individual being bullied won't say anything or that everything is fine. Don't accept this answer; this individual needs your help.

If you witness an employee being bullied and you're a manager, you need to write them up and report them. If you're a younger employee and are afraid to confront the bully, then report the occurrence to HR and your supervisor. If your supervisor is the bully, then absolutely report their behaviour to Human Resources.

Bullying should never be tolerated, especially in the workplace. If you remain silent, others will be a target of this individual.

Do you agree?

Work Lesson #330 – *Saying "Yes" to an opportunity when you're scared, and saying "No" to a bully, both take courage.*

Whether you're standing up to a bully or sticking up for family and friends, never forget that doing difficult things, requires courage.

No one enjoys being bullied and walking on eggshells around certain people.

People who bully others are ineffective leaders and are generally insecure. They prey on the vulnerable, so they can feel strong and in control.

They can't handle people disagreeing with them; therefore, their teams usually operate per dictatorship with nearly zero innovation. Their opinion reigns supreme, and they want your constant agreeance.

This isn't a healthy work environment, and if it continues, it can harm your health. Review my posts throughout this week on how to deal and confront a bully if this isn't an option for you, plan your exits from the situation or organization. You must make yourself a top priority.

How have you removed yourself from a situation with a bully?

Week 38 Theme: Coping with an Unhealthy Work Environment

Coping with an unhealthy work environment is difficult and may not be easy to escape.

Even if the position is temporary, an unhealthy work environment can be straining and stressful, therefore, you must develop coping mechanism to minimize its impact.

This week, I'll be discussing how to find sanctuary away from negative people, how to develop a plan to escape your undesired circumstances and how to recognize an unhealthy work environment, as sometimes it can be settled.

The first step is to recognize an unhealthy workplace and then put in protocols to minimize its impact on you, and this may mean you move on.

How have you escaped an unhealthy workplace?

Work Lesson #331 – If you find yourself surrounded by negative people at work, you'll have to discover your sanctuary away from their influence.

Negative people can suck the positivity out of a room.

Have you ever witnessed a person enter a room, and their mere presence changes its decor? This can have both a positive and negative impact on the room, depending on the type of change. But in the case of negative people, it can be draining, and your health and well-being may be impacted.

If this is the case, how do you remain positive when negative people surround you?

There are a few things you can do:

- Minimize the time you spend around them. Don't go for coffee and lunch breaks with them. Use this time to escape and relax.
- If they sit near you, minimize how much you hear from them, by using headphones and listening to music.
- Set clear boundaries with people and limit the time you need to interact with them. If it isn't work-related, don't carry on a discussion with them, especially if it's a conversation that makes you uncomfortable.
- Personalize your workspace with photos, inspirational quotes etc. that cheer you up and remind you of what matters to you.

You can be influenced by what you're surrounded by, therefore, reduce the time you need to be around negative people.

How have you remained positive around negative people?

Work Lesson #332 – *Concentrating on what's not in your control, has put your focus and attention on the wrong things. This can make you feel like a hostage to your circumstance.*

Remaining focused on the things you can control, and influence may be easier said than done, as your work environment can impact you, whether you're in control or not.

An unhealthy workplace can impact your well-being; therefore, the first step is identifying what's triggering your stress and what's changing your focus.

For example, when working around people you don't like, you must minimize your interactions with them and how their actions impact you. If they sit beside you, maybe listen to music to tune them out. You'll have to put protocols in place to minimize their impact on your focus, stress, work and health.

Part of this is putting rules in place to assist you in remaining in control. You may not control the team you are on or the people you work with, but you control your reactions, attitude and actions. Therefore, if you notice, your focus is drifting onto unimportant matters, don't ignore this, ensure you put protocols in place to reduce these distractions.

How do you ignore the actions of people you don't like in your office?

Work Lesson #333 – *Some work situations cannot improve, and the only option may be to leave.*

Some situations at work can escalate to a level of stress where you're best to walk away. Your health can be directly correlated to your work environment, including your stress level; therefore, you must gauge this level and decide if it's acceptable.

Dealing with a stressful work environment is hard; below are 5 tips to help:

1. To understand the level of stress that is acceptable, you must gauge it. Write a daily journal and keep track of your stress. Do you recognize a common theme? Are things progressively getting worst?
2. Establish your limits and boundaries, for example, how much overtime you're willing to work.
3. Take time to relax and recharge. Don't compromise on this. This can be a simple walk at lunch.
4. Request support. If you're overworked and the pile isn't getting any smaller, maybe it's time to hire additional support. Speak to your boss.
5. Add some fun into your daily task, such as listening to music as you reply to emails.

Stressful work situations may not disappear on their own. You may need to set boundaries and reduce the time you spend with negative people who are impacting your productivity. Regularly review your stress and how your work environment is contributing to it and make changes when needed.

How do you cope with a stressful work environment?

Work Lesson #334 – *There will always be bad days at work, but it's concerning if the days you enjoy are a fraction compared to the miserable days.*

It isn't healthy to dread going to work... Well, it may be the norm for other people, but don't settle for this; be the exception. Don't allow yourself to dread work.

We can spend approximately 70,000 hours at work during our life... that is a lot of time wasted being miserable.

If you're miserable at work, the position is temporary, and you should put together a plan to escape this situation. Some tips:

1. Target an industry, company and position you're interested in.
2. Learn what skills are required to execute this new role.
3. Assess what skills you have that can be transferred to the new position.
4. Develop the skills you're missing through online courses, while you're doing this, network with people on LinkedIn that can help you move into your new career with your potential employer.
5. Sell your qualification to the new employer through posting applicable content online that is visible to the industry and employer you're targeting.

How have you escaped a miserable work situation?

Work Lesson #335 – *No one has the right to make you feel guilty without your permission.*

A work environment that uses guilt to control is unhealthy.

Some unhealthy work environments are discreet and disguised to resemble positive places, but don't be misled. If your intuition is telling you something is wrong, it probably is.

To assess an unhealthy work environment, ask yourself:

- Are you being made to feel guilty? For taking a sick day or not working late?
- Is the office always negative? What's the regular mood on the team?
- Do you find yourself avoiding everyday work situations and people?
- Do you wake up dreading to go to work?
- Are you overstressed continuously?
- Are you always overworked?
- Does your organization tolerate bullying?

If your responses to some of these questions is a yes, your work environment is unhealthy and potentially toxic. You may need to plan your exit from the organization.

What are the signs of a toxic work environment?

Work Lesson #336 – *To maintain perception management during your day to day work, you must be aware of your organization's unwritten rules.*

Every organization has unwritten rules, and to maintain appearances, you must be aware of what they are.

When it comes to unwritten rules, organizations can vary considerably. From having few, to having many in which a company culture can severely be impacted.

If your organization appears to allow unwritten rules to reign supreme, this can be a sign of an unhealthy work environment. One of the significant examples of this is perception. Does your company allow perception to take over? What I mean by this, is what you appear to be doing, is given more credit than what you're actually doing. If this is the case, there is an issue here.

For example, if you take a sick day, is your absenteeism at work being judged as a lack of dedication, when, in reality, staying home, keeps the entire team healthy. If an organization allows false perception to weigh in how your performance is judged, your organization is doing an injustice.

You must be aware of the power of these perceptions to either decide to stay and manage these or to leave.

How have you managed perception in the workplace?

Work Lesson #337 – *To choose an employer that will provide the work environment for you to excel in, you must first understand what will meet your needs.*

To assist in picking the right organization that can help you grow and improve. You must, at a minimum, be aware of your short-term career goals.

If you don't know what you want, at least in the near future, how will you know if an organization can provide what you need?

Having short to long-term career goals will assist in making better choices on where to work and what positions to pursue.

This is valid for pursuing your first position out of school and making a career change.

First start by developing near term goals, then picking an industry, potential companies and positions that you believe can present the right environment to reach your goals.

It starts with you having a plan, therefore, develop one. If you move ahead without a plan, you'll be more likely to make mistakes and waste precious time.

What's your next career goal?

Week 39 Theme: Climbing the Corporate Ladder

Climbing Corporate can be a long and strenuous climb; therefore, the first step is to ask yourself, do you want it? If you do, then don't be naive; this will require your dedication, time and sacrifice.

You don't get to the top of the corporate ladder working 40 hours a week; there will be sacrifices and tough decisions along the journey. This is why I say, ask yourself, do you want it? Many talented employees fall into the trap of chasing dreams they don't want.

They're talented, the right people have taken notice, they get offered a fantastic opportunity, and they say *"yes"* blindly. Then this leads into the next opportunity and the next, never stopping to ask, *"Do they want it? Does this fulfill them? Are they happy?"*

If you do want to climb the corporate ladder, then this week's theme will interest you. All week, I'll be discussing the necessary traits in climbing the corporate ladder.

What traits do you believe are required to climb the corporate ladder?

Work Lesson #338 – *The Corporate Ladder is an incorrect statement... as careers aren't linear; therefore, neither will your ladder.*

A more accurate statement is, *"Careers resemble a game of snake and ladders."*

Careers can have giant leaps, modest steps forward and setbacks, therefore, remember:

Failure is a huge part of success. If you're going to leave your comfort zone, this requires you to enter new terrain, where making mistakes is more likely.

You learn more from your setbacks and mistakes than you do from easy successes.

To move on from a setback, you will need to adjust and try new methods... This can lead to increased learning, which can lead to success and greater confidence in your ability.

Career setbacks can set you up for a career leap.

How have career setbacks moved you forward?

Work Lesson #339 – *You must take full responsibility for your career, and this may mean you create your own opportunities.*

Have you relied on others to open doors for you? If you have, you may not be taking full responsibility for your career.

Taking full responsibility means, regardless of the hand you're dealt, you make the best of it.

- You cannot control the cards you get, but you can control how you strategize your wagers.

- A game of poker isn't based on one set of cards being dealt; it's how you calculate your risk versus reward, gauge your audience and play the correct odds, over many hands.

- Like poker, there will be variables in your career that you cannot control, but you can always control how you react to every hand being dealt and adjust accordingly.

- Create opportunities... You hold the hammer, and you can build your own door.

Are you calculating your wages?

Work Lesson #340 – Be visible to your organization.

Why do some deserving employees don't progress forward in their career?

There can be multiple reasons for this, but the most common I've witnessed is that they aren't visible to the right people to ensure they get credit for their work and promoted accordingly.

You get rewarded by delivering consistent, high-quality results that are visible to your organization. The second part of that sentence is important.

You need to be seen solving difficult problems because when you're seen, you get credit for your work. This can offer protection for your reputation. You don't want to be the proverbial tree in the forest... if no one hears it, did it happen? The same thing goes for being seen, if no one sees it, did it happen?

To sustain long-term career success, you must deliver consistent, high-quality results that are visible to your organization. When you're visible to your organization, people learn what you're capable of, and this can create career growth opportunities for you.

Do you believe that being visible to your organization is essential to career success?

Work Lesson #341 – When people know who you are and what you can do; it's the beginning of building a sellable name.

A sellable name means your reputation has reached a new level.

Not only do people know who you are, but they also know what you're capable of. A sellable name means, your name carries influence and is marketable.

When you have influence, you can persuade, which allows you to sway people's opinions and behaviours.

When you're marketable, you're an asset to your organization, as you're in demand, and your name will be the supply to meet this demand.

To build a sellable name, you must bring something to the table: talent, skills and a network. When you're talented, well know and have access to an influential network, you can often write your own ticket.

How are you building your name and reputation?

Work Lesson #342 – *No one makes it to the top on their own.*

You can be the best at what you do, but you can't be everywhere, to truly open big doors, you'll need help opening them.

Many times, career success comes from who you know, therefore, make networking a priority.

Understanding the type of relationship you want with your new contact will assist in approaching the recruitment process. I caution you by chasing a title and numbers. Think strategically on who you'll need in your network to help make you successful, such as influencers, mentors, trusted colleagues etc.

Always put time aside throughout your career to network as you never know who can open unforeseen doors. A strong network has all levels and generations accounted for; ensure you have no missing gap.

Don't rush building your relationships, as trust takes time to earn. When building an effective network, it's quality that matters, not quantity.

How are you building your network?

Work Lesson #343 – *Ambitious goals require sacrifice, and often this sacrifice isn't witnessed by anyone except yourself.*

Work hard, work smart and rest when required.

When you have ambitious goals, you'll need to dedicate the time to develop the skills of your craft and many times, this happens after your 40-hours of work are done.

Whether you want to climb the corporate ladder or build a business, you'll need to make difficult choices along the journey, and sometimes, this means sacrifice.

You probably won't make happy hour every Friday, and you'll have to say *"No"* to many fun activities that arise over the years... and when you finally make it and have reached your ambitious goals... people may call you lucky because they didn't witness the endless hours behind closed doors that made you the success you are today. Don't let this impact you... luck has very little to do with discipline and working your ass off.

If you have ambitious goals, there is no elevator to the top floor; you'll have to take the stairs. And if you want the Empire State Building, it will take time, training, endurance and hard work to get there.

Do you agree?

Work Lesson #344 – *Understand that working hard requires you to work smart, and sometimes, this means, you rest to recharge.*

Successful people don't remain stagnant, but they can stay still for a time. They do this to rest and regain their energy.

To produce your best work requires you to be healthy and focused.

I know many successful people are regimented in their stress relief routine, whether this is working out, sleeping well, or meditating. They all rest to recharge. They know when they need to say no, and when they are spreading themselves to thin.

Successful people live in awareness of what their mind and body needs, and don't sacrifice this under any circumstance. As they understand, if they become ill, they are no use to anyone, including themselves, their families and their organization.

How do you recharge?

Week 40 Theme: The Art of Communication

Communication is a skill that will never go out of style.

As technology plays an increasing role in our day to day lives and remote working becomes more the norm, being able to communicate effectively has become critical.

You can have a magnificent vision that can change the world... If you can't communicate it to others, for them to see its greatness, you have a problem.

You must be able to listen, control your emotions and be open to other people's opinions to be a strong communicator.

This week, I'll be discussing the Art of Communication from active listening, to controlling your body language and practicing patience.

How important is communication?

Work Lesson #345 – Patience is a vital part of communication. Don't interrupt or assume you know what someone is going to say.

Often, we experience loss in translation when attempting to rush a conversation or make unnecessary assumptions and interruptions.

Even when we are both speaking the same language, miscommunications can easily happen. Now, add in multiple languages, and cultures, miscommunication is more likely.

Many conversations need to run their course and cannot be rushed. Teaching and mentoring entry-level employees may take longer than explaining a process to a senior employee. Providing instruction to someone learning a second language may even take longer. Don't rush your instructions when your audience appears to be lost.

Continually ask them questions to assess their understanding, be sincere in your questions.

Part of effective communication is having the other person feel comfortable enough to ask you questions to clear up any misunderstanding.

Don't assume your team has understood because they didn't ask questions. If you appear to be in a hurry, they may think you don't want to be bothered. Best to be patient and ask clarifying type questions.

Do you practice patience in your communication style?

Work Lesson #346 – *Leadership is a universal language.*

Communication doesn't always come from words. Some of the most effective communication comes from our actions.

Actions can send a clear message to an audience without uttering a word. True leadership is an excellent example of when actions should be clear.

Actions of a Leader:

- Practices patience
- Listens
- Engages with their team
- Shares credit with their team
- Self-aware
- Kind and fair
- Helps and develops people
- Humble
- Practices tolerance

This is a small list of actions of a true leader. When they're practiced, a transparent form of communication has been established. True leadership is witnessed, regardless of the language spoken, or the country and culture you're within.

What other actions would you add?

Work Lesson #347 – *Listening can be a great gift to those who need to be heard.*

Listening is the most important part of communicating and the easiest way to gain and learn information.

True Leaders are strong communicators. They're strong communicators because they possess the two fundamentals of communication:

- **First**, they can translate ideas to their team; and

- **Second**, they listen to the wants and needs of their team.

Part of motivating your team is understanding their needs and creating an environment where they can flourish and reach their goals. You learn this information by observing, asking the right questions and listening.

Strong communicators are good at recognizing problems, building trust with their teams and encourage an open-door policy. They want to hear from their team regardless of the news. The sooner you're aware of a problem, the sooner you can solve it. With this built trust, their team will go to them with any issue and solve it as a team.

Leaders recognize their team members' contributions and provide constructive feedback when required.

Do you believe communication is its most potent when there is an establishment of trust?

Work Lesson #348 – *Never forget, silence is an answer.*

In today's world of ghosting, often, no answer can be an obvious and, at times, painful answer.

If you ask someone a clear and direct question and all you get is silence in return. This is an answer and one that shouldn't be ignored. Never assume because someone didn't speak and provide an answer that you didn't receive one.

The silence, when asked a question, or an avoidance to answer a question, such as changing the topic or never giving a clear reply, are clues that the person doesn't want to provide an official answer.

For example:

"How do I look in this dress?"
Silence...
"Sweetie, how do I look in this dress?"
Looks at the floor... pause... "Honey, we better get going, we're going to be late?"

If a person wants to answer a question, they will. If a definite answer isn't provided, as in the example above, he probably doesn't think you look good in that dress and doesn't want to answer it.

Sometimes silence or avoidance of a reply is your answer.

Do you think silence can be an answer?

Work Lesson #349 – If you're not sure what to say, learn techniques on how to stall.

Sometimes you need a few extra seconds to structure and gather your thoughts on how you want to reply to a question directed at you.

When I find myself in this situation, I generally use three types of stall techniques, depending on the situation.

1. If I don't want to reply to the question, I use misdirection, either by using noncommittal words such as: maybe or changing the topic to a topic I know will distract the person asking the question.
2. I ask a follow-up question, stalling to answer, and learning more information so that I can provide a better, more informed answer.
3. I paraphrase the speaker's words, walk them through my thoughts as I stall, and gather what I'm trying to say.

Lastly, if I don't have an answer because I don't know the answer. I generally reply by saying, *"I don't know, but I'll find out and get back to you shortly."* And keep my promise.

No stalling technique will help you if you don't know the answer, and if additional questions to the people in the room can't help you. Best to let them know you'll get back to them and move on.

How do you stall for more time before replying?

Work Lesson #350 – *Ask questions when you don't understand. Assumptions can often lead to miscommunication and wrong conclusions.*

If you don't understand something, ask questions.

Even if you feel you understood the instructions your boss gave you, best to confirm and paraphrase what they told you and ensure you're aligned on their expectations.

Assumptions can often lead to false conclusions.

"I assumed you were busy last night, so I didn't bother calling you to see if you wanted the extra concert ticket."

"I assumed you didn't want that assignment because you have a young family, and it would require you to move."

Both these examples have made assumptions, potentially incorrect ones unless you asked the person directly, you'll never actually know if you were correct.

Don't assume, best to always double-check with the person before you think you know their reply.

Have you had people assume things on your behalf that was incorrect?

Work Lesson #351 – *Your body language communicates to your audience. Ensure it's speaking the same message as your words.*

Does your body language match your facial expression and words? Have you said *"Yes,"* while nodding your head *"No"*?

Ensure your body language matches the message you're trying to convey, if it doesn't, mix messaging may result.

Body language can reveal your true feelings, as its harder to control than words and facial reactions.

<u>For example</u>, during an interview, you may be smiling and using confident sounding words, but your body may be sweating or mildly shaking, revealing your nerves. Or

Have you said, *"you're comfortable and fine with the decision your boss made,"* but are tense, have folded arms and frowning... your body language isn't matching your words.

An effective communicator doesn't send mixed messages. Their body language, facial expressions and words are all aligned and sending a clear message.

How has your body language impacted your communication style?

Week 41 Theme: The Power of Teamwork

Being a member of a team has been an honour throughout my entire life. From sports teams to project teams, a good portion of my learning and growth has been directly related to being part of a team.

Over the years, I've learned some of my most valuable lessons from teammates, coaches, bosses and mentors.

This week, I'll be discussing teamwork, from being a strong team player to self-improving through your team, to driving innovative ideas through collaboration.

Each of us will be a member of many teams throughout our careers: some bad, some good, and if we are fortunate, some amazing ones.

Being part of a strong team is truly an honour because:

T - Together
E - Everyone
A - Achieves
M- More
(Source: Unknown)

Would you agree?

Work Lesson #352 – *The foundation for building strong teams comes from establishing trust and respect.*

Respect and trust go hand and hand. They bind together to create loyalty.

Loyalty is an integral part of an effective team.

When you create loyalty within a group of people, they feel compelled to help each other. This can come in the form of mentors, friends, partners, and strong supporters.

Strong inner circles of a network are embedded with loyalty. They'll drop what they're doing to help you, and you would do the same.

When you lack either respect or trust in your character, you'll have a hard time building a loyal inner circle, and without loyalty, you'll be trekking through a good portion of your career alone, without true supporters.

We all need help opening doors throughout our careers. A team of one can only go so far. Build a strong character embedded with trust and respect.

What else goes into building a team?

Work Lesson #353 – There'll be a limit to what you can teach yourself. To truly reach your potential, you need multiple avenues and people to learn from.

There is a reason why teams generally outperform individuals. As an individual can plateau faster by themselves than a team.

I remember being in college and doing a coding assignment. I wrote, then rewrote, and debugged my program, yet it wouldn't run. I looked over my code 100 times and couldn't see my error. A peer come over and within five minutes of review, found a coding error midway through, and the program ran smoothly after that.

Within five minutes, my peer solved my problem. They brought fresh eyes to my old problem and were able to solve it.

My point here is that sometimes two minds are better than one, and sometimes, three minds are better than two. We can be limited by ourselves, as each of us has weaknesses, but as a team, other members may have our weaknesses as strengths, and together we are stronger.

There is higher learning and growth when you increase who you can learn from.

Do you agree?

Work Lesson #354 – *To withstand a storm, we reinforce our homes with multiple beams and load-bearing walls.*

An effective team offers us protection and backup. When I get sick and need to stay home, the team and company don't stop progressing; they continue to move forward.

An effective team offers support and growth. The leader builds a team with reinforcement, meaning they're mentoring their successor and ensuring each member of the team is offered development and training.

If you're building a home, you don't leave visible cracks in the foundation, and you don't leave gaps in the roof. One hole in the roof can lead to a leak, if that leak is left untreated, it can lead to structural and foundational damage, impacting the entire house, leaving it susceptible to collapse.

A team is no different. If a team has missing gaps and goes unchecked, the team cannot withstand all storms, leaving their foundation vulnerable to external attack.

For a team to perform ideally, they need to feel protected and safe.

Do you agree?

Work Lesson #355 – *Collaboration is the coming together of many ideas to give birth to one big vision.*

Ideas build off of ideas.

A collaborative environment where you finish often doesn't resemble where you began; as the team together built off each other's ideas and suggestions to get somewhere new and unfamiliar.

A few years back, I had the honour of attending my first Innovation Catalyst Event in San Francisco. During the event, the team was given a tough problem to solve that was plaguing the industry. Over six months, the team worked every weekend, building the solution. Where we ended up was a mere pipedream from that week in San Francisco. Over six months, we built off ideas, off failed solutions to finally end up where we were and where we got to present our solution to our CEO.

My point here is, without a team, we would have never gotten as far as we did. Each of us brought a unique set of skills that could be utilized to come to a solution.

Do you believe ideas build off ideas?

Work Lesson #356 – *It's easier to get up from a fall by offering a hand.*

My 11-month-old son just started walking, and as you can imagine, along with this new skill, there have been many falls.

Some he can brush off and continue to move forward, and some are bad, and they require me to tend to tears.

When I offer him support and a hug, the tears disappear much faster than when I sit back and watch him try to cope.

My point here is, when we try new skills and are leaving our comfort zone, falls and mistakes will happen. If you witness a team member, peer, friend, or family member struggling, offer them support, other them help, offer them your hand.

It's easier to face a challenge when you have a built-in safety net there to catch you. My son knows I'm never too far to pick him up and make him feel better; I'm his safety net.

If you're able, be someone's safety net.

Has someone been your safety net?

Work Lesson #357 – *A bear may go after a wolf but never the pack.*

I'm not a believer in the statement: *"Every man for himself."*

If you live by this statement, then, in the end, you'll be by yourself, with few people willing to stick up for you, and ready to help you.

Yes, there is safety in numbers, we see this commonly in nature, but the true strength in teams is access to greater growth and learning. In teams you're more likely:

- To learn,
- To grow,
- To develop,
- To be mentored, and
- To have support.

A pack of wolves is stronger than one wolf. A pack can attack from multiple angles, where a wolf can only attack from one position, making it predictable.

A team versus an individual is similar; while a team can use each member's collective intelligence and knowledge, an individual can only use their own resources. A team can have access to a vast network of influencers as each member brings something to the table, whereas an individual only has access to their own network.

Throughout your career, a team environment will outperform that of an individual.

Do you agree?

Work Lesson #358 – *An effective team has an aligned vision, clearly defined goals and understands their roles.*

It's a reward, a privilege and an opportunity to be a contributing member of a Team with a common goal and purpose. (Source: Unknown)

There are teams of individuals, and then, there are teams who win championships. The team who wins championships is fully aligned on their purpose, their role and their goals.

This may mean some team members need to check their egos and take a role the team needs versus what they want. Being a member of an effective team often requires sacrifice from each member.

A team needs to fit together like a puzzle. Moulding each piece to build a picture. A complete puzzle doesn't have missing pieces.

Do you agree?

Week 42 Theme: Powerful Career Moments

Careers can span decades, and they'll be filled with both their ups and downs, moments that break our hearts and moments that supply them with joy and happiness.

Since the world needs some positivity, I decided to dedicate this week's work theme too powerful career moments. These are the moments that will be remembered for a lifetime, the moments if we experience them, will fill our hearts; these are the moments that make our careers reach the level of happiness that dreams are made of.

Taking pleasure in your daily habits and responsibility, meeting a mentor that changes your perspective on life, and finding light in your darkest setback, careers are full of powerful moments.

Careers are full of moments, so let's discuss some of the most defining moments we'll experience in our careers.

What's your happiest career moment?

Work Lesson #359 – *If you can't embrace and enjoy the journey, what makes you think you'll enjoy the destination.*

You spend far more time travelling down the path to a career goal then you generally do at a destination. The way you feel about the journey is a strong indication of how you feel once you get to the destination.

My point here is, if you're miserable travelling through the journey, you should stop and ask yourself whether you're genuinely chasing a goal you want. You will have miserable days during the journey, but they shouldn't be the majority. Keep this in mind if you find yourself unhappy; it's a great indication that you may be on the wrong path.

For example:

You're working towards a degree, but hate all your courses, what makes you think you'll enjoy your career?

When I was studying Engineering, I certainly didn't enjoy all my courses and hated that I needed to take so many at once to graduate in a reasonable time frame, but overall, I enjoyed my time at school. Sometimes you have to take courses you don't like to secure a degree you want, but if you hate all your classes, that's a red flag you shouldn't ignore.

Practicing gratitude helped me appreciate the journey. Not every day can be a significant success or a huge event. Finding joy in your daily habits and responsibility can add many beautiful moments to your career.

Are you enjoying your journey?

Work Lesson #360 – Put time aside to enjoy the designation and be present with your accomplishment, you've earned it!

You work your ass off to reach a goal; then, before you recognize it, you're onto the next one.

When you reach a successful milestone in your career, spend some time savouring the destination. Be proud of yourself and your accomplishment.

When you reach the end of your career, many of these accomplishments might feel short-lived because you never spent time embracing them.

If you have dedicated a decent amount of time reaching a career goal or milestone. Do yourself a favour:

1. Stop,
2. Relish in your success,
3. Take that time to recharge, then,
4. Move forward to the next target.

Have you stopped to be present with your accomplishments?

Work Lesson #361 – *Our career's darkest moment can give the spark to our brightest triumph.*

Don't call the winner of the Superbowl at half time.

An underdog today, can be a triumphant winner tomorrow.

Over the course of my career, I've had some significant setbacks, where I could have given up. Given my personality, which is an extremely gritty and determined person, I persevered. I know first-hand that my most significant career moments to date have started as my darkest moments.

A candle can provide light, but it also endures burning... my point here is, when you're in the middle of a setback, you're in quicksand, you're not supposed to feel comfortable.

My advice is, don't panic, don't allow the quicksand to consume you; instead, reach for a branch. This can be in the form of asking for help, reaching out to a mentor, or reflecting on how things went wrong.

When I was working in Mongolia, I had a system completely breakdown, right at a critical time during construction. The pressure was on me to solve it, and when I did, it became my biggest career game-changer, and I was given my first large team to lead as a result. This sent me on a fantastic path in my career.

What has given light to your brightest triumphs?

Work Lesson #362 – *A mentor can be your lighthouse guiding you to safety.*

Many successful careers have had mentors play critical roles...

...but sometimes, you meet that one particular person that changes the course of your career and their influence is powerful that you can't imagine what your career would resemble without them. These types of mentors are a formidable force, and I'm honoured to say I had the privilege of having one in my career.

If I had to pick one person who has had the most significant influence on my career, I would choose my mentor. I chose him, not because of one skill he taught me, but because of how he got me to believe in myself.

A great mentor can influence your perspective, which, in turn, can change how you see your own potential. My mentor played the pinnacle role in getting me out of my comfort zone, stepping up as a leader and motivating others to follow.

If you don't have mentors in your career, keep looking, they can be your greatest supporters.

How has a mentor influenced your career?

Work Lesson #363 – *You have reached a new level in your career, when people come to you, wanting to be recruited into your network.*

When people know who you are and what you are capable of, this is a sure sign you're building a strong reputation backed by a sellable name.

A sellable name means, your name carries influence and is marketable.

When you're marketable, you're an asset to your organization, as you're in demand, and your name will be the supply to meet their demand.

When this happens, people notice... and this is often when people come to you. Some of them will want something from you, but many will want to join your climb up the Org Chart. This is the beginning of you growing a fan club and followers.

When this started happening to me, I missed it and only became aware through reflection. This can be a significant moment in your career, where you officially went from being a high potential employee to a known leader.

No one points out significant transitions in your career, as they're hard to pinpoint, but they happen, and it's often when evidence begins to mount, like people always asking if they can join your team.

What major transition has happened in your career?

Work Lesson #364 – Never think you're not enough. Sometimes, we need to drive a Corolla instead of a Ferrari, but it will get you there.

Humble beginnings are often a great start to a story. If you're learning, trying your best and reflecting on the journey, you'll hit your destination.

Often your perspective of success can interfere with your progress. It's common to look rough as your climbing Mount Everest, but once you finish the climb, hit the peak and have time to rest for your photoshoot, you may look a little different.

By the time we reach our destination, many of us look like a rusty old Buick instead of a nice shiny Ferrari... this is normal. Our war wounds should be worn with pride!

When I was pregnant with my son, I had an idea of what my labour would be, and I can assure you, none of those ideas had my labour end in an emergency c-section. After 34 hours of labour, I spiked a fever that couldn't be controlled by medicine; therefore, we had to make a choice; my son came out then and there.

Yes, I had an 8-week recovery and a permanent 10-inch scar, but it didn't matter; my son was beautiful, happy and healthy. And I was happy and healthy. I recovered from surgery, and my scar is a lovely reminder of the moment I became a Mom.

Scars can be beautiful and help us remember what we needed to go through to have our happiest moments.

Do you agree?

Work Lesson #365 – If you can say you're happy and mean it... then you're successful.

Happiness is an underrated accomplishment.

I've noticed very few people ever ask if you're happy.

If you're not happy with your life? Can you ever be labelled successful?

Maybe by others, but how about yourself? Your own opinion of yourself is what matters.

I remember my Dad turning to me once, completely out of the blue and simply asked,

"Are you happy?"

It caught me off guard because it isn't a typical question I get from him. My competitive nature indeed came from my father, as did my love for setting goals and climbing the corporate ladder. So, when he simply turned to me and asked, I was a little starstruck. And because I was completely caught off-guard, I was brutally honest with my answer, *"No."*

And he said, *"Maybe you should do something about that."*

Maybe I should, and I did. That little question triggered many changes in me. Writing my book was one of them, and fulfilling my love of helping others with their careers was another. The list grows.

I hope this post inspires you to reach for happiness and never settle for anything less.

Are you happy?

Week 43 Theme: Bad Career Advice

Over the course of my career, I've heard some bad career advice. It never ceases to surprise me; how much incorrect information is out there.

What worked for your friend or parents may not work for you. Each career has a unique formula to reach the success you desire. Yes, there are standard variables, but don't be discouraged if something that has worked for others appears to be failing for you.

I think we can all relate to being given bad career advice at some point in our careers, and some of it can be considered a common belief. There is rarely a one solution fits all piece of career advice that can be applied blanketly... lots of advice requires common sense and judgement. And a deep understanding of the unique situation you happen to be in.

So, let's discuss, *"why you shouldn't just be yourself... and just apply for any job... and it's not who you know, but what you know."*

This week's theme focuses on debunking bad career advice and discussing the reality of the workplace.

What's the worst career advice you've gotten?

Work Lesson #366 – <u>Bad Advice</u>: "Just be yourself." <u>Reality</u>: *The work environment requires you to be professional, which means you curb your personality depending on the situation.*

Don't misunderstand me with this post. I think you should be authentic when building relationships and trying to be true to who you are and not fake it...

...At times, you'll need to curb your personality, depending on the audience, situation and culture.

In a professional environment, you need to make adjustments.

For example, if you have a trucker mouth, this won't fly in an office environment with clients present.

If your company has a strict dress code policy, they don't care that you like hoodies and jeans. You'll be sent home, often without pay for violating policy.

So, when I hear people tell young professionals, *"just be yourself."* Make sure you recognize this means, within reason.

What do you think, professionalism or be yourself? Or some middle ground?

Work Lesson #367 – *Bad Advice:* "All things come to those who wait." *Reality: Results often come to highly driven individuals who worked their ass off.*

You'll need to practice patience throughout your career, but practicing patience by not forcing an event to occur is different from merely waiting endlessly.

It's easy to be driven on your good days and after major successes and breakthroughs. It can be an entirely different story to remain motivated after you've failed or experienced a significant setback.

When you've dedicated yourself to your goals, you understand that a setback is simply part of the process, and you don't just sit back and wait for everything to fix itself.

Setbacks are corrected by reflecting on what happened, learning the lesson, and then moving forward with a new strategy. There isn't much waiting there. Reflection may appear that you're at a standstill, but you're not, as you're executing a critical step in your learning.

So, yes, practice patience and reflection, but don't ever be naïve and think waiting will bring you your dreams.

Continuous success is often a result of highly driven individuals that have devoted their lives to the concept of lifelong learning. When you can find a way to motivate and inspire yourself on your darkest day, you're on the path to success.

Do you believe results come to those who wait?

Work Lesson #368 – <u>Bad Advice</u>: "Love what you do, and you'll be happy" <u>Reality</u>: *Happiness is a choice and shouldn't be dependent on external variables.*

I married a business owner who turned his love of scuba diving into his career. He has completed over 1,000 reef surveys and knows more about marine life than most marine biologists.

But the one thing I learned from him and many of my entrepreneurial colleagues, that when you rely on something to pay your bills, regardless if you love it, at some point, maybe not in year one, or year two, but it does turn into work and a job.

Loving your job can be misunderstood... You may LOVE it but not always LIKE it. I've met many teachers and nurses who love their job, yet, they too complain. Working with customers and clients can be draining. Dealing with staff and coworkers can be a nightmare.

Every job has its negatives and shortcomings... my point here is, there is no perfect job that will make you completely happy. Happiness comes from within, from yourself. External variables contribute to your happiness, but they don't create it.

Yes, you can receive enjoyment and fulfillment from your career, which contributes to your happiness. But I caution you if you're relying on your career to make you happy. Careers can span 40 years, and they can be a rollercoaster, as many business owners are experiencing right now with Covid.

Do you love your job?

Work Lesson #369 – _Bad Advice_: "It's not what you know, it's who you know." _Reality: Who you know can open a door for you, but What you Know will allow you to stay in the room._

Many people believe it's who you know and not what you know that makes you successful; I'm not one of them. I'm aware you need both as:

- What you know can lead to who you know; and
- Who you know can lead to what you know.

What you know is extremely important... A network can open a door, open a big door, but you won't be standing in the room for very long if you don't bring anything to the table.

Your credibility as a professional comes from your ability, personality and character... mostly, it's What You Know, Say and do.

Don't get me wrong, you can learn about unadvertised positions from your network, and this can be highly advantageous, but if you can't bring knowledge and ability with you, these advantages won't be utilized to their full potential.

Always and I mean, ALWAYS, bring credibility with you to any opportunity.

How important do you believe _'what you know'_ plays' in a person's success?

Work Lesson #370 – _Bad Advice_: "You have to start somewhere; take the job for experience." _Reality: Career success comes to those who make an informed decision based on a plan. Stick to your plan._

While you need to make enough money to pay your bills and may need to take a job, this doesn't mean you settle for a less than ideal work situation.

Pay your bills, but keep looking and working on your plan.

If you have little to no work experience, well, this requires you to be creative.

Most candidates graduating from University have some experience; you simply need to know how to sell it.

For example, say the job application is asking for leadership experience:

- Was the captain of my University Varsity baseball team, led my team to the State Championship, mentored and developed new teammates etc. or

- Was a camp counsellor accountable and responsible for program development for over 100 children.

Do you have volunteer experience? Such as: running a charity campaign, spending time at an elderly home, camp counsellor etc. Many of these roles can have leadership and time management experience.

Do you have extracurricular experience that is relevant? Sports, write a blog, Social Media business... social media businesses have experience in branding, marketing, and content development. YouTube channels require writing, storyboarding, film editing etc.

It's your responsibility to sell your qualification to an employer.

You do this by linking the skills you have to what the employer is looking for. This may require you to think out of the box and use your sports or volunteer experience to help sell your capabilities.

How did you land your first job?

Work Lesson #371 – <u>*Bad Advice*</u>*:* "Keep applying." <u>*Reality*</u>*: Ensure your cover letter and resume are tailored to the job description and position you are applying for.*

Don't use a generic cover letter and resume and expect an employer to jump all over it.

Generic cover letters and resume tell an employer you made absolutely no effort in applying for the job, so why should they waste time interviewing you, as you're not the right candidate for the job.

Employers want people who make an effort, and because tailored cover letters and resumes take time, they know you can't just simply apply to every advertised position.

Most resumes and cover letters need to be tailored to a position because most employers are looking for something unique. A generic template will have a hard time differentiating you from the competition, especially in the current market.

Be strategic and know what you want. Put a plan together and go after it.

Do you believe a generic resume and cover letter gets you a job interview?

Work Lesson #372 – <u>*Bad Advice*</u>*:* "Put your head down, work hard, and they'll notice." <u>*Reality*</u>*: To ensure career success, your organization must be aware of what value you bring; therefore, make your results visible.*

A great work ethic will benefit you through your career, but only if you use it to work productively and improve.

Throwing hours at a problem doesn't mean you solve it.

If you're not able to:

- Learn from your past mistakes,
- Understand what went wrong and didn't work; then

- Readjust and try again.

Your hard work is mainly for nothing because you haven't improved nor solved the problem... you essentially have nothing to show for your hard work.

Many people tell young professionals to work hard, keep your nose to the grindstone, and you'll be promoted... this may work, but if hard work were the true secret variable to career success, there would be far more successful people.

I know many of us like to think our boss has great plans for us and recognizes our work, but in many cases, this simply isn't true.

- If you're working long hours at the office and no one sees it, did it happen?
- If you're working long hours and have nothing to show for it, did it happen?

You get rewarded for what you're seen doing and for delivering consistent results; therefore, ensure your work is visible to your boss, the team, and the boss's boss.

What do you believe gets you promoted?

Week 44 Theme: Best Career Advice

Throughout our career, we'll receive lots of advice, some good, some bad, some indifferent, but once in a while, we get advice that changes our outlook and perspective.

Sometimes we receive advice right when we need to hear it. We may not want to listen to it, but if we can force ourselves to listen, it can make all the difference.

This week's, I'll be discussing some of the best career advice people have shared with me and what I've received over the course of my career

The purpose of this theme is to share career advice that each of us can benefit from. From having clear set goals and a plan to achieving them, learning how to ask for help and finding effective mentors, careers are built over the years, and each of us needs help along the way.

Last week, I discussed bad career advice; now, let's discuss the best career advice and learn how to apply it to our careers.

What's the best career advice you've received?

Work Lesson #373 – Without a plan, you're shooting darts blindfolded. Never rely on luck to hit the bullseye.

Goals help measure where you are in your career and show that you're going in the direction you desire.

At the beginning of your career and throughout, spend time thinking about where you want your career to go, the path you desire to travel.

Then, put together a career development plan with targeted goals; these goals will serve as stepping stones to accomplish your career aspirations.

When establishing and developing goals, choose check-in points to ensure you're not straying off course.

The path to accomplishing your goals can take many routes. Deviate and pivot when required; goals mature and develop as you progress through your career as priorities change.

Well established check-in targets will assist in measuring your progress and whether a change is required to keep you on course.

Do you set career goals for yourself?

Work Lesson #374 – You will never climb Mount Everest training on your own. Who's belaying your rope?

Continually developing new skills is hard work. The further you progress in your career, the more tested and the greater capabilities you must develop. Gaining these skills will get harder.

You'll need help to acquire these skills, whether from peers, colleagues or mentors; each of us needs help isolating our weaknesses and developing good habits to overcome them.

The further you go, the more you're entering new terrain, and the smaller the group will become. There may be less competition in the form of numbers, but the talent pool will be tight. To remain agile and ahead of the game, you'll need to dig deeper than you have previously. This will require discipline, resilience and a built-in thick skin to listen to constructive feedback to learn when to ask for help.

When things get hard, how you react then, and there can be a difference in building the necessary skills to make yourself successful and continually reach the next level.

When pursuing ambitious goals, ensure you have created the right habits and trained yourself to work through the pain. You don't summit Everest with good intentions; you must put in the time, build the right relationships and train.

Do you ask for help when it's needed?

Work Lesson #375 – *Part of Self-Awareness is being aware of your excuses.*

Self-aware people are aware of their emotions and motives. They understand why they feel them, what they mean and where they originate. Therefore, they never lie to themselves.

The main ingredient of self-motivation is discipline. Relying on motivation to get things done, often results in missed opportunities and ideas of grandeur. Don't allow excuses to overtake your motivation; instead, learn to motivate yourself through discipline.

To continue to grow and improve over the course of your career requires you to understand your capabilities and work on your real weaknesses; therefore, don't fall victim to your excuses.

When I decided to write my book, it took 11 months to write the first draft. I wrote nearly every weekend for a year. If I had waited to be motivated to write... I would have written 15 pages of 300. I never allowed my lack of motivation or excuses to stop me from writing.

I learned to trust the process and hoped that my motivation would creep in after I started, which it usually did. But on some days, it didn't but still kept writing. My book got written because I was disciplined.

How have you remained disciplined when motivation wasn't there?

Work Lesson #376 – *An unprotected reputation is an invitation you want to be lost in the mail; therefore, buy insurance.*

What people say about you may be none of your business, but it's wise to know.

A strong reputation is often protected by numerous factors, making you a hard person to attack through defamation; therefore, ensure you have protected it.

A few tips in protecting your reputation and name:

1. Establish your professional credibility.
2. Deliver on your commitments. Always keep your word.
3. Produce high-quality results. Always exceed expectations.
4. Solve difficult problems.
5. Ensure your high-quality results are visible to your boss and organization.

All five tips will help protect your work and have people connect your name with your ability to produce consistent, high-quality results from difficult problems. This will build a strong reputation that will be hard to defame.

How important is reputation in building a career?

Work Lesson #377 – *Never sacrifice or sell your integrity; its value is priceless.*

Without integrity, you're a boat without a sail, a body without a heart, talent without a team. You can't build a skyscraper when your foundation is missing its rebar. A successful career starts with integrity.

Your integrity is a significant variable in establishing your credibility as a professional. It's your foundation in which you can build a long successful career.

Credibility is your capabilities as a professional; it's your ability and talent. There are three main ingredients to establishing your credibility, character, personality, and ability:

Your **character** is built by your integrity and accountability; without it, your reputation will be susceptible to defamation. Always keep your word and deliver on your promises.

Ensure that your **personality** remains humble as your successes gain momentum. Be kind and fair to everyone you meet. Be generous and help others when you can.

Develop your skills and increase the **ability** you bring to every role. Bring consistent, high-quality results for every challenge and obstacle given to you.

When building your career, start with establishing your credibility, as this will feed your reputation as a high performer who has integrity.

Is there a price for integrity?

Work Lesson #378 – If you limit your mind, you limit your opportunities.

Sometimes, it's our perspective that limits our mind and, therefore, limits our opportunities. You can't shoot for the stars if you settle for the moon.

Your mind can influence your perspective, which, in turn, can change how you see your potential.

Often your own perspective of success can interfere with your success. It's common to look rough as your climbing Mount Everest, but once you finish the climb, hit the peak and have time to rest for your photoshoot, you may look a little different.

For many of us, success will come after many setbacks, failures and obstacles; therefore, never mistake the photoshop photo to resemble the reality of your effort.

At my home, the first photograph I framed of my son, was the photo the nurse took of us as a family in the operations room after 34 hours of labour, which ended in an emergency c-section. I was exhausted, the most tired I had been in my entire life, but our smiles in this photo tell the real story and a story that will never be forgotten.

By the time we reach our destination, many of us look like a rusty old Buick instead of a nice shiny Ferrari... this is normal. Our war wounds should be worn with pride! This is the reward for leaving our comfort zone and shooting for the stars.

Are you shooting for stars?

Work Lesson #379 – *People don't help people they don't like, trust, nor respect.*

Effective and influential networks are built from strong, trusting relationships.

When it comes to a network, think quality over quantity.

Large numbers don't always indicate effective and influential. When it comes to a powerful network, you need it to be effective and to work in your favour.

When people trust you, they usually respect you. With trust and respect, they have faith in your ability and, therefore, are much more likely to help you. Add in, likability, and you have a winning formula.

When you lack trust, you may have a large extended network, you may even be well known, but generally, a mistrusting reputation is also well known. These extended networks don't mean you have a strong inner circle of people that will use their influence to open doors.

Effective networks are built from the inside out, from your inner circle and expand outwards. If you're not trustworthy and it becomes known, the tarnish against your name will be extremely hard to clean, and your network will suffer as a result.

Would you open doors for someone you don't trust, respect, nor like?

Week 45 Theme: Assessing Your Career

Careers go through many stages. Sometimes you leapfrog forward. Sometimes, your learning is exponential, and other times you may feel stagnant where your progress seems to have flattened.

Many times, this is a normal part of the process, but how can you be sure? How can you assess your career to ensure you're still on progress and moving towards your goals? This week's theme will answer the following questions:

- What do YOU want from your career?
- Do you enjoy your job? Are you happy?
- If money and time weren't a concern, what would you do?
- What's the most rewarding feeling you've had in your career? Can it be recreated?
- Are you where you want to be?
- What's your next big career goal? Are you on your way there?
- Have you learned from your past?

This week, I'll be discussing critical questions you can ask yourself to assess your career progression to understand if you're trekking on course with your goals.

Have you done a recent assessment of your career progress?

Work Lesson #380 – What you want to accomplish in your career is an important question and one that requires you to be completely honest in your answer.

Ask yourself: What do YOU want from your career?

A question that must be answered before truthful and realistic goals can be established.

Never lie in answering questions that can impact your destiny and happiness, as they can hurt you and your future.

What you want to accomplish in your career is an important question and requires you to be honest in your answer.

If you're dishonest, you're more likely to travel down the wrong path.

If you begin to be dishonest with yourself, you are more likely to make poor decisions about where and how you spend your time, but it will most likely not result in fulfillment.

When determining career goals, be honest and realistic in establishing targets, so you can have check-in points, to ensure you're on your desired path.

Do you set career goals for yourself?

Work Lesson #381 – *Happiness is an underrated accomplishment, and it's often the only accomplishment that truly matters.*

Ask yourself: Do you enjoy your job? Are you happy?

Happiness can be an overlooked career accomplishment. To amplify my point: how many times have you been asked, what do you do? Now, ask yourself, how many times have you been asked, are you happy?

I've been asked what I do, more times than I can count. I've been asked if I was happy, three times in my entire life and can remember each time.

If you think of your life as a whole, is there any question more important than, are you happy?

Therefore, make it a part of your routine to assess your happiness regularly, this shouldn't be a lengthy assessment, you either are, or you're not; if you're not, then you should be asking why? And What are you going to do about it?

I remember my Dad turning to me once, completely out of the blue and simply asked,

"Are you happy?"

It caught me off guard because it isn't a typical question I get from him. I was a little starstruck. Because I was completely caught off-guard, I was brutally honest with my answer, *"No."*

And he said, *"Maybe you should do something about that."*

Maybe I should, and I did. That little question triggered a lot of changes in me. So, I'll ask:

Are you happy?

Work Lesson #382 – *Dreams are often the big vision that kick starts your plans. Now, execute the heck out of them!*

Ask yourself: If money and time weren't a concern, what would you do?

If your answer is anything than what you're currently doing and it was realistic (meaning: famous musician and can't even play an instrument isn't an answer), you should start putting a plan together to go after it.

There are people on Instagram that make a living posting puppy pictures, so nearly any passion can turn into a viable career with a plan and a desire to work your ass off to make it a reality.

Never underestimate the power in having a plan with targeted milestones and goals. If you're willing to learn, work hard and readjust after setbacks, you can have a winning formula to reach your goals.

Dreams are the start. They create the image and vision in your hard, which turns into motivation for your plan. Your plan turns into actionable steps with check-in points to ensure you are on target. Set goals, readjust when needed and execute the heck out of your plan. Go for it!

Are you working towards your dreams?

Work Lesson #383 – *Careers can span decades and are full of both their ups and downs, moments that break our hearts and moments that fill them with joy and happiness.*

Ask yourself: What's the most rewarding feeling you've had in your career? Can it be recreated?

These are the career moments that will be remembered for a lifetime. The moments if we experience them will fill our hearts; these are the moments that make our careers reach the level of happiness that dreams are made of.

Do you have any moments that can fill your heart with happiness? They can be simple things such as taking pleasure in your daily habits and responsibilities, meeting a mentor that changes your perspective on life, or finding light in your darkest setback.

Discover these moments and learn what it is about them that made them unique. Was it finishing something? Starting something? Helping someone?

Reflect, assess and learn, then try to recreate, if you can.

Understanding what makes you fulfilled at work can help create an enjoyable environment in which you excel in.

Do you agree?

Work Lesson #384 – *Goals help gauge where you are in your career and show you that you're going in the direction you desire.*

Ask yourself: Are you where you want to be?

If the answer is *"Yes,"* keep going. If the answer is *"No,"* then what are you going to do about it? Do you have the right goals and targets set?

Goals assist us in positioning our efforts to hit correct targets, ensuring we are spending our time productively to reach each career milestone.

If you're moving forward with your career without having short- and long-term goals:

- How will you measure your progress?
- How will you know if you're on the correct path?
- How will you know you're using your time productively?

Goals help gauge where you are in your career and show you that you're going in the direction you desire.

Goals are the map, and you steer the vehicle.

What's your next career goal?

Work Lesson #385 – To get to a new location, you need a vehicle, a GPS and the address. Remove one of them, and you're less likely to get there.

Ask yourself: What's your next big career goal? Are you on your way there?

Having short and long-term career goals will assist in creating an accurate and realistic career development plan.

Your career development plan (CDP) will address the critical questions you need to answer to achieve your career goals.

Properly developed goals feed a more detailed CDP.

Your CDP will address where you want to be in your career at certain milestones:

- 1-year,
- 2-year,
- 5-year etc.

And what skills you will need to develop to achieve these career milestones.

If you don't have a Career Development Plan, start today!

Do you have a career development plan?

Work Lesson #386 – *There can be significant growth and learning from reflecting on the past.*

Ask yourself: Have you learned from your past?

Sometimes to understand where you're going, you need to reflect on where you've come from.

There can be significant growth and learning from reflecting on the past.

Reflection exercises can provide a new perspective on an old thought; you can see it through clear eyes. Spending time reflecting on your past can help you see things differently.

When I started my career back in 2006, I had a personal journal. I wrote in it for years, then moved 1,000 km away, and my old journals went into a box.

Four years later, I reread them... and I was shocked at how accurately I recorded the first few years of my career... and voilà... the birth of Work Lessons 101... you never know what you think today; what you write today may turn into tomorrow.

Remember, you must move on from the past but not before you've learned from it. Take your time and reflect, ensure you learn your lessons.

Have you learned from reflecting on the past?

Week 46 Theme: True Leadership

"A true leader has the confidence to stand alone, the courage to make tough decisions, and the compassion to listen to the needs of others. He does not set out to be a leader but becomes one by the equality of his actions and the integrity of his intent."

– Douglas MacArthur

I had the privilege to work for a great leader early in my career. While you can learn a great deal from a poor leader, nothing will compare to the lessons you'll learn under a great leader.

If I had to pick one person who has had the greatest influence on my career, I would choose Rick. I chose him, not because of any one skill he taught me, but because of how he got me to believe in myself.

A great leader can influence your perspective, which, in turn, can change how you see your potential. Rick played the pinnacle role in getting me out of my comfort zone, stepping up as a leader and motivating others to follow. Great leaders ignite your passion, motivation and help you develop into the person you're meant to be.

This week, I'll be discussing true leadership, from learning the traits of a leader to picking out a fraud.

 What are the traits of a true leader?

Work Lesson #387 – Leaders don't mind showing a little dirt on their hands. They serve their teams.

A servant leader leads by example, and they operate under the 5 components of emotional intelligence. They bring the power of knowledge to their team, and they're highly effective as a result.

They're aware of their emotions and understand why they feel them, what they mean and where they originate. They know how their feelings and actions impact their team.

They practice self-regulation and always remain level-headed, calm and in control of their emotions during all confrontation and stressful situations.

They're highly motivated people who set goals and encourage themselves and their teams to reach them. They target goals that will inspire their team.

They practice empathy and can put themselves into someone else's shoes.

They're strong communicators. They can translate ideas to their team; and listen to their wants and needs.

Lower EQ Leaders are usually concerned with leading and getting their desired results. Higher EQ leaders are effective because they don't focus on wanting to lead; instead, they get people to want to follow. High EQ Leaders bring a solution mindset to every problem.

Did I miss anything?

Work Lesson #388 – *Strong Leaders will tell you what you NEED to hear, not what you WANT to hear.*

Your talent is revealed in how you can bring talent out of others.

A sign of true leadership is how they can develop talent in their teams and get average performers to become top performers.

- An effective leader doesn't feed your ego; they help keep you grounded and working on self-improvement.

- You want leaders that will tell you the truth, even if it hurts your feelings as weaknesses can hold you back from reaching your potential.

Strong leaders are rare; therefore, if you find yourself working for a great leader, ensure you listen to them and learn as much as possible.

Have you worked for a great leader? What did you learn from them?

Work Lesson #389 – *A leader can be a candle in the darkest room,*
even if it requires them to endure burning to provide light.

The more resilient you become, the more your mindset will be determined
to succeed. This is often the hidden variable in strong leaders.

Resilience is a trait that will play a critical role in both your life and career.

I have learned this, many times over. I was diagnosed with severe dyslexia
at the age of six and couldn't read until I was nearly nine. I didn't accept
this and eventually became a writer. This helped make me strong, to make
me resilient and to persevere.

You'll have obstacles and setbacks in your career; you'll have the proverbial
road bumps trying to block you from reaching your goals and destination;
work through these. Because as Thomas J. Watson elegantly
stated, *"success is often found on the far side of failure."*

Resilience teaches you to get back up and keep trying. You don't fall, if you
keep getting up, it's merely a stumble. Successful people make mistakes,
but they learn and try again. They've learned that failure is only permanent
when you stop trying, so don't stop.

Are true leaders resilient?

Work Lesson #390 – *True leaders' words are as good as law. Their*
actions match their words, and they deliver on their commitments.

Leaders are honest, transparent and send clear messages to their teams.

Communication doesn't always come from words. Some of the most
effective communication comes from their actions.

Actions can send clear messages to an audience without uttering a word.
True leadership is an excellent example of when actions should be clear.

Actions of a Leader:

- Practices patience,
- Listens,
- Engages with their team,
- Shares credit with their team,
- Self-aware,
- Kind and fair,
- Helps and develops people,
- Humble,
- Practices tolerance,
- Delivers on their commitments, and
- Speaks the truth.

This is a small list of the actions of a true leader. When they are practiced, a transparent form of communication has been established. True leadership is witnessed, regardless of the language spoken, or the country and culture you're within.

What else would you add?

Work Lesson #391 – *Leaders challenge. Even if it's their own beliefs and assumptions, they accept they may be the ones who need to change.*

A leader who cannot handle constructive feedback is no leader.

Some fake leaders can't handle criticism, and they create an environment that isn't engrained with free speech, shutting down anyone who disagrees with them.

Remember, strong leaders allow you to question their decisions and challenge them. Period.

Leaders don't make you:

- Walk on eggshells,
- Feel inferior, and
- Feel you're in the wrong.

Leaders are:

- Strong Listeners,
- Self-aware, and
- Confident in their ability but aware of their weakness.

If a team leader doesn't allow free thought and speech within their team, then they haven't established trust, and when there is no trust, then the leader is only getting a portion of the information the team has access too.

Strong teams can go to their boss with any information, including concerns, mistakes they made and questioning a decision.

Leaders embrace constructive feedback as they want their teams to trust them, and they're aware that they aren't always in the right. It's a sign of a poor leader if they cannot allow their ego to listen to feedback on their performance.

Have you challenged your boss? How did they react?

Work Lesson #392 – *Leaders Listen. They lend their ears and give their time to those who need to be heard.*

Listening is the most critical part of communicating and the easiest way to gain and learn information.

True leaders are strong communicators because they possess the two fundamentals of communication:

- First, they can translate ideas to their team; and
- Second, they listen to the wants and needs of their team.

Part of motivating your team is understanding their needs and creating an environment where they can flourish and reach their goals. You learn this information by observing, asking the right questions and listening.

Strong communicators are good at recognizing problems, building trust with their teams and encourage an open-door policy. They want to hear from their team regardless of the news. The sooner you're aware of a problem, the sooner you can solve it. With this built trust, their team will go to them with any issue, and they'll solve it as a team.

Leaders recognize their team members' contributions and provide constructive feedback when required.

Can you be a leader and not a strong communicator?

Work Lesson #393 – A leader who chooses to follow, knowing they're capable of leading, is a sign of a true leader.

The employees and entrepreneurs who don't *'play nice'* with others have limited career paths.

You can be an extremely talented person, but if you can't get along with others, your career choices will be limited.

There aren't many positions that don't require teamwork, leadership and communication skills.

Talent is a great start, but it isn't enough on its own. You must be able to work well with others and be a contributing member of a team. This requires you to:

- Listen to others; don't interrupt or assume you know what they're going to say.
- Being open-minded and understand you may be the one that needs to change.
- Understand the difference of when you need to lead and when you need to follow.

There will be times during your career when there is someone else that should lead, even if you're capable. It merely means there is a better choice or a greater need.

What are the signs of a true leader?

Week 47 Theme: The Role of Emotional Intelligence in the Workplace

"It is very important to understand that Emotional Intelligence, is not the opposite of intelligence, it is not the triumph of heart overhead. It is the unique intersection of both."

— David Caruso

Emotional intelligence is in nearly everything we do, from effective communication to understanding our motivations; to understand our feelings and the feelings of others.

From popular request, I decided to expand on the theme of emotional intelligence (EQ) from Week 30 and discuss EQ's role in the workplace. The five components of EQ are:

- Self-Awareness.
- Self-Regulation.
- Motivation.
- Empathy.
- Social Skills.

EQ can make an individual highly effective, as they are self-aware, controlled, motivated, care and understand others and can communicate clearly and concisely. These components build the foundation for leadership and how a team can execute efficiently and effectively.

How has EQ impacted your work?

Work Lesson #394 — Self-aware people are aware of their emotions and understand why they feel them, what they mean and where they originate. They know how their feelings and actions impact others.

Self-awareness is a big step in the process of improvement and understanding. How can you correct poor habits, if you're not aware you have them?

The issue with self-awareness is many people think they have it but don't. That's the irony... ignorance is ignorance... when you're ignorant, you're unaware, and often think you're more talented and aware than you indeed are; therefore, let's do a quick assessment.

Ask yourself:

- Can you handle constructive feedback? Do you welcome constructive feedback? Meaning, do you go out in search of it? Asking your peers, bosses and supervisors for areas of improvement?
- Do you remain emotionally calm when receiving unsolicited advice?
- Do you listen attentively when people are speaking to you?
- Do you regularly assess your results and decisions?
- Do you challenge your own beliefs and assumptions?
- Do you accept that you may be in the wrong and the one that needs to change?

If your answers to any of the above questions is a *"No."* Then, there is room for improvement.

Self-aware people understand that they may be the ones in the wrong and need to change to meet their teams' needs.

How have you improved your self-awareness?

Work Lesson #395 – *If you choose to engage in a confrontation, you must always remain level-headed, calm and in control of your emotions.*

You must always remain level-headed, calm, and in control, if you're engaging in a confrontation. Never engage in an argument when you're emotionally compromised.

There can be a great strength in walking away.

Walking away can sometimes be viewed as a weakness, but this isn't always the case. If you have made an informed decision, supported by facts and merit, then walking away can be wise, as sometimes, you should cut your losses.

Remember, not all battles can be won. If a battle is hopeless, and you're up against a person that regardless of how wrong they are, will stick to their stubborn and inefficient ways, then maybe you're best to leave the situation.

Common situations to walk away from:

- There is no benefit by staying to argue;
- The stress of continuing the battle is too excessive and will impact your health;
- If you're emotionally compromised and cannot remain calm; and
- When the battle infringes on your core values, boundaries and limits, certain things shouldn't be compromised.

Learning when to walk away and cut your losses, can save you time throughout your career.

What do you do when you become emotionally compromised?

Work Lesson #396 – Highly motivated people are disciplined even through setbacks. They never stop encouraging themselves to reach their goals.

It's not about having all the answers and never failing. Successful people simply find a way to motivate and inspire themselves in their darkest days. Be your biggest cheerleader.

It's easy to be driven on your good days and after major successes and breakthroughs. It can be an entirely different story to remain motivated after you've failed or experienced a significant setback.

When you have dedicated yourself to your goals, you understand that a setback is simply part of the process.

Failure is a part of success... when you have ambitious goals, you'll enter areas where you lack experience, and therefore, you'll make mistakes by default... this is the reality of the game.

Since mistakes are a part of learning, you cannot rely on others to provide you with the motivation and inspiration for your success. You must find a way to tap into your own motivation and learn to inspire your actions, especially in times of failure.

Remember, continuous success is a result of highly driven individuals that have devoted their lives to the concept of lifelong learning. When you can find a way to motivate and inspire yourself on your darkest day, you're on the path to success.

How do you remain disciplined through setbacks?

Work Lesson #397 – "Empathy is seeing with the eyes of another, listening with the ears of another and feeling with the heart of another." – *Alfred Adler.*

Empathic Leaders can relate to nearly anyone, as they can see the world through others' perspectives.

They understand what people are feeling and thinking and are mindful of how their actions impact their teams.

I believe empathic leaders are the best leaders, and this is why.

Empathic Leaders:

- Show compassion.
- Actively listen.
- Ask powerful questions to understand and learn.
- Fully present.
- Don't judge.
- Don't assume.
- Don't interrupt.
- Care.

- Encourage.
- Develop others.
- Self-aware.

Now, who wouldn't want to work for someone who has all these qualities? Empathic leaders create a safe environment for their teams to grow, develop and learn. Most people in this environment can reach a higher potential, as they're safe to be vulnerable and are allowed to fail.

When you're allowed to fail, knowing your leader and team will catch you... you reach for the stars instead of settling for the moon.

What else did I miss?

Work Lesson #398 – *Strong communicators are good at recognizing problems, building trust with their teams and encourage an open-door policy.*

Strong communicators are transparent and encourage open dialogue. They create a safe and trusting environment, so everyone feels comfortable speaking up.

There is a reason why passive-aggressive people are often considered poor communicators... not all confrontations can be avoided, and nor should they be. Passive-aggressive communication isn't clear and can send mixed messages. <u>For example:</u>

Sometimes, you must be the bearer of bad news, and there is no other option.

If you're leading a team, part of your responsibility will be to provide feedback to your team members and this could mean constructive feedback.

If you have a team member who is disturbing other members with poor behaviour, you'll need to interject. If you choose not to, the situation will get worse, not better, and you may lose valuable team members.

You cannot ignore poor working situations or tiptoe around them and hope they'll improve on their own... this is rarely the case. You'll need to interject if you want the situation to improve.

You can't always escape confrontation, especially if it's impacting others.

Do you agree?

Work Lesson #399 – *Emotionally Intelligent Leaders understand how their reactions, words and actions impact their teams.*

The world is full of poor leaders acting under the umbrella that they're great. Servant leadership is simple: You serve your team, and you have their best interest at heart... meaning you don't need them to stroke your ego or boost your self-esteem.

Poor leaders are easy to pick out if you know what to look for. Remember, words can come easy and without responsibility for some people. In simple terms, they lie, either to you, to themselves and to their organizations.

If you want to learn who the true leaders are, watch their actions.

- Do they deliver on their commitments?
- Do they overpromise and under deliver?
- Do they blame others when things go wrong?
- Do they always have an excuse as to why something wasn't done?
- Do they communicate when they are going to be late?

Strong leaders communicate and deliver on their promises. They understand how their words, reactions and actions impact their teams; therefore, they don't blame their team for the team's shortcomings. If the team failed, they take full responsibility for this failure. This is an evident action of a proper leader.

Have you witnessed a fake leader blame their team?

Work Lesson #400 – *Don't be a hostage to your own emotions. Understand them, enjoy them, and own up to them.*

Emotions have a broad spectrum. We can feel happy and sad at the same time. This can be utterly complex or simple; it's all in our perspective.

Because emotions can be complicated and confusing, the best approach is to embrace them and never ignore what you're feeling.

I understand that there is a time and place to reflect on your feelings, and you can't always embrace every feeling while you have them but never suppress them to the point you no longer feel them.

What I mean:

- **Understand them** – meaning you know why you're feeling what you are and where they're stemming from.

- **Enjoy them** – meaning be at one with your feelings, you don't need to justify your own feelings to yourself. If you're sad, be sad. Many times, sadness and happiness go hand in hand, often giving life to each other.

- **Own up to them** – meaning be honest with yourself and what you're feeling, even if what you're feeling is unreasonable, understand and learn where it's stemming from and why you're feeling it. You don't need to justify your feelings to yourself, but ensure you understand them and are never a hostage to them.

Remember - *"Feelings can't be ignored, no matter how unjust or ungrateful they seem."* – Anne Frank

Do you agree with Anne?

Week 48 Theme: The Power of Diversity

A 2018 study by the Boston Consulting Group (BCG) has found that diversity increases the bottom line for companies. The study found that *"increasing the diversity of leadership teams leads to more and better innovation and improved financial performance."* It looked at 1700 different companies across eight different countries, with varying industries and company sizes. They have found that increasing diversity has a direct effect on the bottom line. Companies that have more diverse management teams have 19% higher revenue due to innovation.[13]

Through my research, I found another seven studies that have concluded the same thing. Diverse teams make more money for their organizations, yet, many companies have failed to integrate diversity into their leadership teams. They have failed to eliminate unconscious bias from their company culture.

This week, I'll be discussing the power of diversity and why inclusion fuels it. Diversity requires different generations, gender, culture, process of thought, to ignite innovation.

How important is diversity to the workforce?

Work Lesson #401 – Diversity of thought is true diversity. We can all look different but think the same, which isn't going to get us very far.

I think we've all seen the poster photos of diversity—both men and women with visible minorities. Companies can pat themselves on the back; they have a diverse workforce. But do they?

True diversity means far more than what a photo may seem to represent.

If your company has a broken chain of command and a lack of transparency and honesty, meaning they don't promote and encourage free diverse thinkers, it doesn't matter if the photo representing your company shows

---

[13] https://www.forbes.com/sites/annapowers/2018/06/27/a-study-finds-that-diverse-companies-produce-19-more-revenue/#7b566d13506f

diversity. You'll still suffer and be plagued by the troubles of groupthink and a lack of real diversity.

Diversity is as much about mindset as it is through visible diversity. If a company has a strict checklist to be promoted, don't be surprised if everyone at the top thinks similar. Over time, innovation and the ability to adapt and change to the market will disappear.

True diversity offers the benefit of different backgrounds and differences of opinions; if you haven't captured this through your promotion process, your company is suffering from a potential lack of diversity.

Do you believe mindset plays a critical role in true diversity?

Work Lesson #402 – Don't be angry with the person who plays the devil's advocate; they often play a critical role in effective brainstorming and ensure all angles have been investigated.

Through the ideation phase, you want ideas to build off of ideas and therefore, you want open-minded thinkers to be a part of this process, but once the ideation phase is over and before you move into ironing out the details, you need to investigate the negatives and the *'what ifs'* of your ideas...

... And this is where the devil's advocate thinkers come into play. The role is critical to ironing out an ironclad plan. No idea is ready to be pitched to clients or higher-ups in your organization without thorough investigation as to why the idea may not work or what could go wrong.

Proper preparation requires you to investigate all sides and angles of an idea and to go over every possibility. This will assist in a smoother execution and implementation phase.

Therefore, don't shun the devil's advocate role; there is a time and place where this role is necessary and critical to preparing for the execution of the idea properly.

Have you had to play devil's advocate?

Work Lesson #403 – *Different generations can provide a natural diversity to a team.*

Generations are born and raised during different times and therefore are shaped partially by these times in history. This can provide a natural diversity in the workplace.

Each generation has gone through their hardships and has had unique opportunities throughout history. When we combine these on a team, it can provide a well-rounded account of knowledge that can be utilized to strengthen the team.

We mentor, but we can reverse mentor as well, where each member of the team can contribute to its whole.

The classic example is detailed knowledge of technology within the younger generation. The use of technology isn't valuable unless you know how to apply it correctly to a process; this is where experience is utilized. Together this can create a winning formula.

I believe the best mentorships go both ways, a two-way street of give and take, where everyone benefits from the team's knowledge and experience as a whole.

Do you believe that different generations within a team provide a natural diversity?

Work Lesson #404 – *Diversity and inclusion go hand and hand. If you aren't invited to actively participate in all aspects of your organization, you won't be able to bring your true unique views to the discussion.*

Inclusion and transparency are required to reap the benefits of diversity.

If someone doesn't feel included, it's not a safe environment, and employees can't be honest with who they are and what they can bring to the table in a setting laced with judgement and bias.

To be comfortable in the room, the room must be welcoming. To truly eliminate groupthink, an organization and team must encourage free thought and create an environment where these thoughts are allowed to bloom.

If someone doesn't feel they belong or are allowed to enter a conversation, you won't receive their full contribution; you'll only receive a portion of it, leaving talent outside the room. To truly reap the benefits of diversity, you must practice inclusion.

How important is inclusion in diversity?

Work Lesson #405 – The power in multiple viewpoints and perspectives fuels innovation. Diversity is like gasoline to a fire; it sets it ablaze (of course, in a good way).

Ideas build off of ideas. Collaboration is the coming together of many ideas to give birth to one big vision. Diversity and inclusion allow the momentum to get started.

A collaborative environment where you finish often doesn't resemble where you began; as the team together built off each other's ideas and suggestions to get somewhere new and unfamiliar.

A few years back, I had the honour of attending my first Innovation Catalyst Event in San Francisco. During the event, the team was given a tough problem to solve that was plaguing the industry. Over six months, the team worked every weekend, building the solution. Our solution was a mere pipedream from that week in San Francisco. Over six months, we built off ideas, off failed solutions to finally end up where we were and where we got to present our solution to our CEO.

My point here is, without diversity, we would have never gotten as far as we did. Each of us brought a unique set of skills that could be utilized to come to a solution.

Do you believe effective collaboration comes from diversity?

Work Lesson #406 – *Different experiences and perspectives foster innovation, change and growth.*

As I've been building my business, I'm learning how precious and effective different experiences and perspectives have helped me.

When it comes to career observations and how to maneuver the internal politics of the Fortune 500 world, I'm good ... but developing marketing graphics, building websites and creating interest in my product has been new for me.

There is only so much you can learn on your own; yes, the experience is a wonderful teacher, and nothing will change this, but this is the long game. To play the long game ideally, you must be an active member in the short game; this helps speed up the full process.

Utilizing diversity as an educational tool can help speed up your long game and create innovation. Building new relationships in the hustle culture in the past year has changed my outlook on business. My learning curve has been exponential, as I've added many entrepreneurs to my network, which has complimented my corporate knowledge.

Together this has leapfrogged me forward, and it wouldn't have been possible if I hadn't added diversity of experience to my network.

Does the diversity of experience within a team make it productive?

Work Lesson #407 – *Our acceptance of diversity can be how we end personal bias and judgment.*

> *"Our ability to reach unity in diversity will be the beauty*
> *and the test of our civilization."*
>
> *– Mahatma Gandhi*

We may not control or influence to change our organizations, but we do control ourselves and our thoughts.

With the power of numbers, we can provide life to diversity and eliminate personal bias and judgment.

As Gandhi so elegantly stated, by accepting the differences in others and seeing beauty in our differences instead of threats or wanting them to change, we can eliminate judgment.

By embracing our differences, we can genuinely be promoted based on our strength of character and merit, instead of how we look or how others have allowed their personal bias to cloud our perception.

How are you overcoming your personal biases?

Week 49 Theme: Paying Your Dues

Paying Your Dues is an old concept that will never truly disappear, as, in many ways, it will always be relevant.

Whether you've entered an organization on your first day, or starting your own business, you'll need to prove yourself. Prove your value and ability; whether, this is to your boss, supervisor, staff or client, people will want to see some form of proof of your ability before giving you real responsibility or their money.

This week, I'll be discussing the concept of paying your dues, from proving your ability to learning the negative aspects and perception around paying your dues.

I'll be discussing some of the negatives: Feeling jolted when you feel you've earned something you didn't get, like a promotion, which can create hostility and negativity within you. Paying your dues can be linked to entitlement, I've worked for 30 years and deserve retirement.

Paying your dues is laced in preconceived opinions that may or may not be relevant to the situation or today's workplace; therefore, let's discuss.

Do you believe Paying Your Dues is an old concept that must be eliminated?

Work Lesson #408 – You deserve to be treated with kindness and respect, but till you're able to bring something to the table, you haven't earned an invitation to sit down.

Entitlement can go both ways regarding Paying Your Dues. Before I explain myself, I first want to say; each employee always deserves to be treated with kindness, fairness and respect. But if you're going to be promoted and invited to influential conversations with your company's leadership team, you'll need to prove yourself as a capable professional. These invitations must be earned, and you merely showing up isn't enough; you must bring results.

You may feel you have earned something based on a recent success or a preconceived notion, and so long as these thoughts are well thought out and reasonable, you may be able to gauge paying your dues this way, but I've witnessed a large spectrum on this topic. <u>For example</u>:

- *"I graduated top of my class. I deserve a job and start ahead of my classmates."* I can see why a valedictorian may feel this way, but because you're a good student, it doesn't necessarily translate to being a good employee. Therefore, you generally start in the same place as your classmates' will. Once you start at an organization, what matters, is what you do from that day onwards.

- *"I worked for 30 years; I deserve to retire."* Did you save money accordingly? You deserving retirement has little influence on actually retiring. I've met 30 years old who are retired. They only worked 10 years but saved and invested to a level where they no longer need to work. There is working hard, and there is working smart; they're different.

The concept of Paying Your Dues is laced with personal bias, ensure you know your own preference and where you stand.

Do you think people need to prove themselves?

Work Lesson #409 – You don't get a participation trophy for merely showing up. Somethings, you must earn.

When I say you should always be treated with kindness, fairness and respect, I mean this in a humanitarian sense. When it comes to respect in the professional spectrum, this still needs to be earned.

Being great at your job, adaptable, and keeping your skills relevant will help you earn professional respect and build a strong reputation.

When you graduate with your degree, it may be an incredible personal achievement, but you're generally untrained and have little experience. You have yet, to bring actual value to your employer...

...Therefore, don't expect to start at a 6-finger salary right out of school. And don't think your degree will offer you job security. Some advanced degrees provide extra protection, but generally, a degree will simply get you in the door, along with every other new graduate. It won't differentiate you.

Don't be naïve in thinking a degree (especially a degree that is primarily theoretical based), will assist you in gaining professional respect, in an environment that requires you to be practical.

If you want to make a name for yourself and build a strong reputation, then deliver results... consistent, high-quality results that solve difficult problems.

People who can provide solutions to difficult problems are the rarest type of employee; be this person.

How have you earned professional respect?

Work Lesson #410 – *Timing can help you, but never rely on luck to get you in the door. Have a strategy and plan.*

Your career will advance faster and be a smoother climb when you're executing a strategy and plan.

I've spoken to hundreds of aspiring professionals in the last year. Paying your dues, essentially means, gaining experience, and often, this can be a hard journey, especially if you're pushing yourself and leaving your comfort zone.

When you're in the middle of a steep learning curve, it is always difficult, but it's much worst when you have no plan. If you're shooting darts blindfolded and hoping to hit a bullseye, you've handcuffed yourself as well as blindfolded yourself. You're relying on luck instead of relying on yourself. This is a huge mistake.

When you're learning and gaining experience in a new field, having goals and plans allows you to set milestone targets, which will help you stay focused and on your desired path. Never strictly rely on luck to get you somewhere, have a plan and execute it.

Did having a plan help you focus on your goals?

Work Lesson #411 – Just because it's your dream job or your own business, doesn't mean you don't need to pay your dues.

I look at the concept of Paying Your Dues, to mean *'prove yourself.'* Whether you're working for an organization or working for yourself, you will need to prove yourself.

When you're a business owner, you still need to prove yourself to both your clients and your staff.

If you want to retain the best talent, you must be a talented boss as well. Leaders lead by example, and if you don't hold yourself to the highest standards, neither will your staff. And it's your staff that generally serves your clients. It's like a game of dominos; one touches the other for a constant linage of momentum. When you remove one piece, the momentum is either slowed down or stopped.

Therefore, even if you're working in your dream job or building an empire, you'll continuously develop your skills to grow and reach new levels in your career.

How are you improving yourself?

Work Lesson #412 – Paying your dues means you need to gain relevant experience for your job. This doesn't mean you need to work for free or settle for poor working conditions.

Paying your dues means different things to different people and organizations. But I've witnessed both people and organizations take advantage of this concept. Here are my two cents:

Do's:

- Gain experience and skills that are relevant to your job and career aspirations.
- Bring a positive attitude.
- Work hard and smart.
- Doing work, you don't want to do, is generally needed to gain more skills, this will require you to leave your comfort zone.

Don'ts:

- Make people work for free (Yes, I'm talking about your unpaid intern positions).
- Treat them with disrespect.
- Believe they need to go to the school of hard knocks.
- Stop believing, *"You had to go through hard dues, so they must as well."* It's a different world now; ensure you change with it.
- If you want to retain talent, treat your staff with respect and dignity and pay them for their job. Offer an environment where training and promotions are available and allow your employees to earn their success through reasonable methods.

Anything I missed?

Work Lesson #413 – *Never underestimate the power of consistency. Consistency can bring trust to your character.*

Of course, I mean, consistency in a good way.

- Consistent results.
- Consistent positive attitude.
- Consistent work ethic.

If you're consistent, people will learn what to expect from you, and they will begin to trust your ability. Allowing this method to help build your credibility and reputation as a professional will help develop a sellable name and becoming a safe bet.

Sometimes, I feel the concept of paying your dues comes from proving your consistency. To succeed over the course of your career, you must bring consistent results and ensure you don't burnout; you must bring these results through sustainable methods. <u>For example</u>:

Working 80-hour weeks may not be a sustainable method that you can sustain over the years, leading to burnout. Being consistent means, you learn the technique in which you can be successful and sustain this success.

How important is consistency in building a reputation?

Work Lesson #414 – If you have ambitious career goals, you'll be paying your dues for life. Every new level brings new challenges and new people to prove yourself too. Get comfortable with this concept.

How long does it take to pay your dues?

A degree, then Medical school, then residency is a classic example of paying your dues. It lasts a long time, and you're constantly tested.

Mick Jagger was quoted saying: *"Always play your best show, every time."*

So, if one of the most successful bands of all time believes you need to perform at your best always, then the concept of paying your dues can be a lifetime commitment. And doesn't need to be negative. This can be a personal positive motivational tool to help you step up and perform your best. It can help create a positive outlook and attitude to challenge yourself to continue to reach for the stars and not to settle for the moon.

If you go out every day to perform your best and bring a positive attitude with you, you'll continually improve throughout your career.

Is Paying Your Dues a lifetime commitment?

Week 50 Theme: Workplace Stress

Coping with workplace stress is difficult and may not be easy to escape from.

Even if your position is temporary, an unhealthy work environment can be straining and stressful; therefore, you must develop coping mechanisms to minimize its impact.

This week, I'll be discussing how to find sanctuary away from toxic people, how to isolate where the stress originates from, how to address bullying and methods to escape undesired circumstances.

The first step is to recognize a stressful workplace and then put in protocols to minimize its impact on you, and this may mean you move on.

What are common workplace stressors?

Work Lesson #415 – *To remove stress from your work, you first must isolate where it stems from.*

Self-awareness is in nearly everything we do. Being self-aware will help you isolate why you're feeling certain emotions and where they're stemming from. Some early signs of stress are:

- Headaches,
- Low energy, fatigue,
- Can't sleep,
- Getting sick more regularly,
- Upset stomach, and
- Anxiety.

Your body will often be the first indicator that you're dealing with stress; don't ignore these signs.

If you're feeling any of the above signs, try to isolate when you're feeling them, as it can help you isolate the cause of them.

- Are you feeling more stressed at home or work?
- Are there certain people that you feel more stressed around?
- Are there specific activities that trigger more stress? (e.g. like going to the bank may indicate financial burden).

Once you can learn the signs of your stress and know when these stresses are heightened, it will help you isolate the cause of the stress. Step two is learning to cope with or eliminate them. This will be discussed this week.

What are some other signs of stress?

Work Lesson #416 – *The Covid outbreak has triggered feelings of loneliness, isolation, stress, and anxiety. These are unprecedented times; embrace what you're feeling.*

Very few people are genuinely comfortable with uncertainty. Uncertainty can be scary. This is something you shouldn't deny, but instead, accept your feelings and directly address your fear and understand where it stems from.

It's perfectly normal if you're scared of the uncertainty in the world at the moment. Being scared is nothing to be ashamed of; it indicates the humanity in you.

Your career is unknown, your health is unknown, and your finances may be unknown. Our future is blurry, and a clear picture has yet to reveal itself.

I'm reminded during times of uncertainty and change that yes, it's a time to focus on the positive and to try my best to practice gratitude, but in my darkest moments, fighting the darkness of my fear and thoughts seems to be battle I cannot win.

If this is where you are mentally, I don't think you should fight it. I think you should embrace it and learn where it is stemming from. For example, if you're worried about your finances, dive into your budget, immediately cut out what's not needed and put together a worst-case budget plan for the next three months. Begin addressing your fear and make preparations that will help control it.

By doing nothing, you allow fear to grow and become a disease. Do you agree?

Work Lesson #417 – *Overworking is a good recipe for illness.*

In our busy day to day lives, we can often compromise our health and not realize the long-term detriment we're doing to ourselves. We tell our self:

- Just grab a quick lunch to go...
- I'll work-out tomorrow...
- I'll catch up on sleep on the weekend...

Even though what we're doing today, may seem more important than eating a home cook meal or skipping out on the gym... if you continue to compromise, over a long period, our bodies will begin to show the neglect.

- Does it take longer for you to get over a cold?
- Do you continue to work through a virus?
- Do you get sick more often?

Don't ignore the signs your body is trying to tell you when you need to slow down and concentrate on both your physical and mental health.

If your health is compromised and you get sick, not only are you unable to provide for your families, but you can't provide for yourself... therefore, your health is nearly always a number one priority and shouldn't be compromised.

Everyone reacts differently to life's pressures and stresses; the secret is to learn these reactions and put protocols in place to cope with these stresses before they take an undesired impact on your body.

How do you cope with stress?

Work Lesson #418 – *Bad bosses can create a stressful work environment, as they are there each day. To remove yourself from their grip, will require you to have a plan.*

You'll be far more likely to be successful in your career when you're executing a plan.

I cannot stress this enough, if you're working in a hostile area, such as, working for a bad boss, to maneuver out of their control discreetly. Keep your plans and moves to yourself.

If you're discreetly removing yourself from their reach and executing a secret plan, you must practice silence, and this means, you don't publicly bash or discuss your boss's poor performance.

You don't want your boss as an enemy, and you don't want them to be aware of your plan, therefore, remain silent about it. Avoid discussing your boss in public.

If your boss is unaware of your plans, then they cannot try to stop it. Just like Sun Tzu stated in The Art of War,

> *"The supreme art of war is to subdue the enemy without fighting."*

The less your boss knows, the easier it will be to execute your plan. Move with lightness in your feet.

How have you removed yourself from a bad boss?

Work Lesson #419 – *If the stress at work is no longer manageable, it's time to move on. This is a time to be taking care of yourself and your well-being.*

It's not healthy to dread going to work... Well, it may be the norm for other people, but don't settle for this; be the exception. Don't allow yourself to dread work.

We can spend approximately 70,000 hours at work during our lifetime... that is a lot of time wasted being miserable.

If you're miserable at work, the position is temporary, and you should put together a plan to escape this situation. Some tips:

1. Target an industry, company and position you're interested in.
2. Learn what skills are required to execute this new role.
3. Assess what skills you have that can be transferred to the new position.
4. Develop the skills you're missing through online courses, while you're doing this, network with people on LinkedIn that can help you move into your new career with your potential employer.
5. Sell your qualification to the new employer through posting applicable content online that will be visible to the industry and employer you're targeting.

How have you escaped a miserable work situation?

Work Lesson #420 – It's perfectly normal not to enjoy confrontation, you're not supposed too. Unfortunately, it's required throughout your career.

When confronting a bully, you must be direct and transparent in your message. This isn't a time to be subtle nor passive-aggressive.

Dealing with confrontation can be uncomfortable; therefore, don't be too hard on yourself if this is hard for you. It's perfectly normal not to enjoy confrontation, you're not supposed too. Unfortunately, it's required throughout your career.

There will be times during your career where it will be best to walk away. Generally, this is not the case with a bully. Bullying tends to continue till you deal with it, as it rarely disappears on its own, therefore, below are a few tips in confronting a bully.

- Mentally prepare for the confrontation. Your well-being is critical and therefore, prepare emotionally for the confrontation.

- When a person is bullying you, stop them, interrupt if needed and tell them how their behaviour impacts your work and present clear instructions on your future expectations. Make your boundaries clear. Potential wording, you can say, *"Please don't talk to be that way."* With a firm voice.
- Remember, bullying is rarely about you. It feels incredibly personal, but it's rarely personal from the bully's perspective, therefore, confront them. No one has the right to make you feel inferior.
- If it continues, ensure you document the bully's actions and words, then report it to your higher-ups if required.

Any tips on confronting a work bully?

Work Lesson #421 – To bring the best out of your team, to retain great talent, people must feel safe and, in an environment where bullying is tolerated, is not safe.

Bullying should never be tolerated. It creates a poor work environment, as people may fear coming to work or stating their opinions.

To bring the best out of your team, to retain great talent, people must feel safe and, in an environment where bullying is tolerated, is not safe. If you witness an employee being bullied, you must take action.

Sometimes, you'll need to interject immediately and stop the bullying from occurring; this will most likely require you to interrupt, ask the individuals what's going on. Ensure you maintain full eye contact with the bully. Generally, the individual being bullied won't say anything or that everything is fine. Don't accept this answer; this individual needs your help.

If you witness an employee being bullied and you're a manager, you need to write them up and report them. If you're a younger employee and are afraid to confront the bully, then report the occurrence to HR and your supervisor. If your supervisor is the bully, then absolutely report their behaviour to Human Resources.

Bullying should never be tolerated, especially in the workplace. If you remain silent, others will be a target of this individual.

Conclusion

What if you promised yourself that you'll be in a specific place a year from now? What if you decide to commit, to truly commit to your goals, what would happen? If you commit and dedicate yourself to your goals every day for the next year, where will you be?

One year ago, I decided to fully dedicate a year to building Work Lessons 101. I used each day to slowly grow my business and to become a better writer. Every day was a step forward in self-improvement. Just like when you set out to run a marathon, each mile completed gets you closer to your goal, even if you don't notice the distance you're completing, you're getting closer and building momentum to get to the finish line.

Some miles in my marathon were harder than others, fighting burnout, working through writer's block, recovering from surgery, sleep-deprived new mom, dealing with trolls... in retrospect, these were mere stumbles along my journey. I finished the race and succeeded.

On July 22, 2019, my goals were to post a work lesson each day for a year and build a social media following that would impress a major publisher and help me secure a book deal. What I gained and learned along the way became much more valuable than my original plan.

I succeeded and posted content each day on my social media platforms for one year, which has grown to be over 40,000 followers and 600 pieces of content, which included:

- 421 individual Work Lessons including 50 different work topics.
- 48 Episodes of my Work Lessons 101 Q&A Show.
- 10 Episodes recording my journey to building a business.
- Over 80,000 words written.

The compilation of Work Lessons within this book was written over an entire year and is a direct result of dedicating myself to my goals.

Once I started, I got going and gained momentum. What began as posting daily content online grew into a large following and then began to produce other avenues for my business. I began to move into career coaching, guest blogging, running workshops and appearing on podcasts.

By July 22, 2020, Work Lessons 101 offered a full range of career services from:

- Career coaching,
- Resume writing and review,
- Interview preparation,
- Career development plans and goal setting,
- Leadership Development,
- Speaking events, and workshops.

What started as a simple goal to grow a following to secure a book deal, has grown into a full-fledged business. With a broad audience, I have been able to get a literary agent to represent my upcoming career development book (Coming in 2021). I'm currently finalizing my book proposal to send to the market.

Next year's goals are to secure a publishing deal, continue to write and post content, keep networking with wonderful people, and help people build successful careers through Work Lessons 101. I love helping people. Please reach out to me if you have career concerns and need a guiding hand.

Committing yourself to your goals may not seem like you're moving and making progress day-to-day, but days add up, and over a year, you can make a leap forward. Baby steps can add up to become a giant leap. If you're in doubt, remember Warren Buffett's quote:

"Someone is sitting in the shade today because someone planted a tree a long time ago.

Are you planting your trees?

Start today, commit to your goals for the next 12 months and write to me to describe the lessons you learned on your journey.

Believe in yourself because you are worth believing in; be your greatest advocate!!!

Acknowledgement

To the Work Lessons 101 Community for making this all possible.

Where we start in life can influence where we go. I'm grateful to have won the lottery with my parents. They taught me from the moment I entered this world, that love and friendship are true wealth, leading to the foundation of a happy life. Thank you, Mom and Dad, for loving and guiding me through life and always being my ultimate safety net. It's easier to reach for the sky when I know you are there to catch me shall I fall. You have always been there for me, my number one fans.

To my brother Chad, my first mentor and friend. My big brother taught me how to get up from a fall, that life can throw you unexpected curveballs, but that you're better to learn to catch them then run away. Whether it was teaching me my multiplication tables, helping me work through my dyslexia to always having my back, you were a calming trusting voice that always punctured my stubborn hard head. Thank you for your patience, for your love and friendship. Thank you for marrying such as wonderful women in Anke, and making me an Aunt, with a couple of the loves of my life in Emilia and Max. Having your family in my life has brought me more happiness, I cannot quantify. I love you all so much.

To my extended family, in-laws, and friends who have created a loving support structure that, regardless of what I'm going through, has been there for me over and over. This has given me laughs, love and knowledge. All the support has contributed to my success in ways I cannot describe. An extra thank you to Marlene and John for their feedback and constant support.

To Rick, for being the best mentor of my career. Your belief in me got me to see my own potential, and the goals I set out for myself after this discovery is a direct result of your guiding hand.

To Karine and Tim, thank you for being my first set of peer mentors. Your guidance helped me climb the first few steps of my career, which sent me in a direction that got me where I am today.

To Sean and Michelle Danielson, thank you for welcoming Mike and me to Calgary. You helped make it a home. You two were the first people to help me establish my reputation in a new office, and I'll always be internally grateful for your kindness and guidance.

To Hannah, you're an amazing friend, colleague and brainstorming partner. Thank you for your constant support of Work Lessons 101, you're a strength I can rely on. Your words in the Foreword were touching, and together, we'll continue to build our business towards the future.

To Ally, Arpana, Arvind, Brian Elliott, Cecil, Chanel, Christina, Don Costco, Dustin, Enrique, Keith, Matt Glass, Matt Dina, Michelle Lee, Mikel, Morgan, Susan, Tahir, Vivek and all the wonderful colleagues I've met through my career... so many memories have come from your amazing friendships.

To Brian Johnston for taking a risk on me and giving me my first professional position. I couldn't have asked for a better first boss. How you empower women in the engineering field allowed me to feel safe and strive towards higher goals.

To Ricardo, Jonathon, and Jaakko for teaching me the ropes of being a Process Engineer, it all started there.

To Peter Oosterveer, who taught me the true meaning of Leadership. You are the example; I model my own career after.

To Jason and Raj, thank you for your support, guidance, and wonderful mentorships.

And lastly, to Mike, the love of my life. Work Lessons 101 would have never happened without your constant encouragement and support. Everything that is within this book is for you. You have been by my side, day in and day out, and your support has never, not once wavered. Last year, when we welcomed our son, Quinton, to the world, you not only were an amazing husband but became an amazing father. Our family is what gives me motivation, even in my darkest days. Your love and support give me strength. I know life has been kind to have you and Quinton by my side. Thank you for being my best friend.

About the Author

Sabrina Woodworth, P.Eng, has worked in the corporate environment for over 14 years. She started her career as an entry-level process engineer in training and quickly rose to prominent leadership roles. Her career has included multiple industries and business groups, comprised of numerous positions and leadership roles, demonstrating her ability to adjust to change and furthering her well-versed foundation in corporate operations.

Her career has taken her overseas to Mongolia, to several major cities, including her Canadian corporate headquarters in Calgary, Alberta. Now, as a Project Manager and Founder of Work Lessons 101, Sabrina's career has a proven track record of strategizing, manoeuvring, and being promoted through the hurdles of the corporate world.

Sabrina has navigated the career ladder across two business lines inside a Fortune 500 company. She has worked with dozens of different functions, including managers and executive leaders while working within the office and on construction sites. Sabrina has led multiple teams, worked closely with client organizations and built strong, lasting relationships. Sabrina is an experienced project manager with extensive knowledge of the corporate environment. With this knowledge, Sabrina founded Work Lessons 101, an organization that focuses on sharing experiences from the work environment by assisting, guiding and teaching people the essential work lessons to empower success within their careers.

Sabrina has spoken to both Universities and Corporations on the foundations of building successful careers and has built a large following on her social media platforms (40,000+), which receive over 3 million views each month. You can learn more about Work Lessons 101 and their services on their website: www.WorkLessons101.com.

Follow Work Lessons 101 on their social media platforms:

- Instagram and Facebook: @worklessons101
- LinkedIn: Sabrina Woodworth, www.linkedin.com/in/sabrinawoodworth/
- YouTube: WorkLessons101